REFLEXIVE WATER
The Basic Concerns of Mankind

REFLEXIVE WATER

The Basic Concerns of Mankind

A. J. AYER and ARNE NAESS
SIR KARL POPPER and SIR JOHN ECCLES
NOAM CHOMSKY and MICHEL FOUCAULT
LESZEK KOLAKOWSKI and HENRI LEFÈBVRE

FONS ELDERS

A CONDOR BOOK
SOUVENIR PRESS (EDUCATIONAL & ACADEMIC) LTD

First published 1974 by Souvenir Press (Educational &
Academic) Ltd,
95 Mortimer Street, London W1N 8HP
and simultaneously in Canada by
J. M. Dent & Sons (Canada) Ltd,
Ontario, Canada

ISBN 0 285 64742 3 casebound
ISBN 0 285 64749 0 paperback

Printed in Great Britain by
Northumberland Press Ltd,
Gateshead

Contents

Preface by Fons Elders

Philosophy is one of those words which most people find difficult to define. Even those who have been professional philosophers for years often find it difficult to give a clear and concise definition of it. During a visit to Rudolph Carnap some months before his death in 1970, I was struck by the gaps which divide philosophers from each other. Carnap told me that he didn't understand why Arne Naess, for whom he had considerable respect, even though he didn't agree with him on many points, had written about both him and Martin Heidegger in one and the same book, *Four Modern Philosophers*.

Different conceptions about such fundamental issues as truth or human nature, can result in two philosophers being unable to recognise each other as such. The very differences of opinion on fundamental issues, which are so characteristic of Western culture, make for confrontation between philosophers, each of whom is trying to develop and then to systematically articulate a coherent theory.

Although most people wouldn't know what the word "philosophy" means, it doesn't mean that they are not concerned with questions which belong to the domain of philosophy: such questions as how truthful is our knowledge, or whether we are living in a just and free society are asked in many different ways by millions of people each day. I realised this shortly after I had begun to visit different philosophers to ask them to debate with each other before a Dutch television audience about issues central to their own philosophies. At two o'clock in the morning, on Broadway in New York City, I found myself taking part, with eight other people, all of them strangers to each other, in a passionate but entirely rational discussion about the meaning of Christianity. As the traffic rushed by, we tried to explain what we thought and why we didn't agree with each other. Several times I could hear the arguments put forward by Bertrand Russell in his essay, "Why I am not a Christian".

Our nighttime discussion on Broadway didn't differ essentially from the debates which were broadcast on television by the Dutch Broadcasting Foundation (Nederlandse Omroep Stichting: NOS) on four late Sunday evenings in 1971. On each occasion, two prominent contemporary philosophers were brought face-to-face for two hours of debate in either English or French. The philosophers debated in the following combinations: Sir Alfred Ayer (England) and Arne Naess (Norway): "The Glass is on the Table: an empiricist versus a total view" (in English, at the International School of Philosophy at Amersfoort); Sir John C. Eccles (United States, Australian-born) and Sir Karl Popper (England, Austrian-born): "Falsifiability and Freedom" (in English, at the Binnenhof in The Hague); Noam Chomsky (United States) and Michel Foucault (France): "Human Nature: Justice versus Power" (in English and French, at the Technical High School in Eíndhoven); Leszek Kolakowski (England, Polish-born) and Henri Lefèbvre (France): "Evolution or Revolution" (in French, at the Lutheran Church in Amsterdam).

The debates, which were shortened to one hour long each for the television broadcast, and were interrupted occasionally with short expositions by Professor L. W. Nauta of Groningen University, were preceded by fifteen-minute profiles of the participants which took the form of film biographies by the Dutch film-makers Milo Anstadt, Louis van Gasteren, and Vincent Monnikendam. The supervision of the series of debates in this International Philosophers' Project was in the hands of NOS producer Kees van Langeraad, L. W. Nauta, Professor J. J. A. Mooy, also of Groningen, and Professor Emeritus Karel Kuypers, of the University of Utrecht. The idea behind the project was originated in 1968 by Gerard J. P. Rijntjes, the former head of extra-mural education at the University of Utrecht, who then developed the plan further in close colla-

boration with Leo C. Fretz, at that time director of the International School of Philosophy at Amersfoort. They suggested
that several philosophers from abroad should be invited as
guest lecturers at various Dutch universities. To begin with,
the project was purely academic: however, the NOS became
involved and the idea of televising the lectures was put forward.
The next step followed on naturally, namely that the possibilities of television should be used to take philosophy out of
its ivory tower and bring it, in the form of televised debates,
into the living room. Needless to say, the plan was not worked
out in one day: amendments, additions, and differences in
emphasis were all brought to bear on the original idea.

I was then asked by the planners if I would be responsible
for setting up the actual debates. My three major responsibilities
were visiting the philosophers to ask them if they would co-
operate, interviewing them for their profiles, and presiding over
the debates. My role in the project grew as the emphasis shifted
from a programme of guest lectures to a series of television
debates; however, the lectures retained their significance.

The reason for the shift is clear. When two philosophers,
surrounded by cameras, debate the basic ideas of their own
philosophies, they are faced with a completely new situation.
They speak to a public they would otherwise never reach, and
one that on the whole knows them by name only, if at all.
Furthermore, debating on television serves to illustrate a basic
principle of philosophy: one can doubt everything and believe
everything provided that one is prepared to defend one's doubts
and beliefs with as many arguments as possible and to listen
to other and opposite arguments.

I believe that this is one of the most remarkable books to
have appeared in the last few decades, both in the originality
of the philosophers and in the dialogue form used. What seemed
an obvious approach for Greek and medieval philosophers,
namely that attempts should be made to reach the truth
together, or at the least to discuss it and to take each others'
arguments seriously, has been revived in the NOS Project and
in this book; a fact that becomes all the more important when

one realises how fundamental are the theoretical differences among these eight philosophers. Together they represent most of the basic philosophies of Western culture. I am most grateful to them for giving their permission, notwithstanding all the difficulties, for the publication of the integral texts, amended only by necessary corrections.

I also thank the NOS for the rights of publication of the text and for the loyal co-operation which I always received from them. For the typing, editing and translation work, I have been helped by Karel van der Leeuw, Willem Daub, Riet Bonnemayers, Jacqueline deJong and especially, Judith Gray, in the way that only friends can help.

FONS ELDERS

ALFRED AYER
and
ARNE NAESS

The Glass is on the Table:
an empiricist versus a total view

The Glass is on the Table

ELDERS:
Ladies and gentlemen, I would like to welcome you to a debate which will, I suppose, be of interest in many respects. I would like to lose as little time as possible in beginning this philosophical contest, in which you will see an avid football fan, Sir Alfred, and a lover of boxing and alpinism, Arne Naess, debating with each other on central issues of their own philosophies. First of all, we have to discover what kinds of philosophical views both philosophers have. Sir Alfred and Mr. Naess, would you each explain to the audience what you consider to be your tasks as philosophers? Sir Alfred?

AYER:
Well, I suppose to try to answer a certain quite specific range of questions that are classified as philosophical questions—and are very much the same questions that, I think, have been asked since the Greeks, mainly about what can be known, how it can be known, what kind of things there are, how they relate to one another.

In general, I would think of philosophy as an activity of questioning accepted beliefs, trying to find criteria and to evaluate these criteria; trying to unearth the assumptions behind thinking, scientific thinking and ordinary thinking, and then trying to see if they are valid. In practice this generally comes down to answering fairly concrete specific questions.

And I hope, in a sense, to finding the truth.

ELDERS:
And you, Mr. Naess?

NAESS:

Well, I see it a little differently, I think, because I would rather say that to philosophy belong the most profound, the deepest, the most fundamental problems. They will change very little, and they have not changed much over the last two thousand years. So we have different conceptions of philosophy, but we agree that the epistemological question, "what can we know?" and the ontological one, "what main kinds of things are there?" belong to philosophy. As I see it, they are among the most profound questions we can ask.

AYER:

Yes, but how do you measure the profundity of a problem? I mean, a problem may often look quite trivial and then turn out to be profound. In a sense, you try to answer what you're puzzled by. Now this may be something very profound, it may even look quite superficial, then turn out to be profound.

NAESS:

How do we measure? Well, that's one of the most profound questions of all. How do we know? I suppose it will vary with cultural and social circumstances. It involves fundamental valuations, not only investigations of fact or logic.

ELDERS:

Sir Alfred, would you give an outline of a sceptic?

AYER:

Well, I was going to talk about this. It seems to me that, perhaps not so much in ancient philosophy, but certainly in modern philosophy since Descartes, a lot of problems have arisen out of a certain very characteristic sceptical argument. I should say that a sceptic is always someone who questions one's right to make certain assumptions—often assumptions about the existence of certain kinds of things—on the ground of their going beyond the evidence.

I mean, a very obvious and classical example would be scepticism about other minds. People will say, well, all you observe is other people's behaviour; all you observe is their actions, the expressions on their faces. How do you know that anything goes on behind? How do you know that everybody isn't a robot, or whatever? And so you get scepticism also tied up with a certain neurosis, I think. It has also a certain emotional tone.

Or again take the classical example of the scepticism of David Hume, the scepticism about induction. Hitherto, when you lit a cigarette, it would smoke, and so on; when you have walked on the floor it has supported you. How do you know that this will happen in the future? How can you extrapolate from past evidence to future occurences? And then you are proving that the argument is, in a sense, circular, always presupposing something that you can't justify. And a lot of philosophy comes out as the posing of arguments of this kind and the attempts to find replies to them. And you could even characterise different sorts of philosophy by their different ways of meeting the sceptic. Now, I think one mark of a philosopher, why I think that Arne Naess is a profound philosopher, is to take scepticism seriously. Would you?

ELDERS:

But in *The Problem of Knowledge* you are quite critical about scepticism.

AYER:

I think I rather cheated in *The Problem of Knowledge*. It seems to me that I gave scepticism a good run, and then in the end somehow some little strong John Bull common sense came out in me and I took away from the sceptic the victory he had won, like a referee in a boxing match.

NAESS:

I had the same impression when I read your book. Ultimately

you would say: "Hm, no! Common sense, after all, tells me there is something rotten here, so there is something rotten." But ... well, I don't know your mind.

ELDERS:

Speaking about this common sense, Sir Alfred, has it something in common with what the Germans call *Gesundenes Volksempfinden*?

AYER:

I don't know whether it has or not, because I don't know really which Germans you are talking of, or what they would mean by this.

ELDERS:

But what do *you* mean by common sense?

AYER:

By common sense I mean what Hume calls natural belief. For instance, take the case of the past. Now, in fact, you can't justify any belief about the past, because any attempt to justify it will be circular. The most you can do is check one memory by another one, one memory report by another one; or check in the records, and this again presupposes the reliability of memory, because how do you test the records? So you really have no non-circular justification.

So it's perfectly true to say, as Russell said, that for all we can *prove*, for all we can demonstrate, the world might have begun five minutes ago, with people already fully grown who delusively remember a totally unreal past.

Now I suppose, Naess, you want to leave it there and say: I really don't know. But I'd say, well, the argument for it may be circular, nevertheless I'm going to assume it. This will be what I would call common sense. At a certain point I say, no, no, no, this is carrying scepticism too far: to hell with it.

And possibly that is a remarkable weakness in a philosopher: I should be more heroic. I mean, are you more heroic, more heroic in this way? Would *you* say we have no reason to believe that the world has existed for more than five minutes?

NAESS:

I think it is reasonable to say that it has existed for a very long time, and that it is reasonable that we should assume this. But that still leaves open the question of truth. Reasonableness does not rule out mistakes. Our concept of known truth is such that you must have a guarantee. But are we ever justified in saying that our research is over, we need not bother to test our beliefs any more, fifty thousand years ago there were people living on this earth? We do not have any guarantees—or do we? I have not found any. The more I think about this, the less I come to feel that I know. That's a feeling you don't have every time you take a tram or walk on the floor. But in the moments when, as Heidegger would say, you live more authentically, that's to say you ...

AYER:

Let's keep him out of this. [*Laughter.*]

NAESS:

I knew it, I knew it, and therefore I had my small pleasure!

AYER:

We ought to maintain certain standards.

NAESS:

Well, a man whose name begins with H and ends with R thinks, and other philosophers also, that we are more or less concentrated and integrated. In moments of high concentration and integration, not at the times when I am merely functioning, I have this feeling—and it is not just a feeling—that we don't have any decisive arguments for any conclusions whatsoever. That is, when the conclusion starts with "It is true that ...".

AYER:

And yet there is something peculiar here, in the way I view it, because we have got all the evidence. It's not like a palaeontologist, who might be doubtful about dating some fossils, because perhaps more evidence will come in; perhaps some day more archaeological work will show him in which way his dating is wrong.

But with sceptical questions, in a sense there literally isn't any more evidence to come in. No experiment could be made that would show us, one way or the other, that we *were* justified in assuming the existence of other minds. No psychoanalyst is going to still our doubts on questions of this kind. They are in a sense logical doubts; in a sense all the evidence is there.

NAESS:

There are so many conceptions of logic and of intelligibility, and of what an argument is, and of what is evidence. I feel that in questions of conceptual analysis you can never say: now we have all the evidence here, now the cake is complete. Who knows the baker? Even in logical questions our situation resembles that of the palaeontologist: we do not have all the evidence about the evidence. I am also against the idea that the collecting of evidence should always be a kind of collecting of the results of external experiments. Experiments should also be made with our logic and ourselves. What does the I, the ego mean? We use the distinction between the I and the rest—what does it mean? Philosophers have many, but doubtful, solutions, and I will probably go on trying to collect evidence until I die.

The mysteries that we "know" include those of "I", "know" and the link between the knower and the known.

AYER:

Yes, I'm not dissenting from what you say, I'm merely trying to get at what's behind what you're saying. Do you think we might discover any quite different criteria even of validity; I mean that we might suddenly say, no, we don't want to use this logic? That you envisage even finding a different form of logic?

NAESS:

Yes, I expect the future here will resemble the past: continued modification of the conceptions of inference, criteria and evidence. I don't think that in the year 2000 we will have a completely different conception of what constitutes evidence. But sometimes you add or subtract some kinds of evidence; and in a most unexpected way. As, for example, the concepts of proof in mathematics.

AYER:

Indeed, indeed.

ELDERS:

Mr. Naess, I think we're still speaking a little evasively, because we can also formulate the problem of the past and the present in our own terms. Perhaps Sir Alfred will tell us how certain, how convinced he is that we are here now; and perhaps you could also speak on this question.

AYER:

Yes, I would say, if I were in a law court, I was convinced beyond reasonable doubt. [*Laughter.*] I wouldn't say it's certain; it's certainly logically conceivable that I should wake up and find myself back in my bed in London; that I've dreamt the whole thing. Although, of course, *that* experience might be the dream one. In that case, however, the question would be how things went on from then. But I would be convinced beyond reasonable doubt. I would bet on it. I would bet at least as much as you're paying me, for instance. [*Laughter.*] And I think Naess would too; he's more sceptical than I am, but he will keep a bet.

NAESS:

A little less willingly than you, I feel.

AYER:

But of course it's not simply a question of the fact of our being here: it's also how you are going to interpret that fact. We say we are here; but what are *we*? I mean, are these just bodies or do they have minds too; what's meant by their having minds? Are we going to regard them just as little bits of atoms, or are we going to regard them in a common sense way as being consciousness looking outward? All these questions come up.

Just saying "We're all here", represents, I think, something that you are pretty confident of. How, then, are you going to analyse that? What ontology do you envisage? This is again disputable.

NAESS:

You are now speaking as a sceptic here, Sir Alfred. We don't disagree on a single point here. But an important thing in scepticism is this: that anything can happen somehow, and that perhaps all things are somehow interconnected. Perhaps no question can be solved in isolation.

The question "Is this a glass?" is somehow irrelevant in relation to the basic problem that all things are interconnected. The particular question "Is this a glass?" evades the fact that there are several different ways of looking at the glass, that there are different relationships between human beings and a thing, and that all these interconnect.

ELDERS:

But you still presuppose the entity of the glass.

NAESS:

If you say "presuppose" an "entity", that raises a tremendously difficult question. Do I ever presuppose?

AYER :

Well, of course, an enormous number of presuppositions are
built even into the language we are using. If we talk about
our being here at all it presupposes, first of all, an assumption of human beings, in some sense or other; a whole spatio-
temporal system; the glass you're looking at; even the very
terms we're talking in. But I wanted in fact to ask you : how
serious is your scepticism? You say anything can happen.
Now I perfectly agree that it is logically possible; there is no
contradiction, no formal contradiction, in the idea of all
these people turning into swans, and even Jupiter coming—
I think Jupiter is going too far, but some human analogue
of Jupiter coming in—and behaving as he did to swans. This
is logically possible, but you don't envisage it as a serious
possibility.

ELDERS :

As an empirical possibility.

AYER :

I mean, it seems to me that although one admits the logical
possibility, one doesn't think it will happen. One's scepticism
in actual life, in one's actual beliefs, in the way one plans
one's life, is pretty narrow because of the extreme force of
what Hume called "natural belief".

We are conditioned to make certain assumptions, to take
for granted that things *do* go in regular patterns. A really
serious scepticism might be represented by someone who
really would refrain from taking action because, after all,
the man that I shake hands with, *might* suddenly explode;
therefore, he says, I won't go near him. This is, if you like,
an armchair scepticism, but I would not for this reason say
that it was not serious, for I think that purely intellectual
problems are serious. But it is, in this sense, theoretical.

ELDERS :

You agree with this sharp distinction between logical and
empirical possibility?

NAESS:

Well, this is not as important as certain other things which were said at the time, if you will excuse me.

I would say that sometimes I'm just functioning. When I buy a ticket to Groningen I neither assert anything nor deny anything; therefore I do not presuppose anything. I just walk, talk and go. I don't quite feel a philosopher at such moments. I do not assert the truth or falsity of any proposition: I just function. I act with a certain *trust*. A trusting attitude in walking and buying things for paper money. I think it's a trust towards things, not propositions. And that's different from making an assertion; this *is* true and the other *is* false. That's one point.

The second point is this, that I could easily imagine that a certain lady here in the room might become a swan at any moment. I also tend to think something completely different —so many different, incompatible things, that they must collide with each other.

Therefore I'm not afraid that we shall explode, for if anything and everything can happen, you're no longer afraid. You may explode but it may not hurt you. If you only think something dangerous will happen, you're afraid; but if anything can happen, you simply calm down. And that's how I feel.

ELDERS:

So as a sceptic you are less afraid than Sir Alfred?

AYER:

I think that if I thought anything could happen I should be afraid, yes. Anything whatsoever.

NAESS:

Well, that may be because you have had some bad experiences, but I have mainly had good experiences.

AYER:

No—I think it's just because I have a more feverish imagination.

NAESS:

Basically I have had good experiences with other people.

AYER:

But in *this*, you see, you're now doing exactly what you ought not to be doing: you're generalising from past experiences. You say you've had good experiences, therefore you expect only good things to happen. But this is not just allowing anything to happen, it's allowing only what has happened to you to happen.

NAESS:

That's a misconception of scepticism.

AYER:

It's in your natural belief.

NAESS:

This is a first semester scepticism. Not generalising and using a lot of "perhaps'es". In the second semester you utter generalisations, because you do not strongly resist your own tendency to utter what strikes you. So I say something about all people and I don't believe it to be a truth in the sense that I'm convinced it is true in the moment I say it. But if you say, "Oh, Mr. Naess, you are generalising and speaking about all good experiences with all people", then I would say, "Yes, yes; I generalise quite naturally, but I couldn't give a good argument for the truth of what I am saying."

So, generalising is okay for a sceptic; if he is relaxed as a sceptic he will make a lot of generalisations, but *without taking them too seriously. [Laughter.]*

AYER:

Yes, I mean, every moment it's true; of course, you're taking generalisations seriously now in reaching forward confidently and drinking your orange juice. You're taking generalisations seriously because a huge amount of theory goes into this. Theories about the behaviour of the glass, about the liquid that's in the glass, about your own body, about the behaviour of your neighbours, deciding that they will not suddenly go mad and start to be violent, all sorts of theories. Every minute you're making an enormous number of assumptions of this kind.

NAESS:

But do I assume the truth of any proposition? Scepticism has to do with claims about the truth. During the war and during the Hitler regime, and when I meet people who are really convinced that what Marx says is true, then I feel the importance of a sceptical attitude; these people take the attitude that what they're saying just couldn't be false, an attitude of unshakeability and incorrigibility. This I fight. I can be shaken and I wish others to be able to be shaken! The stand against incorrigibility somehow becomes generalised until it colours one's total view. But I think one of the roots of unshakeability and incorrigibility must lie in political and social conflicts.

ELDERS:

Well, will you try to apply what you are saying now to the concept of democracy?

AYER:

That's a big jump!

NAESS:

Well, I have, for instance, discussed and published more than three hundred different definitions of democracy, in order to undermine politicians who say that democracy requires so and so; Soviet theorists who say that *they* breed "real" democracy; and British democratic politicians who say that "real" democracy is very different. But I only undermine, not accuse of error. The British traditions go back to certain authors in the Greek world and the Soviet conceptions go back to Plato and Aristotle. So they all have a "big shot" behind them. What I do is merely to make it complicated for propagandists to monopolise the term.

AYER:

Ah, something I was interested in: you used the phrase "real" democracy and I think this brings out an interesting, indeed philosophical point, namely what Stevenson called "persuasive definitions". When you say real democracy, the word "real" here is, as it were, an okay word, it's trying to capture assent for your conception of democracy. Not essence, I'm not saying that I mean there is no essence of democracy; the word "democracy" means what we choose it to mean.

And you're therefore trying to capture assent for a certain definition of the word, and of course not simply assent for a certain use of language, but trying to gain adherence to a type of behaviour that is associated with the language. Someone might say, well, real democracy consists not in the right to vote, but in economic equality, shall we say. What he's then doing is trying to capture the favourable word "democracy" for a policy that he advocates. And I think that with questions like how you define democracy, what they're really asking is not in the least how you define the word, they're not asking questions of lexicography, they're asking you for some kind of political programme; the word "democracy" now being one that has got favourable sentiments attached to it. And presumably you arranged your three hundred definitions in some order of desirability. I mean there were some you wanted to be accepted more than others, that even reflected your own political opinions, presumably.

NAESS:

Sure, to do that is very tempting. So far, I have only undermined the use of the slogan "democratic". But, I'm sorry to say, in some ways I feel miserable to be defending scepticism now, because there is a very tragic conflict between the attitude I hold in my integrated and concentrated moments, which is more or less sceptical, and the requirements of consistent action. For instance, when we believe that we really must do something about some terribly pressing problem, we must somehow narrow down our perspective. The vast plurality of possible words—and how do we know in which world we live—are suddenly not only irrelevant, but contemplation of them undermines the willingness and capacity to act. Most people are only willing to act forcefully and consistently when they have a belief in *the* truth and close their minds to all else.

AYER:

But I should have thought this was a field in which a certain kind of scepticism anyhow was very desirable and fruitful. It's very healthy indeed not to listen to the rhetoric about democracy, but to look at the facts. Look and see what actually happens: see how people live their lives, see what is actually done in the law courts, look behind the words to realities. This is in a sense a formal scepticism, although you're not sceptical about the words that we use to mark them with. And I would think there that your approach is thoroughly sceptical and at the same time constructive in this field.

NAESS:

Yes, it's desirable that people should be like you in this way, but mostly they seem not to be like that. The students say that we must get rid of particular textbooks of Naess because they undermine convictions and will undermine collective action now and over the next five years. And this is real; it is a tragedy, because they need rhetoric and dogmatism, I think. Scepticism breeds passivity. I do not feel that way, but the students do.

ELDERS:

But, Sir Alfred, if you are stressing this point of the relationships between certain philosophical schools on one hand and certain values on the other hand, do you see any relation between your empiricism and your role as director of the Humanist Movement in Great Britain?

AYER:

Yes, I see some relation. I don't see a relation in the sense that I would be able to deduce my political or my social views from any set of metaphysical or epistemological principles. I don't think that, in this sense, I have a coherent system or that there can be one. But of course I think that there is some relation, inasmuch that if one has an empirical, even sceptical temper of mind, then one will be hostile to rhetoric, or at least one will look for the facts behind the rhetoric.

I've been a humanist, for example, partly because I could see no reason to believe in the existence of God. And therefore I would be opposed to people who not only maintained this, but also based political or social programmes on it.

I would be a humanist inasmuch as I think I would be professionally opposed to humbug of any kind: the kind of humbug that you too often find in people in power, in judges and people of that sort. And, in a sense, I would expect an empirical philosopher to be radical, although if one looks at history, this isn't always so: Hume, who was the greatest of all empiricists, was in fact, if anything, a Tory. This was partly because of his scepticism. He was so sceptical about schemes of human improvement.

ELDERS:

Like Schopenhauer.

AYER:

Yes. But in general it has certainly been true in the last century or so that there has been a close association, *so* close an association between empiricism and radicalism that it couldn't entirely be an accident. But I think it's a matter of a certain habit of mind, a certain critical temper in the examination of political and social as well as philosophical questions, that is responsible for this, rather than some deduction from first principles.

ELDERS :

Yes, but these are not really arguments, but merely a piece of history.

AYER :

I'm giving you an explanation. You asked me what I thought the connection was, and I ...

ELDERS :

The historical explanation. But we're talking now on the level of arguments about the relation between empiricism and humanism.

AYER :

But it's slightly more than this, because I think a certain habit of mind, a certain critical temper that you would develop if you did philosopy in the sort of way that Naess and I do it, would on the whole tend ... after all, you bring the same intelligence to bear on any of a wide range of problems, even though they aren't necessarily the same problems, and this would, I think, tend to have the effect of making you a liberal radical in social and political questions. This would be more than just an historical accident, as it might be if I happened to be both protestant and have brown eyes; it's not as accidental as that. There is, I think, some causal connection of a very close kind.

But I don't think that I can, from any kind of empiricist premises, deduce a political programme. I mean, you can't get rabbits out of hats that don't contain them. Do you agree ?

NAESS:

Well, no! First of all, you expect that as philosophers we should somehow be able to deduce them, whereas I would say our responsibility is to connect our views—our ethical and epistemological as well as our political views—in a fairly decent way so that we get a coherent whole. The connections may be looser than ordinary scientific connections, looser than deductions. I think we disagree here on how we conceive of our roles as philosophers. I consider myself a philosopher when I'm trying to convince people of non-violence, consistent non-violence whatever happens. That is a fairly fantastic doctrine, considered descriptively or empirically. I must therefore make clear, to myself and others, what kind of normative principles I also make use of, and derive from them the special norms and hypotheses characteristic of Gandhian strategy of conflict behaviour. I think I believe in the ultimate unity of all living beings. This is a very vague and ambiguous phrase, but I have to rely on it. It is a task for analytical philosophy to suggest more precise formulations. Because I have such principles, I also have a programme of action, the main outline of which is part of my philosophy. So I might suddenly try to win you over to consistent non-violence and to persuade you to join some kind of movement—and this in spite of my not believing that I possess any guarantee that I have found any truths.

AYER:

I can see you might indeed try to persuade me of this, but I don't think you'd persuade me of these methods. The ultimate unity of living things: I mean ...

ELDERS:

Is this metaphysics, in your opinion?

AYER:

Well it could be an ordinary scientific statement. In fact it would include not only living things but also inanimate things, if they are all made of atoms; in this sense they are homogeneous. Then I suppose there is more homogeneity between organic things, although the difference between organic and inorganic is so slight.

It doesn't seem to me that on any scientific basis of this sort, one is going to build an ethical view. After all, civil wars take place, and the people who fight each other in them don't deny that they're each human beings and even belong to the same nation: but it doesn't stop the fighting.

So, in fact, this alone is not going to be sufficient. You have to put up some moral principle, which is not going to be deducible from any factual or metaphysical one; that it is wrong to take life of any kind. But do you then extend this to all life, mosquitoes and the like, or just human life? I'm not saying this ironically: I think that it's a perfectly defensible position to be vegetarian and so on—I'm not, but I think ...

ELDERS:

But will you try, Mr. Naess, to give the metaphysical foundation for your belief in non-violence, about which we can speak later? We are still at the level of principles and arguments for or against metaphysics.

AYER:

And it's partly political too, isn't it? It's not just metaphysical. How well Gandhi did against the British, he would have done less well against the Nazis.

NAESS:

Yes, metaphysical and political and anthropological, all at once, all in one: therefore systems are unavoidable. Gandhi as a leader in Germany? Perhaps one million Jews killed before 1938, none after. He advised resistance, not submission. The metaphysical principle here of course belongs more to the Indian than to the European tradition.

AYER:

Yes, I would say so.

NAESS:

But the ecological movement may change the European tradition. The formulation "all living beings are ultimately one", is neither a norm nor a description. The distinction between descriptions and norms and even imperatives can be put in afterwards, semantically speaking. It is the kind of utterance you make in support of something I would call an intuition, by which I do not mean that it is necessarily true. In moments of concentration you are aware of vast perspectives: yes, that is the thing, ultimately life is one!

And then you start to ask yourself how you can argue for this and what does it mean; and at this moment you need a norm, a system of ethics and an ontology and plenty of hypotheses in many fields covered by the sciences. And you say: a mosquito and myself are obviously not biologically the same, so I must mean something different from it. For instance, something like: if I hurt you, I hurt myself. My self is not my ego, but something capable of immense development. Think of a picture from the war: a young man is just going to throw a grenade and there is another young man, the so-called enemy, very similar to him, also intending to do the same at exactly the same moment. It's a case of "him or me"; but they are also obviously aware of the fact that they are the same kind of being and that to throw grenades at each other is really nonsense. They are one.

AYER:

Well, I share your moral sentiments, but I think what you've been saying is very largely just false. It's like the schoolmaster who is going to beat the boy and says "This is going to hurt me more than it'll hurt you". That's an absolute lie; it isn't going to hurt the schoolmaster at all—on the contrary, in only too many cases it's going to give him pleasure.

NAESS:

The boy also if he's a masochist.

AYER:

The boy also if he's a masochist, yes. But, in fact, what you are saying simply isn't true. I mean, not only I and a mosquito, but even you and I are not one. Of course, if I sympathise with you and you are hurt I shall be sorry, but I shan't be hurt in the same way. It's indeed true, empirically true, that to a rather limited extent human beings sympathise with one another; with people they know and like, and people they feel in some way close to. But to say that they're one is in any literal sense just false. I'm not identical with you, and it would be a terrible thing if I were, in a way. [*Laughter.*] I mean, this discussion would be very difficult.

ELDERS

Or it would be much more easy.

AYER:

Ah, well, yes, it would be. It would be even more solipsistic than it sometimes tends to become.

ELDERS:

Growing more and more together.

AYER:

It seems to me that clearly, if one takes these things literally, they're false; and therefore you take them metaphorically. Now, it's just when you take them metaphorically that they become moral principles of a perfectly respectable kind: that you ought to treat other people as though they ... I mean, if you like, as in the Christian way of thinking.... I mean, deal with other people as you wish them to deal with you. They wouldn't necessarily have the same tastes, but in a sense one should treat other people as if they were as important to you as yourself. This is a perfectly good moral principle. But why pretend that we are identical when we are not?

ELDERS:

Now you need some whisky, Mr. Naess?

NAESS:

No, no. You are too rash.

AYER:

He doesn't want to identify with me too much, does he?

NAESS:

Too rash, you are too rash. First of all, there is no definite literal sense of an utterance like this in relation to its metaphorical sense. You have to analyse it from a great many points of view. Its so-called literal meaning is hardly exemplified in any available text; what is the literal sense of the identity of all living beings?

AYER:

Well, I mean it in the sense in which the Evening Star is identical with the Morning Star; in the sense in which the Young Pretender is identical with Charles Edward Stuart; in the sense in which the author of *Pickwick* is identical with the author of *Oliver Twist*: this is what I would call the literal sense of identity. Now it's up to you, since you're not using it in that sense, to define a sense in which you are using it.

NAESS:

That's right.

AYER:

And now I subside.

NAESS:

Good. That's better. [*Laughter.*] Have patience!

When we say that we are the same, three concepts may profitably be interconnected. The ego, the self with a small s, and then this great Self, with a capital S, the atman, which you hear so much about in Indian philosophy, but also, of course, in certain Western traditions. If you as a boy had had a very much wider development, your self, what you take to be part of you, would not only include your body, it would include everything that's yours, so to speak; so what is yours would have been much wider.

This justifies the tentative introduction of an entity, the Self, with a capital S, the power of which gradually increases. You might still say your limits are those of your body, but there you would have to include units of your central nervous systems such as, for instance, those corresponding to the Milky Way and the Andromeda nebula in so far as you have sensuous or other bodily interactions with them.

And in this kind of philosophy they ultimately believe that human beings can develop in such a way, that in a sense their selfs include the other selfs in a certain way.

AYER:

But in *what* sense? In *what* sense does my self include Fons'? Or could it ever, however much I thought of him?

NAESS:

Now you are too impolite. Fons is not utterly different.

ELDERS:

I should like that.

AYER:

I'm sorry, but I don't know, I ... Fons would like it.

NAESS:

Philosophy is just this; that you develop something that

I've started and gradually you introduce preciseness from different directions. Then you breathe three times, reinforce your intuition, and go a little further towards precision. But there is no hurry, this process will take a long time. And of course sometimes intuitions vanish for some of us; for instance, those of "absolute movement" or of an absolute "voice of conscience".

I suppose you would say that the limits of the self gradually increase from infancy to puberty; and the sense in which it increases is, I would say, what you are concerned about. What you identify yourself with ... the norms you internalise.

AYER:
Ah! Now that's, yes ...

NAESS:
And concern in the sense in which you say *my*! You use the possessive term, my—*my* mother, for instance.

ELDERS:
I think in a biological sense we form a chain of divisions; so for example, in this sense, you can use the meaning of the greater Self, against the small self or ego.

NAESS:
Yes, biologically we are just centres of interactions in one great field.

AYER:
But why put things in a portentous way when they can be put in a simple way? Why not say that as you grow older you come to comprehend more things; your knowledge perhaps increases, and then after a certain point, I'm afraid, diminishes again. But up to a point it increases. Perhaps your range of sympathy is greater; perhaps you identify with more things and sometimes again with less.

Again, one can't always generalise; some people differ in this respect, some people narrow themselves in the sense of concentrating more on themselves. When one has a fairly precise method, a precise way of describing all these facts, why does one have to make such portentous statements about one's self expanding and including everything. It sounds romantic, but it's quite superfluous when what you mean can be put quite definitely : that these things happen, and these things are empirically testable. I would say that what you're describing is true of some people, not of others.

NAESS :

Well, what is portentious depends on at which university you are studying.

AYER :

Portentous. I did not say pretentious, that would have been rude, I said portentous.

NAESS :

I meant portentous also : and that depends on the university. If you had been at Oxford or Cambridge at the time of Wittgenstein, it would have been a different thing than what it was at the time of Bradley and of the Hegelians. Trivialism is portentous if carried to extremes. But let us go back to the belief in the pervasiveness of the "I". Well, people then used certain terms about which we now would say "Oh, my God, don't be so portentous". So this is completely relative, I think. There are a million things to be said : must they all begin with "I"? Spinoza introduces the "I" in part two, not in part one, of his system. Do we have a definite ego all the time? Isn't that a weird construction? A Cartesian prejudice? "I developed from this to that" or "Now I am developing more in this direction" or "I was very different when I was thirteen from when I was twelve", and so on —I, I, I!

Must we think that there is such an entity? I wouldn't

simply think there is a definite entity there. Without this scepticism I would not feel "all living things are ultimately one" to be a good slogan.

AYER :

I don't think I disagree with you there. I certainly don't want to postulate any sort of Cartesian substance, anything of which the ego could be a name. I'm very puzzled about this, I don't at all know the answer to it, but I'm inclined to think that you can't find a personal identity except in terms of the identity of the body.

But of course, if that's right, if you can only define personal identity in terms of bodily identity, then your thesis that one's identity could include other people would become false, except if some kind of bodily identification were to take place. I'm not very positive about this, but let us take, say, the relation between you and me. We're about the same age, your self and my self are sitting here now, and two small boys went to school so many years ago. Now clearly there is a physical relation, in the sense that there is a spatio-temporal continuity between these bodies and those ones, and there are also certain causal connections. I mean that what we are thinking now is causally dependent upon what happened to those bodies then. Whether there is more than this I would be inclined to dispute—except for memory, but that again could be held to be a function of physical stimuli.

So I'm inclined, I think, to equate personal identity with bodily identity, but I'm not sure about this.

But even if this equation were shown to be wrong, as it easily might be, I wouldn't want a Cartesian substance. I would want something like a Humean theory of a series of experiences linked by memory and the overlapping of consciousness and so on, so that in this sense I don't want to attach too much importance to the I.

But I think I wanted to say that in whatever way you define the series of experiences which are properly called mine, they are always exclusive of those properly called yours. I don't think that series of experiences from different persons can logically intersect. Although paranormal psychology might produce phenomena that one might want to describe in this sort of way, I don't want to be at all dogmatic about this.

NAESS:

I'm genuinely glad to hear this. I agree concerning the term "experience". Its logic is subjective: insisting on using that term, you are caught in the same trap as Hume.

Perhaps before the year 3000 there will be "hardware" people, let us say people who have abandoned their brains, taking in computers instead. Collectivists may prefer this: it might herald the end of egos. But it couldn't be quite the end, and is perhaps not central to what we are speaking about. More central is the fact that, as a philosopher, I think I have a kind of total view, which would include logic, epistemology and ontology, but also evaluations, and that I do not escape from the relevance of them at any moment. When I'm saying who I am, so to speak, I cannot avoid indicating what kind of evaluations I make, what kind of priorities or values I have, etc. And there it seems to me that we get into a metaphysical area, a "portentous" area, because only there do we realise just how many different conceptions of fact and experience are possible.

I have a feeling that the empiricism that I suspect you are inclined to accept is too narrow, in the sense that you do not admit a commitment to statements which are untestable empirically. I am inclined to say "your thinking is too narrow". Would this hurt you slightly? If I hurt you I hurt myself, which means that if, for instance, I now said something to you and the next moment I thought that it had been unfair of me to say that when I realised that it had hurt you somehow—not that you couldn't easily win an argument—but if it had hurt you, I would have a moment of identification. Phenomenologically there would be "one" hurt, which was not yet "my" experience. I expect you now to jump into psychology and say that when you identify yourself with somebody else this is a matter of psychology, not philosophy, and that we have the empirical evidence from more or less good experiments which can show us to what extent we identify with each other. It has no ontological consequences. If A identifies with B, he remains A.

But for me it is more a question of what in German they would call *Einstellung*; it's something that is not reducible to empirical psychology, because whatever the psychologists find, I would stick to it probably. They are committed to a definite conceptual framework from the very beginning.

AYER:

Yes, I wasn't going to take that move, because I don't think these labels matter all that much: these are classifications for librarians. I think we should be free to say what we like in every field if we like. I was rather going to take up what you said earlier about this question of who I am. I think when I was arguing before I was using it more in what could be called a "passport" sense; for example, who is Arne Naess? I would say that he is someone who answers to such and such a description, whereas you were clearly using it in a wider sense than this. You were meaning by "who am I?" something which has to do with your own conception of yourself. When you said that hurting me would hurt you, this means that it would in some way be injurious not to your identity as the passport Arne Naess, but injurious to your conception of yourself, injurious to the sort of man you like to think of yourself as being. And possibly also if you hurt me it would have repercussions on your own character, and therefore in this sense you've injured yourself. You wouldn't literally feel the pain that I felt, but you would be damaging yourself; which means that you are, in a certain sense, identifying with me, because you regard it as part of your conception of yourself that you don't gratuitously or voluntarily or deliberately hurt other human beings.

Now there seems to be no quarrel here whatsoever. But I think that if there is a difference between us, it is that I make a sharper distinction than you do between what's descriptive and what's normative. I would say that this was simply an announcement of what rightly, to put it in this way, could be called a policy.

I mean, it is perhaps not quite right, it's somehow not so deliberate as that, and it's more important to you than that. But this is a form of life that you're adopting, and something that goes very deep, and you put this forward, if you like, for me either to imitate you or disagree with you.

But, I think that a mistake could only arise, and I should only have a quarrel with you, if you tried to prove it by deducing it from what masqueraded as a statement of fact. If you accept what I have just said as what you mean by "you and I are one" or "you identify with me", then we are talking in sympathy. It's only if you say that you have this policy *because*, and then make this appear as a factual statement, that we then quarrel on intellectual grounds.

ELDERS:

So, in fact, the central question is the relationship between metaphysics and morality.

NAESS:

A norm or a moral injunction should not masquerade as a description; but neither should a statement involving description, for instance factual description, masquerade as a norm. "All living beings are ultimately one" admits partial interpretations or analyses in various directions, descriptive and normative. None seem to be exhaustive, which is typical of good old metaphysical formulae.

Incidentally, the distinction between fact and norm, or injunction, is ultimate: it is not that I think the norms are less normative, but that the descriptions are less descriptive.

Description presupposes, for instance, a methodology of description. A methodology includes at least one postulate, at least one rule. A change of postulates and rules changes the description. This makes the notion of description as opposed to norm a little shaky: therefore I no longer use the term fact. It suggests independence of postulates and rules.

ELDERS:
There we go, Sir Alfred.

NAESS:
I am sorry, I would feel badly if you were to take me as just a Heideggerian or some kind of ...

AYER:
No, no, on the contrary, I mean, I wouldn't ...

NAESS:
I'm not so sure I'm not. I'm quite near Heidegger in a certain sense.

AYER:
Nonsense, nonsense, nonsense!

NAESS:
Yes, we are *Geworfen*. I feel very much that I have been thrown into the world, and that I am still being thrown.

AYER:
Now *why* do yourself this injustice? Why spoil it? Now leave him out, keep him out. How do you know we are thrown into existence. You may have had a very difficult birth for all you remember.

NAESS:
How do I know? How do I know the relevance here of knowledge?

AYER:

Thrown into existence, nonsense.

NAESS:

Perhaps you use the term "know" too often.

AYER:

This should be eliminated.

NAESS:

Let's get away from being thrown into existence ... Yes, I shall try to trust you when you say that I am not thrown!

AYER:

Okay, but I take your earlier point, which I think is an extremely important one, about the vulnerability of the notion of fact.

I think we need the notion of fact, because we do need a distinction between fact and theory at some level: we need some kind of distinction between the deliverances of observation and the explanation for them. But of course it is not a sharp distinction. And if you like to say that what we call facts are already theory-laden, I would say it is a fact that there were more than two glasses on this table, and I should agree that an enormous amount of theory has already gone into this.

And I would share your scepticism about anything that might be called "pure unadulterated fact". I think probably that doesn't exist, that there is already some conceptualisation here, and if you like, conceptualisation is already to some extent normative; pragmatic considerations have already come in, in the way we classify things, since the classifications are based on what we find it useful to do. So I quite agree that the distinction isn't an absolute one. The only question is whether it's relatively strong enough to bear the sort of weight I want to put on it. And I'm again hesitant about this.

NAESS:

I'm glad you are hesitant. But of course, when you say we need a concept of fact, of hard fact, I say some need it sometimes. But who, and when? It's not the great Self, it is the small self that needs limitation: it is when I'm functioning in tough practical situations, but not when I'm deciding what it is worthwhile doing in life, when the very widest perspectives are involved and when one is concentrating and meditating.

AYER:

One needs to make certain distinctions in order to move forward a little bit. You must take certain things for granted in order to make a further step, and then possibly you go back and question other things; otherwise you never start.

NAESS:

Yes, I agree. But it doesn't help you when you're saying that we need a concept of fact, e.g. that this is a glass.

I do not think we need a concept of fact, and we do not even need a concept of knowledge, in what I would call fundamental philosophical discussion. After a lengthy discussion, when we really get down to subtleties and refinements and also fundamentals, the term fact no longer occurs in your speech; neither does the term "I know" occur in mine as far as I can see. But there is this kind of vanishing—somebody said that the state would vanish, though they say it less and less now, I think—and I would talk about the vanishing distinction between description and norm, fact and non-fact: the vanishing distinction, not vanishing facts, but the vanishing distinction ...

AYER:

Well, the vanishing distinction between truth and falsehood?

ELDERS:

No, between fact and interpretation.

AYER:

Well, then I would say I would need the concept of fact to maintain the distinction between truth and falsehood, to maintain some notion of truth as stating *what is so* and falsehood as stating *what is not so*, and using "fact" as a purely general term to cover *what is so*.

NAESS:

But you don't need the term fact in order to maintain the very general distinction between true and false ...

AYER:

I don't need the actual term, but I need some term doing that work.

NAESS:

I don't think so.

AYER:

You don't admit—you do?

NAESS:

Well, not in order to uphold the distinction between true and false. There is a need for the term "fact" in everyday trivialities, like when I pick up this glass and ...

ELDERS:

Well, but in a logical sense you don't need any fact ...

AYER:

No. You could certainly do without the actual term fact, because one can talk of propositions as being made true by states of affairs, by events, by things having certain properties, or whatever. But I still think you need something to stand for what stands on the right-hand side of the equation. You have an equation: such and such a statement is true, if and only if ... and then you assert whatever it is. For instance, "you and I are sitting here" is true *if and only if* you and I are sitting here. Then you want some generic term, it seems to me, to describe these states of affairs that in the last resort verify or falsify all the statements that we make.

I do want some residue of realism, I want something out there that in the last resort makes our statements acceptable or not acceptable: in the end one can't say that anything goes. It's all very well my wanting to believe that I have a thousand pounds, or a million pounds in the bank. I go to the bank and I try to draw it out and it's a fact that the cashier doesn't pay it to me.

And in the last resort one wants some, I don't mind what term you use, but some term, it seems to me, to characterise, in any philosophy, really this ... the brutishness of things, the hard thing you stub your toe against. Yes this, like Dr. Johnson. [*Strikes his fist on the table.*]

NAESS:

Excellent. But it is highly characteristic, I think, of your monumental tradition of empiricism in England, in Britain, I should rather say.

AYER:

England I prefer. I'm not a Scot.

NAESS:

I would say British: the Scots were wonderful empiricists. But when you need a term for something, if you say this: it snows, it does not snow; this is true if something, something ...

AYER:

That's right, the actual stuff.

NAESS:

... then you get the idea: ha, facts. No, that is British, [*laughter*] that is not universal. The Bengali seem never to get the idea, think of Tagore and others ...

AYER:

If it were British, alas, we should be in a much more powerful position than we are. I'm afraid it's becoming American.

NAESS:

Well, I learnt from housewives and schoolgirls another way
of putting it. They say that something is true *if* it *is* so.
Marvellous. It is a little wider than "it *is* so", and much
wider than "it *is* a fact". It's true *if* it *is* so, it's false *if* it
isn't so. Marvellous. But very little is said, of course, concerning testability.

AYER:

But "it's being so" is what I call a fact.

NAESS:

"*If* it *is* so"; we have a conditional there, and there we agree.

AYER:

Yes.

NAESS:

It is only true "*if* it *is* so".

AYER:

Certainly.

NAESS:

But what *is*? What *is* there? And here we must be terribly
comprehensive, if we are to include all living ontological
traditions. And to narrow it down to facts, is to narrow it
down to the British Isles first of all.

AYER:

Oh no, no, no, you mean, only in the British Isles anything
is so? I'd be very sorry to hear this.

NAESS:

No, on the contrary, "anything is so that is so" is more, is broader than "what is a fact?" And the British tradition, which politically speaking is sometimes, I'm glad to say, very good in comparison with the opposite German attitude ...

ELDERS:

With the Labour government or with the Conservatives?

NAESS:

Both, they are identical as far as ...

ELDERS:

Do you agree, Sir Alfred?

AYER:

They're much more similar than I care for.

NAESS:

Yes, and very British.

AYER:

No, when the last government was in power, I thought these are no better than the Conservatives. But now that the Conservative government is in power, they are worse.

NAESS:

When you say "they are worse", would you add: well I just talk like this, it is not part of my philosophy. Personally I would say: this is part or should be part of both our philosophies. "They are worse", you should be able to say that ...

AYER:

I do say that, constantly.

NAESS:

But you might do more than say it, you might take it as part of your personal philosophy, or your *total view*. And there we are; the total view, which is considered unclear, un-empirical, metaphysical in a bad sense. Because if you have a total view, somehow it hangs together and you always see the facts only as structures within a great body of hypotheses.

AYER:

You can't seriously maintain, can you, that every opinion that I hold, or every emotional preference that I have, must be tied up with my philosophy. For example, I'm a lifelong supporter of Tottenham Hotspur, a football team: it is absurd to say this is part of my philosophy and that, had I happened to support Arsenal instead of Spurs, I could not be the positivist pragmatist that I am, but some sort of absolute idealist.

This is being ludicrous. I have lots and lots of opinions about all sorts of things: political opinions, aesthetic opinions. If you like, they're all unified in the sense that it's the same person who holds them; and possibly some very clever psychologist could trace some connection, could realise that there was something in the Spurs type of play that would appeal to philosophers of my sort possibly more than something, shall we say, in the play of Manchester United. But why do we have to go so far? Why not leave me in my compartment?

NAESS:

No, not today. No, if you say "they are worse" and you think of a Labour government, or any other government, you do not mean worse as football players, you mean worse ...

AYER:

I make a moral judgement, yes, certainly.

NAESS:

Partly moral, partly political and economic.

AYER:

Mainly moral.

NAESS:

And to me that means that you are already involved in philosophy. There are degrees of philosophical relevance. Not all moral judgements are part of your system, but all moral judgements of yours should hang together within the framework of your philosophy; let us distinguish frame and details. So every moral judgement you make is relevant to your philosophy without being part of it. The mythical fall of the apple which struck Newton is not described in a physical system, but it is a physically relevant fall.

AYER:

In this sense I don't think I have a philosophy.

NAESS:

I suspect you don't have.

AYER:

I don't think so, no. I don't think that anyone *should* have in this sense.

NAESS:

Should! Another ethical judgement.

AYER:

It seems to me that I have an intelligence such as it is that I....

NAESS:

Here is a moral issue for you. I shouldn't have such a

philosophy—your general statement included me.

AYER:

I think it tends to confuse your thought. I think you'd be a better philosopher if you did not have such a philosophy.

But I don't know, it is such a silly question: are you speaking as a philosopher? What does it matter? Am I speaking as an Old Etonian, am I speaking as a former member of a regiment and so on. I mean, it's irrelevant. The question is: what are you saying and what are the grounds for it and how would you defend it? But this "are you speaking as a such and such?" seems to me to be somehow a red herring. I'm not speaking as a fisherman, I am not a fisherman in fact ... not even of souls. [*Laughter*.] The point is to say: well all right, you hold these principles about the Conservatives; why do you think they're so bad? And then I would say something about the dislike of the kind of businessman's outlook they seem to represent, this "let me make as much money as I can" that is the true characteristic of many of them. This, in a sense, is the theme that runs through their policy and attitudes.

And then you say: "Are you speaking as a philosopher?" I don't know how to answer this if you mean "Do you deduce this from your views about the problem of perception?" No, I don't. If you mean "Is this in any psychologically recognisable sense the same person as wrote those books?" Yes, it is. What more do you want?

NAESS:

I wonder, if you said ...

AYER:

Or was it already enough?

NAESS:

... you shouldn't have a total philosophy; you would be a better philosopher ...

AYER:

I don't say "you should", I say you haven't got a total philosophy.

NAESS:

But you said "you should" ...

AYER:

I also shouldn't have ...

NAESS:

I do not forget it. You said, "I shouldn't have it".

AYER:

Yes, I will maintain that. I'll maintain "you should not". Liking you as much as I do, I change this to "you do not".

NAESS:

Too late!

AYER:

But I'm prepared to maintain also "you should not".

NAESS:

We probably agree that a dogmatic view of all things lacks value, even if it were possible to work it out. But implicitly we pretend to coherence, implicitly we pretend to have methods of how to establish views, empirically or otherwise. In short we implicitly pretend to have views relevant to whatever we say. And those views are personal, not something found in libraries.

I'm inviting you to let us get hold of more of you; and not psychologically or socially, as Mr. So-and-So or Sir So-and-So, but to get to know how you perceive the world, its relation to yourself, the basic features of the condition of man as *you* experience them.

And I call this a philosophy and approximations to a total view.

AYER:

Oh, no, no, no.

NAESS:

Now you try to take that back?

AYER:

No, no, no.

NAESS:

You have said "I don't have".

AYER:

No I don't take it back. Let me put it this way. I don't think that the term "total philosophy"....

NAESS:

Total view.

AYER:

... has any very useful application. What would having a total philosophy imply? Assuming that you do and I don't, in what way, in what concrete way, do we differ? I mean, I also have opinions about politics, ethics, aesthetics and and express them and act on them. But these are not part of a total philosophy in your sense. How would I have to to change, either in these opinions or in the meta-language, in order to have a total philosophy in your sense?

ELDERS:

May I try to formulate a question by which you could per-haps illustrate your point of view? Does your offensive non-violence, Mr. Naess, imply that you would prefer to be killed by someone else rather than kill someone else? Is it part of your philosophy?

NAESS:

It would be more than a preference, actually. It might be that I would *prefer* to kill the other person, but I value the preference negatively. Norms have to do with evaluations, with pretensions to objectivity, rather than preferences. Let me formulate it thus: I hope I would prefer to be killed by someone else rather than to kill, and I *ought* to prefer it.

ELDERS:

And this is a part of your philosophy?

NAESS:

Yes. And it has empirical, logical, methodological, ontological etc. ramifications, like other philosophical issues. It belongs to a greater unity of opinions which *in part* are derived from certain principles of descriptive and normative kinds.

ELDERS:

And how is it for you, Sir Alfred?

AYER:

I should, I think, disagree. Although it's a very difficult question I can imagine situations certainly in which I should prefer to kill someone rather than be killed by them, in which I should in fact try to kill someone rather than allow him to kill me.

After all we were both, I assume, in the war and there these situations arose. But I don't see in fact how this fits in. Because supposing I gave a different answer from the answer that he gave or indeed suppose I gave the same one, how would this in either case be part or not be part of a total philosophy?

It might of course in some situations be an extremely

important concrete moral question; but what I am denying when I reject that sort of philosophy is that the way either of us answers a question of this kind has any relation, any logical relation, to our views, for example, on probability or on the theory of knowledge, or on the mind-body question, even on such questions as the freedom of the will. Whatever our theoretical views about the freedom of the will, I can't see that they would settle a question of this kind one way or the other. I mean, we might both be determinists in theory and yet take different views about this; or we might one of us believe in free will, the other in determinism and take the same view. When I was sceptical and said you shouldn't have this total philosophy, what I meant was that I can't see what the links are supposed to be to make the totality.

But of course I have opinions on all these matters and very strong ones, although in this particular case I think I would probably dissent from you. I think I'm not a total pacifist. I haven't been in the past, and I think I can imagine circumstances in which I shouldn't be in the future. I think if something like the Nazis were to reappear, I would want to defend myself against them as I did then.

NAESS :

There is a relation between not wanting to kill somebody else, even in a fight, and epistemology; because any question which you answer implies a methodology. And this also holds good for the question "Would you prefer to be killed rather than to kill?" In order to answer this I must have a kind of methodology to find out whether I would. All fields of inquiry are interrelated, therefore we implicitly must pretend to cover them all when giving any answer whatsoever. We presuppose a total survey from mathematics to politics.

AYER :

May I put this concretely? Suppose that either you or I held a physicalist's view of human beings, something like Gilbert Ryle's *The Concept of Mind*. Suppose you were a behaviourist and thought of the mind as the ghost in the machine and so on, do you think that this would then entail an answer one way or the other to your question? Do you think that Ryle, for example, is in some way logically committed to giving a different answer to this question from the one that you would give?

NAESS:

No, I don't think it would entail this. But I think that certain views cohere more or less and that it's the business of a philosopher today to try out to what extent they cohere; to what extent they're not only logically consistent, for that would leave us too free, but also coherent in their non-logical aspects.

AYER:

Do you think that this view of the mind would even favour one answer to this moral question more than another? I mean, could you deduce simply from Ryle's book, other than psychologically, even in a semi-logical way, what moral position, what view he would take on this moral question?

NAESS:

I think that if you made different combinations of interpretations, it favours, so to speak statistically, the acceptance of violence. But we would be capable of reconstructing it in such a way that it would not favour violence. And this is an important thing. A book like Ryle's leaves things implicit: presuppositions, postulates, methodological rules. No single, *definite* set can be said to be presumed, therefore there will be a plurality of interpretations and a plurality of reconstructions.

And I agree with you, it is too easy to talk about a total view and to say "I have one". I detest questions like "What is your total view?"

AYER:

Yes.

NAESS:

Yes.

AYER:

Well, there you see how much I sympathise with you.

NAESS:

We cannot have a total view in the sense that we are somehow inescapably linked to certain definite opinions; nor can
we behave like a general surveying an army of possible
views and pick out some, saying these are my views—the
relationship between ourselves and our views are too inti-
mate.

AYER:

I should have thought, in fact, that your general philosophical position, with which I sympathise, went entirely the
opposite way, and that the tendency would be to see each
question independently on its own merits; not to feel that
you were committed by your answer to this one, by any
answer to that one.

NAESS:

Not any longer.

AYER:

Not any longer?

NAESS:

No, because I feel that as a philosopher I am an acting
person, not an abstract researcher. Even this discussion is not
really some kind of a contemplative affair; it is also a kind of
continuous action all the time.

AYER:

Indeed, indeed. In certain things you then require more
coherence in action than you do in theory. You don't mind

your theories being incoherent, but you want your actions to be coherent.

NAESS :

In research I tend to adopt an almost playful attitude in the sense of looking at and pleasurably contemplating more combinations of views than anybody else. More kinds of common sense even! But as an acting person I take a stand, I implicitly assume very many things, and with my Spinozist leanings towards integrity—being an integrated person as the most important thing—I'm now trying to close down on all these vagaries. I am inviting you to do the same.

AYER :

But, why should I ...

NAESS :

As a person you may have such a high level of integration that if you took some years off and tried to meditate a little more, you would be able to articulate some of your basic evaluations. These are more than inclinations; Jaspers calls them *Einstellungen*. They determine or at least express an important part of what would be your total view.

AYER :

It's not a prospect that I find at all desirable. Failure to be articulate has never been my problem, I think.

NAESS :

I think so.

AYER :

Well, there are hidden problems perhaps, I don't know.

NAESS :

Too fast, you're too fast.

AYER :

Yes, but I say a lot of things twice, that's alright, I catch it on the second time round.

I don't know; why should integrity demand consistency? One thinks that it does, but why shouldn't one judge things differently when the circumstances are always different? Why shouldn't one have the same flexibility in one's moral and political judgments as one wants for one's theoretical ones? I suppose one thinks that people are insincere if they don't maintain similar opinions in similar cases; but then the question of even what cases are similar is theoretically difficult.

I don't know: I dislike what you have just said—I think it's really the first thing that you have said at all, that I *have* disliked. This seems to me to be really a conception of, well, I don't mind if it's called philosophy or not, and I don't mean that someone's trying in all honesty to solve problems that he thinks important, theoretically important or even practically important, but that somehow this represents a kind of deep narcissism, a digging down into oneself, contemplating: I'm not concerned with this. All right, it is possible that if I spent a year meditating I should perhaps dig up some very pleasant things; I don't know, I don't care. I've got better things to do in a way. I've got this problem, that problem, the other problem, I've got a certain intelligence, I'm going to use it for as long as it lasts. And perhaps, when I'm gaga I'll start contemplating in your sense.

NAESS :

Too late!

AYER :

And of what interest will that be to anybody?

ELDERS :

I'll ask the same question, but not on a personal level. Would you say Mr. Naess, that in your total philosophy intellectuals have a special responsibility at this moment?

NAESS:

Yes, because they are highly articulate. They are trained at universities in situations where they have at least three-quarters of an hour to think what could be argued against this, what could be argued against that; they get to be narrow and clever, too clever. I think that intellectuals might consider their intellects in a more Spinozistic way, as *intellectus* in the Spinoza way, and cultivate *amor intellectualis*.

ELDERS:

Can you translate it?

NAESS:

Amor intellectualis would be a kind of loving attitude towards what you have insight into, while considering it in an extremely wide perspective. And intellectuals might do this without making the terrible mistake of becoming sentimental or fanatical. They would be able to say things to people in a more direct way and to articulate evaluations, their attitudes—*Einstellungen* or total attitudes—in a very forceful way while at the same time using some of the, in a narrow sense, intellectual training they have acquired in the universities.

They should be able to make us feel that to elaborate total views that are not expressive of something like "I am more clever than you are" is neither portentous nor necessarily favours some kind of fanaticism. When I say that you are, perhaps, deficient in articulation, it is because I feel you jump too fast to particular opinions on so-called facts, instead of taking a broad view and letting yourself say things which sound portentous and which might make you sound like a rhetorician or a politician, or even a prophet.

In this way I think that the intellectual of today, and especially the philosophically educated one, has a larger and

wider function than that of being analytically minded. I'm
sorry I use that catchphrase.

AYER:

Well, I don't disagree with you on the question he asked.
I do think that intellectuals obviously have a responsibility
to do their job as they see it, and as well as they can do it;
and also, I think, a social responsibility. I'm not a believer in
the ivory tower at all; I think that anyone who has the
capacity to think and to reason and perhaps believes, rightly
or wrongly, that he can see things clearly, *should* try to
contribute to social and even to political questions, so I
don't in the least dissent from you there. I don't think that
we quarrel at all about what we should be doing. What
I think we may quarrel about is perhaps *how* we should
do our job, and you might think that I do it in the wrong
way.

NAESS:

Well, couldn't you send me a copy of a speech made by
you about a political situation?

AYER:

Indeed, I could send many. I mean, I'm constantly doing
this; I've even stood for office, but I lost. I've stood on soap-
boxes on street-corners....

NAESS:

And there you use descriptions and norms.

AYER:

Ah, mainly normative, my language is then pretty emotive.

NAESS:

May I ask for instance, could you act as if you were now
on a political platform? Say something real, "Bang!" like
this.

AYER :
Well, I think that you can't. Political speeches are not made
in the abstract. But if I knew local politics, I daresay I could
make quite an effective political speech. I would point out
how one side was acting in its own interest, more than the
other, and how such and such a measure was perhaps an
attempt to preserve privileges, or was associated with cor-
ruption, and all this would be highly charged emotionally.

Of course, we have to have facts behind it; it's no good
saying so-and-so is corrupt, unless you produce some
evidence. But these two elements are mixed, obviously; and
political speech has got to be factual, but with emotive
overtones.

ELDERS :
What's your attitude towards the Common Market?

AYER :
This I regard as a factual and technical question. I'm
emotionally in favour of it, in the sense that I'm in favour
certainly of larger units, against nationalism.

But economically I simply don't know; whether from the
point of view of the ordinary English man in the street the
economic price will become too high or not. And the
economists are totally in disagreement. So, as a rational
man, I suspend judgment. But I myself, if you like, feel
European. I am by origin not purely English, I have some
French blood, even on my mother's side Dutch, and therefore I'm emotionally in favour of a larger unit.

But I think this is partly a question of fact where I acknowledge ignorance. Whereas Naess, with his total
philosophy, brings in different little facts. If he doesn't
believe in facts, then why should he joke about them in
this issue?

NAESS :
This is rhetoric, isn't it? (*Laughter.*)

AYER:

Of course it was, yes.

NAESS:

You shouldn't immediately give up so quickly in this way. Behind the rhetoric there are sets of value judgments.

I'm in a fight against Norway joining the Common Market. And one of the main things I'm against is putting larger units in place of smaller ones. I think that the larger units achieve greater technological advances and larger units of production instead of getting together with other people in a nice personal way. We will get bigger markets, more standardised products, and we will take over some clever ideas from British universities instead of using our own less clever ideas about the university.

AYER:

I would think that some ideas from Norwegian universities might even be more clever than the ones I get at Oxford.

NAESS:

I doubt it, really. On the whole we are not clever, but we are provincial in the good sense of living our own way undisturbed by pressures from the great centres.

For me the question of whether to join the Common Market is not merely a factual and technical question. I am trying to connect my fight against the Common Market with basic evaluations. What are our value priorities? I see other people without analytical training taking up a philosophical point of view. I try to help them articulate their implicit systems in order to connect their ways of feeling with ways of asserting and evaluating things. Doing this I still feel myself to be philosophical and intellectual, whereas you would say it's more emotional, it's my emotional inclinations.

AYER:

No, I don't think so: on the contrary. I just said I thought it was partly a rational question, but I suspended judgment because I don't believe I have enough evidence. I mean I don't let my emotions dominate me here, because emotionally I'm attracted to the idea, but I suspend judgment as I'm not convinced of it intellectually.

ELDERS:

So you couldn't be a good politician?

AYER:

I'd be a rotten politician, yes.

NAESS:

Just a minute. You couldn't be convinced intellectually? There I think you again use too narrow a concept of intellect....

AYER:

No, I mean that if I were to take a final decision, it would depend, in part, upon the answers to certain economic questions, to which I don't think I know the answers.

NAESS:

Well, again you are displaying something narrow, I think— no, not narrow, but something peculiarly empirical—when you talk of a final judgment. But I can't make a final judgment about anything political, in a sense, because all the time that I am acting and being acted upon here all my judgments will be provisional.

But in spite of being decidedly against the Common Market, I could say that the range of facts known to me is probably narrower than yours, I know perhaps less about the Common Market. Decisions cannot wait until all the facts are gathered: they are never all available.

AYER:

Well, I hope the judgment is only final in the sense in which the reaction might be irreversible.

ELDERS :

Irreversible, yes. Well, perhaps I could now ask my final and I think most difficult question; a question about the audience : do you think we have managed to get through to the audience, both here and at home?

AYER :

Yes, I think, in part. I mean, how can one possibly tell? I do think that we have got through to the audience here, in the sense that nobody walked out, and nobody threw things.

But inasmuch as we were both talking seriously and saying things we believed and things that interested us, and on the whole not trying to score off one another but trying to get at what truth there is in these matters, then I should hope that this at least would get through.

And perhaps, when one looks at two philosophers talking, this is what one wants to get through : the idea that these questions are important, some idea of what sort of questions they are, and some idea that one can really seek the truth about them without, perhaps, any notions of personal advancement.

ELDERS :

And you, Mr. Naess?

NAESS :

I trust that we have got through to a limited extent, of course. I feel sure many people have turned off and are looking at something else.

ELDERS :

Well, may I now suggest that we have a short discussion with the audience? Perhaps we could agree about time; I suggest a discussion of half an hour.

AYER :

It has taken very long already.

ELDERS:

You would like to relax a little?

AYER:

I must say it was not an easy passage of time.

ELDERS:

Yet you have not walked out, Sir Alfred, after an hour and ten minutes. Well, may I have the first question?

AYER:

Get one done, yes.

QUESTION:

In the beginning, Sir Alfred, you gave a definition of philosophy which was entirely a negative definition. Philosophy is a kind of criticism, a criticism of belief and a criticism of knowledge, but I feel a certain tension between that kind of definition of philosophy and the opinions on everyday matters that you have, and which you derive from what you call natural belief, or what is part of natural belief.

AYER:

Or common sense.

QUESTION:

Well, what is the relation between that positive conception of a rational belief or a rational certainty of the world that you have, and your negative definition of philosophy? And that question is related to another one—and here I feel that perhaps Mr. Naess would have another opinion—namely that natural belief is a thing which for itself has a criterion; you have criteria in order to be certain about certain things. But there can be different kinds of certainty, and so different kinds of natural belief. Why do you have *this* kind of natural belief and not another?

I don't know if this is perfectly clear, but I could elucidate this by giving an example. For instance, I imagine that

I believe in ghosts, or I believe in the existence of Australia, where I have never been. I could give criteria for believing in ghosts, as I could give criteria for believing that Australia exists.

They would be the same kind of criteria. I've never seen either of them, never perceived them, never heard them, but I've read about Australia, and I've read about ghosts.

And I think that if you conceive natural belief in that way, then it could be possible to have another kind of natural belief; for instance in werewolves. I could be instantly afraid of you, for instance, because I saw a certain glance in your eyes which would be for me an indication that you were a werewolf.

ELDERS:

Is the question clear?

AYER:

Yes, it's clear to me, I think. On the first part, I didn't intend my definition to be a purely negative one, and wouldn't in fact think it to be so. I mean that in one's questioning of accepted beliefs, or really of the criteria underlining accepted beliefs, one's attempt to clarify concepts, one can quite often come up with a positive answer. And I think there are examples in the history of philosophy; for example, Hume clarified the concept of cause, and I think that as a result of Hume's work one understands much better than people understood before what is involved in causation. I think he showed that the popular concept of causation was, to a very large extent, if you like, super-stitious; but that there is then a residue remaining which can be clarified and be made quite precise. And I think, for example, that the concept of truth has been clarified, first by Aristotle and more recently by Tarski and so on; and, at present, I am myself working on the concept of probability, and other people have worked on it. And I think that through this, one often arrives at something positive.

I don't at all want to say that one has to come to rest in scepticism, but only that scepticism was a kind of challenge posed to the philospher, one which sometimes he didn't need, sometimes he left alone, but sometimes at least it provoked him into providing an answer, which was at least provisionally acceptable. I think I agree with Naess here that it's always only provisional.

I think the second half of your question was in fact very important and profound, because I think there is a kind of relativism here that is in a sense inescapable. The reason why we all believe in Australia when many of us haven't been there, is that it fits in with our general conceptual scheme; there is nothing surprising to us that there should be a country on the other side of the world. We have a spatio-temporal framework into which you fit things: we already have a scientific, and after all, very fine, well-tested belief that the earth is round, so that there should be a country at the antipodes is something that comes quite naturally to us, so that here we accept testimony; we could go there and see for ourselves, but we don't bother to.

Now ghosts, even though they might be well-attested— let's assume, for the sake of your question, that the evidence in favour of apparitions is even stronger than it is, or, much stronger than it is—there we become more cautious because it doesn't fit into our way of organising the world.

Now you might say, why not? After all this has been true of some primitive peoples, so why don't I see you, not just as another man, but as, potentially, a werewolf, a being with all sorts of magical powers and so on?

Now, this could be a way of organising my experience and it's a way in which people of other communities have, to some extent, organised their experience; and, in a sense, I can't refute it, except by begging the question against it; except by assuming all sorts of metalogical criteria which are inconsistent with it.

So, in the last resort, I think, the answer here is pragmatic, in the way that it seems to me that, with a system of explanation of the sort I have, I explain phenomena more satisfactorily, I make more successful predictions, than I do with an animistic system.

But if someone likes to see the world animistically, I don't think that I can refute him, because, as Naess pointed out in our discussion earlier on, the notion of fact is itself a dubious one, itself infected by theory. And I could say, well ...

ELDERS:
You've nearly converted him.

AYER:
... in a sense I'm more successful with my type of theory than he would be with his.

ELDERS:
Well, Sir Alfred, he has nearly converted you.

NAESS:
No, no, what I would say is that I listened with pleasure, because there you used some kind of a concept of *total view*. And so I congratulate *you* for making Sir Alfred show in practice that he is very near to thinking in terms of a total view.

AYER:
Oh, in this sense, if you like to think of one's language and what's implied by one's language and one's general method as a total view, then certainly. I think connections are much looser within the conceptual system than you're making them out to be. But to this extent, certainly.

ELDERS:
Ladies and gentlemen, this has to be the end of this debate.
Sir Alfred, Mr. Naess, thank you very much for your total, clear discussion, on behalf of the audience, here and at home.

SIR KARL POPPER
and
SIR JOHN ECCLES

Falsifiability and Freedom

Falsifiability and Freedom

ELDERS:

Ladies and gentlemen, I welcome you to a discussion between Sir Karl Popper and Sir John Eccles.

Sir Karl has become famous three times in his life. The first time was in 1935, when his *Logik der Forschung* was published. The second time was in 1945, when *The Open Society and its Enemies* appeared. And the third time was in 1959, when an English translation of *Logik der Forschung* was published under the title *The Logic of Scientific Discovery*. And perhaps, Sir Karl, the fourth time will be this evening.

Sir John is a famous scientist, who received the Nobel Prize in 1963 for his investigations in the field of neurophysiology and medicine. He is a scholar who is deeply convinced that all sciences have a philosophical foundation, which is in fact common to all sciences and to all discussion.

Sir Karl and Sir John are close friends on a personal and philosophical level. Nevertheless there are substantial differences between them in some fields, particularly in philosophical anthropology.

I hope and anticipate that this combination of the philosophical and the scientific approach to problems will make this discussion an intellectual event of the first order.

Sir Karl, one of the dangerous pitfalls in this kind of philosophical debate is the clash between the expectations of the public, who regard philosophers as old, wise men—wiser, at any rate, than other men—and the theoretical discussions of philosophers, who often deny that they are wiser than other men, but still have enormous pretensions. What is your opinion of yourself as a philosopher, and other philosophers, in relation to the expectations of the public?

POPPER:

I certainly do not think that I am wise.

I became a philosopher more or less without intending to do so. I started as a cabinet-maker, and it was while working on a delivery of two dozen writing-desks that I was more or less converted to philosophy ... and to writing-desks. (*Laughter.*)

I think that we are all philosophers; that we all accept certain philosophical theories, if only unconsciously. Many of the theories we accept are very poor, and we are often not aware that we have accepted them. In my view, the main task of philosophy is to examine critically the philo-sophical theories which people—and I include myself—are liable to accept uncritically.

Let me give you a simple example of such a philosophical theory which is uncritically accepted by many people. It is the following. Suppose something goes wrong in society; that something happens which we recognise to be unfor-tunate; suppose, say, that there is a period of high unem-ployment or of inflation, or that there is a war. People will often assume that someone, or some group of people, must have *intended* that it should happen; that everything that happens in society is the result of someone's, or some group of people's, *intending* that it should occur: that there is a kind of *conspiracy* behind it. I have called this view the "conspiracy theory of society", and I have often criticised it. Not only do I not believe in it, but I think it is a dangerous, not to say a mischievous, theory. While, of course, *some* things happen because people intend them to happen, many things—for example the delay that occurred in our discus-sion's starting tonight—occur without any conspiracy's being responsible for them, and even when everyone in-volved does not want them to happen.

ELDERS:

And what is your opinion about philosophers, Sir John?

ECCLES:

Well, I suppose I should also start off at the beginning, like Sir Karl.

When I was a medical student aged seventeen or eighteen, I suddenly came up against the problem: What am I? What is the meaning of my existence as I experience it? And I proceeded to read quite a lot about what the philosophers, the psychologists, and people like Freud had said. I spent my spare time as a medical student reading all this literature and was profoundly dissatisfied with it. So I decided that I didn't know enough about the brain, and the brain was the essence of all my consciousness—of everything that I knew myself to be, my memories and imaginings and so on.

So what did I do? I decided that I would learn something about it, so I decided to become a neural scientist and went to Sherrington at Oxford and worked with him. I thought in a few years I could know enough about the brain and how it worked; and then I could come back and attack the philosophers and the psychologists on their own grounds. And my life has been a matter of progressive postponement of the philosophical commitment, because I became so intensely interested and involved in how the brain works.

But I have ventured into philosophy in the last few years, and last year some of my lectures were produced as a book. That's why I am here, I suppose, because I did write a book on philosophy. It's a personal philosophy and it gives you my thoughts now. I'm sure that it is going to be very unfashionable with most philosophers, and I don't mind. I don't mind being out of fashion. Every age has people in it who are out of fashion in that age, but they may matter for the next age. I have hopes that I may ... matter. (*Laughs with a little sigh.*)

ELDERS :

Sir Karl, can you explain in a nutshell the meaning of your famous falsifiability criterion, and its relation to your critical philosophy?

POPPER :

The term "falsifiability criterion" is in itself a technical term, and I could just as well do without it. I do not like discussing terms, or words, or concepts, for it is theories that are important and their relation to the problems they are put forward to solve. Terms or concepts are merely instruments we use when stating theories. I will explain the problem I was concerned with.

In 1919, when I was seventeen—about the same age as Sir John when he came up against the problem he has described to us—I was struck by a problem somewhat similar to his. It concerned the tremendous difference between the attitude of some phycisists towards physics and some psychologists towards psychology.

What interested me so much was the following. Some psychologists (I have in mind particularly Adler and Freud) had at this time gained quite a reputation. They had put forward theories about human behaviour, and they gave us accounts of case histories which confirmed their theories; and it was generally accepted that the theories were scientific. Einstein also became famous at this time because of his prediction of an unexpected effect during solar eclipses. He had predicted that if you observe the sun during an eclipse, then the stars near the sun that become visible would appear to be further removed from each other than when they are not in the same part of the sky as the sun.

Now what struck me about Einstein was not only that he made predictions, but that he said that if the predictions should be unsuccessful, then his theory would be false.

But consider the theories of Freud and Adler. Here there is a striking difference, for it is difficult to think of any action a man could perform that could not be explained in terms of their theories. Suppose that a man jumped into a river in order to try to save the life of a drowning child, putting his own life at risk. An explanation of his action can easily be offered by a proponent of Freud's or Adler's theories. But consider a man who pushes a child into a river, drowning the child. Again, an explanation in terms of either theory is at hand. In fact, it would seem that, *whatever anyone does*, both theories would be able to explain it. There is no action which we could not explain in terms of those theories.

To bring out the contrast, let us suppose that the glass on the table in front of me began to hop along the table. Suppose that we investigated it, and found that there was nothing unusual about the glass, and that other things in the room stayed much the same as before. In that case, we would have to consider many theories—Newtonian theories and Einsteinian theories—to be refuted. There are a great many things, in fact an infinite number of things, which could happen which are incompatible with Newton's and Einstein's theories. But let us suppose that our Chairman began to hop along the table. It would not be difficult to provide a psycho-analytic explanation of his behaviour.

These reflections led me to put forward the following suggestion: a theory is empirical and scientific only if it is refutable. That is to say, the theory in question must say, at least in principle, that certain things cannot occur; and a theory will be the better the more daring it is, the more refutable it is. Thus, I argued on these grounds that the theories of Freud and of Adler were not good scientific theories (although it is my view that Freud's ideas are very interesting and that they may well, eventually, be developed into testable scientific theories); I have also argued that the vague predictions of the astrologers should not be counted as being scientific. One point which follows from my approach is particularly worth stressing. It is that we should not be impressed by positive evidence for theories unless this evidence was obtained in situations where the theory in question was taking a risk of being wrong. Thus, if *any* behaviour will confirm a psychological theory, then we cannot invoke evidence from the explanation of behaviour in support of our theory. And if our astrological predictions are so vague, or so commonplace, that they take no risk of being wrong, then we cannot claim that their success in any sense supports our theory. But even if a theory *is* scientific, we should remember that it is always possible that it will in fact be refuted the next time we test it. As a result, we must not suppose that even "genuine" confirmations or "corroborations" of a theory give us grounds for supposing that our theory is certain, or even probably true.

If a theory is refuted, it retires to the realm of theories which were, at one time, scientific, but which are no longer scientifically accepted. Thus, there is a difference between the refutation of a theory and its refutability or falsifiability.

ELDERS:

But can you demonstrate, Sir Karl, the superiority of your falsifiability criterion over the verifiability criterion or principle of the Logical Positivists of the Vienna Circle?

POPPER:

I was born in, and grew up in, Vienna. While I was living there, a discussion group or "circle" of very interesting people—scientists, mathematicians, logicians, and philosophers—was formed, and crystallised around the philosopher Moritz Schlick. This group is usually called the Vienna Circle. Under the influence of another philosopher, Ludwig Wittgenstein, who has since become very famous, its members tried to solve a problem similar to the one that interested me. They were interested, as was I, in distinguishing between science and metaphysics. However, there was a most important difference between the problem that they tried to tackle and the one that I was interested in.

The difference was this. The members of the Circle were primarily interested in finding a criterion of sense or meaning. They were opposed to all traditional philosophy, and they hoped to establish that it was actually *nonsense*. Their view was that only science makes sense, and their problem was to find a criterion which would enable them to call science sense and philosophy nonsense. The criterion that they suggested was *verifiability*. This, incidentally, happened years after I had had my idea of falsifiability, an idea which I had not, at the time, thought important, and which I had not published despite the fact that someone had suggested that I should. I was very young, and I thought that everyone must know something that seemed rather obvious to me.

The view at which the Vienna Circle arrived was this. Language falls into two parts. One part is nonsense. Not only, they claimed, does this part include such babblings as "be-ba-bo", but also the whole of philosophy. Their view was that only science is meaningful; only science, as opposed to philosophy, is capable of producing real sense. They said that the criterion of sense is *verifiability*, and they claimed that you can establish the truth, and even the certainty, of scientific propositions by verifying them. If you had verified something, you would, in their view, have in your pocket something that was certain, something that was both *science* and *sense*.

There were really two differences between my approach and the approach of the Vienna Circle. First of all, the problem that I wanted to solve was that of the difference between *science* and *non-science*, rather than between *science* and *nonsense*. I did not want to say that an astrologer was talking nonsense : I would readily admit that he was talking sense. *My* contention was that he was not talking science, as he might claim, but pseudoscience. This was one difference between my views and those of the Vienna Circle.

Secondly, I did not want to say that all philosophy is non-sense. My view was that philosophy is non-scientific, at least in so far as it cannot be refuted. The part of philosophy which cannot be refuted is certainly not science, but this does not mean that it is bad, and has to be rejected. I must emphasise that refutability or falsifiability is *not*, in my view, a criterion of sense. There can be good philosophy which, although it cannot be refuted, can be rationally discussed. For example, if a certain philosophical view has been proposed to solve a particular problem, you can ask : does it *solve* the problem? If it does not solve the problem it was produced to solve, or merely shifts the problem without contributing anything towards solving it, then this constitutes a criticism of the philosophy. Thus it may be possible to criticise a philosophical thesis even if it is not falsifiable. If, on the other hand, the philosophical view in question offers a solution of the problem, then it is *perhaps* a good philosophy.

So, unlike the Circle, I was not against all philosophy; neither was I a philosopher of sense and nonsense. The Vienna Circle made the distinction between sense and nonsense its central interest. And it so happens—and here is the similarity between our problems—that they said that their criterion of sense was also a criterion of scientific character: verifiability was to do both jobs. I said that the criterion of scientific character, which is *not* a criterion of sense at all, is falsifiability.

However, there arose what may be called the Popper legend. It assumed that since I came from Vienna, and the members of the Circle were in Vienna, and since both I and the members of the Circle were interested in science, I must have been a member of the Vienna Circle. In fact, I was never a member of the Circle. I was never present at a meeting of the Circle, although I should have gladly gone had I been invited.

The second point of the Popper legend was that certain difficulties arose within the Vienna Circle about their verifiability criterion of sense, and that I was responsible for proposing a change from a *verifiability* criterion of *sense* to a *falsifiability* criterion of *sense* in the hope of avoiding these difficulties.

If you have followed me so far (I am afraid it may seem a

little abstract) you will see that not one word of the legend is true. Not only was I never a member of the Vienna Circle, but the difficulties that beset the Vienna Circle were pointed out by me, as a result of my criticism of their views. I discovered the difficulties and showed that their criterion of sense was not practicable. And I did not try to rescue them from these difficulties. Rather, I thought that the problem that they had set themselves, the problem of sense and non-sense, was a mistaken problem, a problem which it was a mistake to take seriously. My falsifiability criterion was a solution to a different problem. My problem was not to find a criterion which would enable us to kill traditional philosophy by saying that it was nonsense; my problem was to make a distinction between Einstein and Freud; or between Einstein and, for example, the astrologers.

Thus, there were different problems and different solutions, and the difficulties of the verifiability criterion were not the *reason* why I introduced the falsifiability criterion; rather, it was the other way round. It was the falsifiability criterion which enabled me to discover the difficulties of the verifiability criterion. That, roughly, is the story.

ELDERS :

Sir Karl, I have an impression that the difference between your falsifiability criterion and the verifiability criterion is also relevant to the question of the meaning of life and death. I would suggest that the falsifiability criterion explicitly implies the idea that life and death are intrinsically interconnected, while the verifiability principle is more one-sided, that is to say, only life-directed. Are you of the same opinion ?

POPPER :

You may be right, but it is a tremendous jump from what we have just been discussing.

In order to try to fill the gap between your question and what I have said, I might perhaps mention that the falsifiability criterion is generally connected with what, following Pierce, I call "fallibilism"; with the fact that all men are fallible.

This idea of fallibilism is of great importance, for it suggests to us that we should always be critical of our ideas and ready to spot mistakes in them. It is also at odds with the idea that we can attain certainty in our knowledge. I believe that we can only attain certainty in a few, very limited, areas of knowledge. The proponents of the verifiability criterion, however, went all out for certainty.

There is perhaps a very loose connection between the question of life and death on the one hand and the questions of fallibilism versus certainty and of falsifiability versus verifiability on the other. The connection is that life is one of those things which are very uncertain; we are all bound to die, and death could come upon us at any time. My emphasis on the fallibility of human knowledge, and on its uncertainty, is, I think, more in accord with this aspect of the human situation than is the attitude of those who seek certainty.

ELDERS:

Well, I expect we will make more such jumps later in the evening.

Sir John, your first encounter with Sir Karl in New Zealand was a great, perhaps even a decisive influence on your scientific method and your philosophy of science. Would you explain what your scientific method was before and after your meeting with Sir Karl?

ECCLES:

Yes! It is very nice to remember an occasion like this.

I had grown up, as I mentioned, in Oxford with Sherrington, and had accepted the ordinary philosophy of science there, namely that you do experiments, you do enough on one problem and you publish the results, then you go on and do some more on the next problem and so on. You have a good main stream of investigation; and as a good scientist, you should not be wrong. To publish something which turned out to be wrong and to espouse some view which later on had to be retracted, was in fact a very serious thing for a scientist.

So, I had gone on as a young man fighting for a view of transmission between a nerve-fibre and a nerve-cell at the synapse or between a nerve fibre and a muscle fibre, believing with others that this was essentially electrical. The impulse runs down the nerve fibre by an essentially electrical process and we believed that it also jumped by electrical action across the synaptic gap and so goes on.

Dale and Loewi, for example, had proposed alternatively the idea that transmission across the gap was a chemically mediated action. That, when the nerve impulse reached the synaptic gap, it caused the secretion of acetylcholine, a special chemical substance which acted across the gap and started the electrical responses on the other side.

I accepted this chemical transmission for slower actions, but not for something as fast as when a nerve-impulse excites a muscle fibre across the gap, where it takes only half a thousandth of a second. I thought that it couldn't be done with such finesse and speed by chemical transmission.

In the 1930's I developed these views with many other people. I think about half of scientific opinion was for the electrical and half for the chemical explanations of the fast transmissions. We admitted the chemical transmission for slower actions. Dale and Loewi were awarded the Nobelprize in 1936 for their work on chemical transmission. However I still fought against it for the fast transmissions, and in Sydney I did further work with Katz and Kuffler. I still believed that it was electrical, but I was getting more and more concerned that I may have made a terrible error and that I was almost, you might say, a failure in science. This causes you to suffer very much.

Then a little later in 1944 I met Sir Karl. He came down from Christchurch to Dunedin, a little university town in the South Island of New Zealand.

At that time he was at Christchurch and he came at my invitation to give a course of lectures about falsifiability. He inspired me enormously, because then I realised for the first time that there are two essential things in science: one is to have imagination, to dare, to adventure, to go with ideas beyond what you know, and the other is then to test those ideas in the most rigorous way. You put up your brain-child and you try to shoot it down. And in that way you can advance most effectively in science.

He inspired me with this, so I immediately developed my rather vaguely formulated electrical theory of synaptic excitation and published it in a quite precise manner, and later I developed another electrical theory for synaptic inhibition that was also published. So there were now clearly formulated electrical theories challenging refutation. And I myself refuted them some years later. In 1951 these clear expressions of what would happen on the electrical theories were shot down by our own observations in one night in Dunedin and of course by many subsequent experiments.

POPPER:

I may perhaps interrupt here to say that in about 1951 I met a very well-known scientist in Oxford, and I mentioned to him that I was a friend of Eccles; he said: "Eccles? A very good man, but, you know, the man must be a bit crazy; he actually refutes his own theories." [*Laughter.*]

ECCLES:

Well, you know, it's not so bad. In life you want a reputation for something, to be known as distinct from everybody else. I got a great reputation, you may say, for refuting my own theories. And not only for refuting them, but I was even attacked because I enjoyed refuting them. That was supposed to be a perversion, a very bad scientific perversion, to enjoy refuting your own theories.

But this is what Sir Karl teaches us: that we have to

enjoy it. We should enjoy it, because what we've done is we've discovered something. You put up a scientific idea, if you can shoot it down, then you know that that idea is false and that you have to move into other ideas; and that is scientific progress, that is the way science develops.

As it turned out, I even shot too well. I immediately rejected all electrical transmission and got onto the Dale and Loewi bandwagon of chemical transmission. That is what I got the Nobel prize for—not for my electrical view, but for my subsequent work, after I'd given it up and had espoused the new chemical transmitter theory.

But it turned out that I had rejected too much. The electrical story was not all wrong; it was wrong where I had postulated it to be the case. But now many other examples have been discovered since that time, of both excitatory and inhibitory electrical transmission, working in the way I had described, or nearly so. It wasn't so silly, you see. [*Laughter.*]

So, in the book I wrote in 1964 I had two chapters on electrical transmission. It has come back. It's an example of the way science grows.

ELDERS:

I think you ought to receive the Nobel Prize twice. [*Laughter.*]

ECCLES:

I didn't discover the new electrical theories at all, but I was quite happy to see them being discovered. I had rejected electrical transmission completely, but when it was re-established in special cases that represented further scientific progress. It's all in the Popperian view of science—that the testing and falsification of ideas leads to scientific progress.

ELDERS:

But, Sir John, how do you see the relation between science and technology?

ECCLES:

Well, it's very easy, as long as you don't think somebody is just a scientist for his life, or a technologist for his life. I am both. I put on different hats. I put on a scientific hat and can work as a scientist, and then I can put on a technological hat and work in technology. I know what the difference is.

A scientist is trying to understand nature; he is using all kinds of ways of proving and investigating, but the essence of what he does is to understand the phenomena by understanding the principles of operation. He does this by developing theories of a more and more general character, and testing them experimentally.

A technologist is interested in using science for some purpose or other that he wants, or that society wants. For example he can use a new pharmaceutical agent, which has been discovered by scientific investigation, in order to cure diseases: this is technology. If you are using it at the same time to investigate how it's working on the disease, then you are a scientist again. But if you are just using it on patients, who are treated and get better, then it's technology.

It's the same way, you know, with electronics; this is all technology, everything that is being displayed here with the TV cameras and the camera-men. They're looking at us, taking and shooting and presenting us on the air to the public. This is technology; but extremely fine scientific discoveries are used in the building of these machines for TV display.

ELDERS:

And what about space travel?

ECCLES:

Space travel is almost entirely technology. The scientific content of space travel is quite small and not at all worth the expense. What we get from it are certain measurements of the moon, or about the earth orbit and they can get back some rocks and investigate them and so know something about the moon's history. That is good geology and so on, but it's *nothing like worth the cost*.

The cost of space travel isn't justified by the scientific discoveries. It's justified by adventure, by political values, by man's feeling, which is sometimes silly, that he wants to go places and to get somewhere or other; if there is no adventure left on this earth he will try something else rather similar. But that is not science, that is adventure.

ELDERS:

Sir Karl, what do you think about the growing influence of politics on science?

POPPER:

I apologise for not answering this question, but there was something mentioned a little while ago that I would very much like to go back to. It is just that I should like to emphasise that what really matters in science is theory, which we arrive at by thought, and by understanding the problems that we have to solve. We aim, in science, to discover the truth about something that interests us, to discover true explanatory theories. Contrary to what is often supposed, we do not arrive at explanatory theories by making experiments. Experiments, of course, do have a vital role in science, but their role is primarily *critical*. Of course, most of the theories we will think up as possible explanations will be false, but this should not discourage us, for if we discover something to be false, we do, at the same time, discover something that is true. Furthermore, the discovery that a certain line of approach is not successful will be a valuable addition to our understanding of the problem that we are trying to solve.

I think that it is a myth that the success of science in our time is mainly due to the huge amounts of money that have been spent on big machines. What really makes science grow is new ideas, including false ideas. This point is in tune with fallibilism, but at odds with any preference for verification.

False theories, and the discovery that they are false, are important steps in our progress towards the truth. Sir John has given us some examples of this, and I therefore want to make only a small addition to what he has said. It is this. We often make the mistake of thinking that a scientific theory is good only if it is successful. But this is a mistake. Even the greatest scientists, those like Galileo, Kepler and Newton, who put forward theories of immense power and interest, have not, ultimately, been fully successful, though they have had some success. For even their successes have been superseded. Einstein was well aware of this, and after he had developed his theory of gravitation, general relativity, he told us that the theory could not be true, and himself gave reasons why it was not true. His only positive claim was that his theory was a better approximation to the truth than previous theories.

Science is open-ended: it is always possible for us to ask for a further explanation of any explanatory theory. And it is important to remember that, in the history of science, theories have frequently been corrected by those theories which superseded them.

In this connection, it is interesting to remember that even Newton, the developer of a theory of incredible power which was one of the most successful theories ever, was unhappy about his theory. His theory indicated that gravitational attraction acted between bodies at a distance, through empty space. Newton wrote, in a letter to Bentley: "that gravity should be innate ... and essential to matter, so that one body may act upon another at a distance ... is to me so great an absurdity that I believe no man who has in philosophical [that is to say scientific] matters a competent faculty of thinking can ever fall into it." And Newton made many attempts to find a further explanation of the gravitational attraction postulated by his explanatory theory.

I would also like to very briefly comment upon the

question you asked Sir John about scientists and technologists. It is just this. I have stressed that scientists are not seeking for certainty, and that our best and most fruitful scientific explanations are always liable to be superseded. When technologists use theories, however, they tend to think that they have the truth in their pocket, and that what they do is certain. Now I should like to make two comments about this. First of all, when we have to *act*, we have to choose, and to prefer one theory to another. When we do this, we should always remember that while our choice may be reasonable, the theory we are using is *not* certain, and be aware that things may not turn out as we expect them to. The other point is that we should not be misled by our feelings of certainty—they depend on the *situation* we are in; and things which we accept as "certain" and act upon in one situation we may wish to scrutinize carefully in another.

ELDERS:

Sir Karl, you have just mentioned the notion of truth. Can you explain a little bit more what you mean by truth?

POPPER:

Yes, I can; but it will seem very trivial to most of you.

First of all, I should remind you that I think that notions are not very important; *concepts* or *notions* are only means which we use to formulate *theories*. What is important is the *theory* of truth, rather than the *notion* of truth.

The theory of truth I am going to explain was first introduced as a philosophical theory by Aristotle. But by around 1900 it had fallen into disrepute: had you taken a poll of philosophers in 1900, you would have found, I suppose, that most of them did not accept it. And they would have given arguments why they thought it was not acceptable. In 1930, however, Aristotle's theory was rehabilitated by a great logician and philosopher of mathematics, Alfred Tarski, who now lives in Berkeley in California. And I had the good fortune to be converted by Tarski in 1935.

Now I will explain the theory to you. But I am afraid you will be disappointed, as it appears to be so trivial. It is: a statement is true if it corresponds to the facts.

What Aristotle was unable to explain was what it means to say that a statement corresponds to the facts. And it was this problem that lay at the bottom of most of the criticism of the theory that I have mentioned. In Tarski's theory, however, one can explain how it is possible that a statement can correspond to the facts.

So the theory of truth I accept is that truth means correspondence to the facts—and I think that this is *the* common-sense theory of truth.

Now I hold that very many of the statements that we believe to be true are true, but that many of the statements we believe to be true are false. It is a consequence of Tarski's theory that we can have no general *criterion* to distinguish between true and false statements. One can actually prove in Tarski's theory that for any fairly rich language—one, say, like Dutch or English, where we are not unduly restricted by the language as to what we can say in it—there cannot exist a criterion of truth and falsity. This is, in fact, the deepest reason for human fallibility. While we can sometimes give *fairly good* reasons why something is true or false, we can never give *conclusive* reasons why anything, outside of certain areas of logic, or finite mathematics, is true or false.

This does not mean that we should not try to find the truth, and it does not mean that we may not, if we are lucky, find it, or at least get nearer to the truth. But it does mean that we cannot know for sure that we have got nearer to the truth, or that we are making progress. And, above all, we can never be sure that we have actually reached the truth. This is very important.

Aristotle's theory of truth, which is often called the correspondence theory of truth, is an absolute theory of truth, as opposed to a relativistic theory. It was, as I have already mentioned, unpopular at the turn of the century. One of the reasons for this was that the people who believed in it usually also believed that they had a criterion of truth, and that they could tell for sure that some things were true and others false. This belief, not surprisingly, made them unpopular amongst those who were rightly aware of human fallibility.

Now I accept the correspondence theory of truth, and I agree that it says that truth is absolute—that it is not, say, relative to time or to what people think about it. But at the same time, I think that we can prove that nobody possesses the key which will, with certainty, unlock the truth. Truth always remains a *problem*, except, perhaps, in certain parts of logic and mathematics; and I would also be prepared to admit that it is not a major problem in matters like the perception of simple objects or coloured blots and so on. There are many trivial questions where truth is not much of a problem, but wherever truth becomes interesting, there truth becomes problematic.

ELDERS:

Sir John, does your conception of truth agree with Sir Karl's? I am thinking especially of his reference to colour. You believe that colours only exist in our brains, don't you?

ECCLES:

Yes, of course. I am a neuro-physiologist, and there are certain statements that scientists who investigate the brain can make without fear of contradiction, insofar as they are statements approximating to the truth. At least we know where the problem is; the problem has got two different levels, shall we say. Scientifically there are certain levels at which you work, and you gradually go to levels beyond levels. Having established a firm base you can go further.

Now the remarkable thing about what a neuro-physiologist says is that all of our knowledge of the world, everything including knowledge of our own bodies, comes to us through the senses in the first place. We have memories, of course, and each of us has been gradually building up ways of interpreting our experiences through our whole lifetime. But everything comes in this way; and how does it come? It comes purely by physical or chemical means that excite receptor organs: by wavelengths of different character; by pressure-waves in the atmosphere; by chemical molecules; by heat and cold on special receptors; and through touch and pain and so on from my body. Information from all of these receptors is flowing in all the time into our brains.

Now when it comes to the perception of colour, we have to recognise that it is based on coded information initiated in the first instance by certain wavelengths of radiation which are absorbed by pigments in the cones of the retina. From these receptors there are special pathways up to the visual cortex. In this cortex there are cells responding selectively to the wavelengths that give a red sensation and not to green for example. But this still doesn't explain how the red colour is perceived as such. The problem now is beyond the visual cortex. We have moved into the whole problem of the brain and perception. It's a problem like what I call Sherrington's problem: how does brain activity, where there are only nerve-cells firing messages to one another, how does that patterned operation of immense complexity give us perceptual experiences?

We now return to the question: how does it come about that I recognise an object as having a red colour? First of all, it is not just my first experience of red. For example, if I had been blind from birth with a congenital cataract, I could suddenly be given vision by an operation on my eyes. Many examples of this have been very well reported by Von Senden in his book, *Space and Sight*. For example an intelligent person in his teens is suddenly given vision in this way, but he doesn't know anything of what his eyes observe. Hitherto he has had a "felt" world built upon senses of touch and movement, but with no sight and no colour. It takes many weeks of trial and error effort before he can identify what's coming into the perfectly normal visual apparatus that he now has, including the recognition of colour. We do most of this learning, of course, as babies; we don't remember much about these early learning experiences; nevertheless as neuro-biologists we can state that all of our richness of perceptual experience comes about in this way.

This concept is something that I find missing so much in philosophical discussions, for example in Austin's book *Sense and Sensibilia* or Price's book *Perception* and so on. They miss the scientific knowledge we have now as neuro-physiologists, especially the sensory physiologists. We have now a large amount of sure knowledge up to the level of the specific coding of sensory information and its input into the cerebrum, and the learning by experience. Beyond that there is the great unknown of the brain-mind problem.

POPPER:

Our Chairman wanted a topic on which we do not entirely agree ...

ELDERS:

Oh, no ...

POPPER:

... and this is a subject where I do not quite agree with Sir John.

ELDERS:

I want to ask you a totally different question, Sir Karl, about the high value you place upon rationality. Can you explain to us why it is such a high value and can you also give some arguments about the foundation of this value?

POPPER:

No, I won't be put down so easily! My point relates to the previous question, and I would say that where I deviate slightly from Sir John's views on this matter is on the following point.

It seems to me that Sir John at least sometimes takes our immediate experiences, or what is immediately "given" to our consciousness, as something secure, or at any rate as being something much more secure than our knowledge of the external world. This is a view which I do not accept. Of course, I believe that we should take our so-called immediate experiences seriously, and I think that they are important. But I do not think that they are always secure, or that they form a secure starting point for knowledge, for I believe that they may sometimes mislead us. I take this view because I believe that everything we experience is in some way saturated with theories; and my point is that our theories may always be mistaken.

I see even our physical bodies and our sense organs as being, for the most part, something like frozen theories. Our sense organs, and our physical bodies, are the result of a process of trial and of error elimination. The process of trial and of error elimination characterizes both the evolution of our bodies and sense organs, where the error elimination is by natural selection, and the growth of our knowledge where elimination can take place by means of critical discussion.

Now about this there is, I believe, no disagreement between Sir John and myself. And it is quite well known that theories are built into our sense organs and the sense organs of animals. Thus the eye of a cat makes use of principles of selection which differ from those built into the eye of a rabbit. Each can be said to incorporate theories about the external world, and the theories relate to the differences between the problems facing cats and rabbits in their respective environments. For example, the eyes of a rabbit are constructed so as to enable it to discover dangers coming from above; those of a cat enable it to pay attention to its prey, mainly things that come from below.

ECCLES:
Do you want me to react to that?

POPPER:
Certainly, if you like ...

ELDERS:

Please do, Sir John.

ECCLES:

Well, of course we develop sense organs appropriate for survival during the whole evolutionary story. We have sense organs for this and for that and we know that other animals have sense organs with different receptor capabilities; some have electrical detectors, others, like the bat, can detect very high frequency sounds, a kind of radar detection. But I am not now concerned with all those exotic receptors. What I'm interested in is not all this detail, but the essence of the problem: how *do* we receive evidence from the external world, using our sense organs, what does it give us and how do we react to it?

I agree completely with you, Sir Karl, that all the time it gives us a probable picture, if you like a hypothesis. You are driving a car down the street, and you see patterns changing and getting bigger; your hypothesis is that this pattern is due to another car approaching; and you react appropriately. We're always reacting, all through life we are reacting; life depends on it.

A small child doesn't know this, he has to learn. But all the time we are using our sense organs for the purpose of practical living. We become extremely skilled in this. It's absolutely fantastic to think of what's involved in a ballgame, or what is involved in any skilled performance that we do.

This is all something which is learned all the time. We are continually learning to react. But there is more than that: we're also learning in a much more subtle way as human beings. No animal knows anything about beauty and art and design. No animal knows anything about the creative activities that we enjoy so much as we participate in the plastic arts or in music or in literature, or in science. It isn't just for survival that we use our sense organs; we also use them for all cultural activities and experiences, which are much higher than mere survival.

POPPER :

Here we largely agree; and we also agree in stressing detection, the role sense organs have in detecting what is outside. But I stress their theory-dependence *perhaps* a little more than you do.

ELDERS :

Perhaps I could say, for the benefit of the public, that you are being a little evasive, because if I remember correctly Sir Karl, you gave a talk last year on the subject of why red colours look red, and Sir John writes that red colours don't exist in the physical world.

ECCLES :

Of course.

ELDERS :

And there is some relation here, I think, to things which are more important and more interesting. I am thinking particularly of philosophical anthropology; in other words, our conception of man. Sir John, in particular, has an interesting dualistic view of the relation between brain and mind. Perhaps you could try to explain it to us briefly ?

ECCLES :

This is a long story. It's my story of my life, trying to understand myself. Now I won't apologise for this, because I believe that everybody does it, but not all admit it, at least not in public! Nevertheless they don't spend their lives questing, questing, questing for an answer to this problem, or for the satisfaction of some partial answer. As I've said, I've been obsessed by this problem from when I was seventeen or eighteen years old right through to now, trying to understand the very nature of my existence. And that is why

I speak of sensory experiences as given in perception and of experiences of action.

But, more than that, I want to think of myself as an existing being; I have a kind of philosophy which you might call personalism. I believe that everything is centred on me. This is not solipsism, because I believe it's true for every one of you. We are all the same, in essence, and the life of society consists in understanding and appreciating the unique personal existence of each individual. The life of your own self consists in trying to make the most of what you've got, of all your wonderful talents, which incredibly some people won't even recognise or value. Just imagine this marvellous gift of perception with vision and hearing; just imagine the appreciation you can have of sounds and harmony and melody; just imagine the memories that you are given, how you can remember so many things ... your whole life is one long texture of memories; imagine how you can act as you will, wish to do this or that, and so develop your life, within limits, as you wish. This is the essence of personal existence.

We can ask how it comes about that all this is brain-centred? How can we explain the fact that, as we work more and more on it, we see that our whole conscious experience is something which is in fact in the brain and nowhere else? The rest of the body is merely a pumping apparatus with some metabolism to keep the brain going and with input lines from receptors to the brain and output lines from the brain to muscle so that will can eventuate in action. But the essence is in the brain.

And then you ask where in the brain? The answer can be given as a consequence of the study of the effects of brain lesions and injuries and of electrical recording or stimulation of the brain. The cerebral cortex is especially concerned in conscious experiences. Where then lies our real problem? It's not how information comes into the brain, pouring in from the sense organs as coded information of impulses at various frequencies in the millions of afferent fibres; and so into this tremendous patterned organisation of the brain, where it goes through the most complex spatio-temporal patternings written in space and time at a fantastic, unimaginable speed.

It is at the next stage that the intractable problem arises: how, as a result of these brain actions, you have an experience, you see a light, you feel a touch, you hear a sound, or you have much more complex blended experiences. Somehow what is going on in your brain, which we understand up to a point, turns into a perception. This is a tremendously important problem, beyond any present solution, yet nevertheless a real problem.

All these manifold perceptual experiences give one side of the brain–mind problem. The other side also concerns the experiences that we all have of free will, but it is customary to deny it for some strange reason. By taking thought I can make this glass hop, you see. [*He makes a glass hop, like Sir Karl.*] I've never done that before, but just because I practised doing it in my mind after Sir Karl showed it, I can do this, or anything trivial that you like. Just by taking thought I can make my muscles do this. How does it happen? Somehow I had the desire to do it, I worked it out, and in no time I find that I can do it, I can make it happen.

ELDERS:

But, Sir John, can you also explain the relation between your thought and your actions?

ECCLES:

No, that's what I'm trying to say! I can't explain it, but I believe it occurs, just the same. Don't ask me to explain everything. I can only tell you that this is a real problem, the problem of how taking thought and wishing to do something, makes the nerve-cells in my brain change the patterns of their activity so that discharges occur down my pyramidal tracts and so to my muscles in order to make this happen.

We all know we can do that, every one of you. Yet most of

you, I suppose, will argue against free will, because (a) you believe it is against physics, and (b) you think it's against physiology. And the answer is, of course, that this is a silly situation.

The fact is, that physics and physiology are far too primitive yet to explain how thought can give rise to action. We have to remember that we're only at the very beginning of physics and physiology, which are enormously more subtle than we yet know. We are still primitive investigators. But I *do* believe that the problems of brain and mind are real problems, and that we can make progress in them. We can now define the problems much better with respect to the neural counterpart of consciousness; but still the essence of the problem eludes us.

But that is what man's position is: the challenge in life is to live with problems, not to deny their existence. Some philosophers want to deny the existence of problems in order to simplify philosophy, but I think in science our task is always to be defining problems, and to see them as complexes which you can attack here or there or there; so that gradually, as in assembling some jigsaw puzzle, we come to understand more and more.

ELDERS:

Sir John, you not only believe in free will, but also in the immortality of the soul, and in the existence of God. Are these ideas of the same status as your ideas about the relationship between a thought and an action? Are they just statements of a personal belief, or can you give some kind of a neuro-physiological basis for your beliefs?

ECCLES:

Ah, no. I think you've been reading more into my book *Facing Reality*, which has just been published, than in fact is there. I read parts of it even this afternoon. There is a subtle difference in what I state there. What do we know of ourselves? We wake up to life as a small baby, as we can know from our earliest memories, and gradually through life our self grows with this stream of memories which gives us our unique character and our own personal existence. Everybody has a self like this. And so in retrospect we seem to come from some oblivion, and we find ourselves existing and going on through life, and then at the end we know that death and destruction of the brain follows. Does this mean that life is but an episode between two oblivions? Does the problem of ceasing to be require us to face up to the inevitable end? I would say not necessarily so. This is going beyond the evidence. As scientists we have no explanation, as yet, of what our conscious self is. What is this conscious experience, with all its immediate perceptions and all its memories and passions and desires; what is this that we know ourselves to have? We don't know. It's of course dependent on the brain. But I would say that the brain is a necessary and not a sufficient explanation of our conscious self.

And therefore it is World 2 that we should be discussing. Sir Karl will talk about his development of what he calls World 2, with which I agree, the world of conscious experience. This is *not* a material thing. It is, of course, related to the brain, and to brain action, but we don't know how, and we do not know how it came to be in the first place related to *this* brain and not any other brain. It's not just your genetic coding and your inheritance, as I have argued in my book. This will not explain to you the uniqueness of yourself. You are more than that. Evolution and genetic inheritance do not explain me to myself; they explain how my body and my brain come to exist, but they do not explain the existence of my own conscious uniqueness.

And so it comes to this: coming into being is a mystery, how I came to exist and find myself with this body as a conscious being. And then the body disintegrates. Am I to believe that's the end, and no meaning more than that? I don't know. As a scientist I must be agnostic because I have no explanations of how I came to be, how I am and how I experience, and therefore I cannot refute the possibility that there is some more meaning and some waking up from the oblivion that follows after death. I don't know.

ELDERS :

What is your opinion, Sir Karl, about this problem ?

POPPER :

I was not only a failure as a cabinet maker, but was also a failure as a physicist (although I might say that some of my views in this field have recently been revived). You should not, therefore, expect too much from me on the difficult problem of man's free will, which involves a view of the openness of the physical world and thereby of physics. How-ever, some of my ideas on this topic are similar to Sir John's, although I should perhaps formulate them slightly differ-ently.

We can think of there being at least three different "worlds". There is, first of all, the physical world, the world of objects like, say, the glass on the table in front of me, of our bodies and our brains, and of physical forces and fields of forces. I call this physical world "World 1". Then there is the world of consciousness, of our awareness of things, of our psychological dispositions and expectations, and our feelings of pain and pleasure. I call this psychological world "World 2".

Now there are many physicists who believe that World 1 is closed. Consider, for example, all the movements that I have made during the course of this discussion : my gestures, the movements of my lips, of my tongue, and of my vocal chords. It would be the view of these physicists that my movements are fully explicable in terms of the laws of World 1. This view implies that *if* World 2 exists, then it exists as a sort of shadow, running parallel, perhaps, to World 1, but not able to act upon it. It would be their view that if, say, I make the glass in front of me move, then it is my brain, some-thing belonging only to the physical World 1 (rather than my intention, which belongs to the psychological World 2), which is responsible for making the glass move. Now I do not believe this story. I do not believe that the physical World 1 is closed towards the psychological World 2; and if the physical world is open, then physical theory should not be closed or self-contained either. Thus I do not believe that it is possible to explain everything that happens in purely physical terms. Rather, I believe that there is a physical World 1 and that there is also a psychological World 2, and I believe that these two worlds *interact*; that they influence each other. But in addition to these two worlds, I believe that another world exists; I call this world "World 3".

World 3 is the world of the products of the human mind, the world of the *contents* of thought. If I think of a certain thing, and Sir John thinks of a certain thing, and our Chairman also thinks of the same thing, then it is clear that while our psychological *thought processes* (and our physical *brain processes*) may well be very different, the *content* of our thought is the same. Suppose, for some reason, that we were all to think, "Three times three does not equal twelve". There is no reason to suppose that our thought processes are the same: our Chairman may have even "thought" in Dutch, Sir John in English, and I myself in German. But the *content* of our thought, the World 3 object of which we were thinking, would be the same in each case.

Among the inhabitants of World 3 are theories, for instance scientific theories, problems, mistaken solutions to problems, arguments, and discussions. World 3 can also, in a wider sense, be taken to include other things such as artistic objects and social institutions.

Now World 3 influences World 2 very strongly (and its existence constitutes an argument for the existence of World 2) and through World 2, World 3 also influences World 1. Suppose, for example, that you were to see a new machine. It would be a World 1 object, a physical object. But machines are designed according to plans and on the basis of theories. These are members of World 3. But before these theories can affect World 1 they have to be grasped or understood, that is to say, they have to become part of somebody's World 2. The physical World 1 is constantly being changed by interaction with World 3, particularly by the world of science. Sometimes this may result in improvements, sometimes not.

World 3 is also important for the old problem of determinism and indeterminism. It is my view that an issue which lies behind much of the discussion of determinism is the problem of the openness of World 1 (for which indeterminism is a necessary, but not a sufficient, condition). It is my view that World 1 is not complete; that it is indeterministic, and that its openness to World 3 plays a great role in this.

ECCLES :

Yes; but I want to come in and add something to that. At the present time I'm engaged in a dispute about what is called reductionism : can everything, including life and mind, be reduced to physics and chemistry? This is the claim of the physicalists who want to put everything into World 1; pure materialism, with everything explained by energy and matter going about all their various known motions.

Now, when I'm presented with this theory, by somebody saying : everything, including biology and mind is reducible to physics and chemistry, I always ask : pray, tell me, what is physics and chemistry?

This startles them quite a lot, because they don't know what to say! So you try to help them there : physics and chemistry isn't just matter in itself or any kind of physical experiment or apparatus; it isn't even all the books of physics and chemistry, not as such. In the end, what it turns out to be, is the thoughts and ideas of physicists and chemists in explaining natural phenomena, and in trying to get nearer to general explanations of what is happening in the natural world, which would include the world of biology and even the world of brain activities. In this latter respect physics and chemistry is looking only at the material side of happenings in the brain.

POPPER :

That is, physics and chemistry in World 2; but there is also physics and chemistry in World 3.

ECCLES :

Yes, I agree completely. But if they don't accept your World 3, they're in trouble. If they only accept World 1, they have in fact got themselves into a stultifying position. They have described everything as being in the world of physics and chemistry, and the world of physics and chemistry turns out to be the world of ideas and thoughts and theories of physicists and chemists, which is certainly not what they want. And so they are driven into accepting these other worlds as you described; there is no way out.

POPPER :

If I may, I should like to come back to a point we have just left.

All of you know of the interesting problem of mirrors standing opposite each other. We see the image of one mirror in the other mirror, and this image is then reflected in the first mirror, and this goes on for ever. In principle there is no end to it. If it does come to an end, it is because the mirrors are not very good. But with ideal mirrors it would go on for ever, and the series of reflections is never complete.

Now my view is that physics and chemistry, and more generally, science and knowledge, can never mirror themselves completely. Here also you reach an infinite regress. If you want to describe or explain completely our present-day knowledge, then you have to make a step beyond our present-day knowledge. But this means that you have some new piece of present-day knowledge, and to describe or explain that you would have to make a further step, and so on. You have an endless sequence of problems; and so the explanation or description is never complete.

All this has one very interesting consequence for those who believe that *only* World 1 is real. For, in their view, knowledge is part of World 1. Now if scientific knowledge is necessarily incomplete, and unable to describe itself fully, then this, in their view, is a property of World 1, and World 1 is therefore in this sense incomplete.

My own view is that all three Worlds are incomplete, and that they interact with one another and are thus open towards one another. And it is this which can, I believe, help us to understand theoretically, at least some of the problems raised by the idea of free will.

Now the term "free will" is very commonly used, but nobody knows exactly how to describe our free will. While we all experience it, and while we all believe that we have it, we have, as it were, no scientific theory of the will. In my view, it is, perhaps, best to avoid discussion of free will as such; for I think that we can be misled by our *feelings* of free will, and that as a result our discussions may be sidetracked and may even degenerate into verbal problems.

I believe that the *real* problem here is whether the physical World 1 is open to Worlds 2 and 3. Our idea of free will has been called into question most strongly by those who assert that the physical world is deterministic, and that we are, for this reason, never the creators of, say, new theories or works of art, but are simply doing things physically determined years before we were born.

Now, as a first step, I believe that we have good arguments for the view that the physical World 1 is indeterministic, among them arguments related to the problem of describing or explaining our knowledge. And I further believe that we have good arguments for the view that all three worlds exist, and that they are open towards one another.

Now this gives us a *reason* to trust our feelings of free will, as it undermines the most powerful assault that has been made on them. It also has another important consequence. For it enables us to see that by our thoughts and our actions we can contribute to World 3. World 3, the world of the products of the human mind, is a world to which we can all contribute, and in which we all participate. I even take the view that the best work in science or the arts or humanities is done when we forget about ourselves, and concentrate on World 3 issues as much as we possibly can. If our discussion here today is any good, the reason will be that we have been able to forget about ourselves and to concentrate on World 3 issues.

ECCLES :

And now I must object. I think it's a great mistake to forget about yourself. I think that is part of the trouble today, that people are trying to lose themselves in one way or another. I want to do both things : I want to live consciously, deliberately, introspectively as well as objectively; I believe in the full range of all this. If I appreciate something, I want to try and analyse it : why do I like it, what is the point of this, what is the meaning of this. I always want to bring it into my conscious experience and then to give it expression in speech or writing. It's the same in science, you know. I've been in science because I enjoy science.

POPPER :

In fact we agree on this point. It is only that I believe that people think about themselves too much. I am therefore referring to those people who do not think about themselves, but rather think about what they are doing in World 3.

ECCLES :

Yes.

ELDERS :

I think that you are both aspiring to a certain kind of immortality, only the difference is that Sir John considers it in a more personal way, namely in terms of the immortality of one's own soul, and that you, Sir Karl, are suggesting that it occurs independently of one's existence, in your objective World 3.

POPPER :

Yes, at least in the sense that when we make a contribution

to World 3 we can never know what its consequences will be, how far they will reach, and how long they will continue to be important. But there is also another point that I should perhaps mention. I see World 3 as being the object of human activity or human endeavour, and as being the *product* of human activity. Here I disagree with Plato. He thought that there was a World 3 of Forms or Ideas in themselves, and that they were independent of man. But Plato's World 3 contained only things which are true. My World 3 contains problems, mistakes, and theories both true and false; and it contains, more generally, the products of the human mind.

ECCLES:

Yes, I will add something, just to make it concrete for you. A stone axe made by palaeolithic man is in World 3.

POPPER:

Yes.

ECCLES:

This is a message to us, from palaeolithic man, to say that he was able to design and sculpt stone for purposes; and he often made things of great beauty. As you go through history, the archaeologists have done tremendously valuable services to us by studying and displaying the whole story of man from primitive times. Unbelievably magnificent things were made so many thousands of years ago.

This is the story of man creating; this is the story of how man made World 3, the world of culture and art and criticism and science and literature. Everything that you can imagine to be worthwhile in life, the whole of civilisation and culture is World 3. And that is the essence of living, that we all have the chance to partake, participate, appreciate and also add to World 3, according to our abilities. This is the adventure of living, as I see it, for civilised man, and this is what universities are about; they're about nothing else.

POPPER :

Again I would agree; but again I wish to add something. In my opinion, what is most characteristic of man, of the human World 3 and of most human products, is human language. And perhaps the most important moment in the emergence of human language was the moment when man was able to *tell a story*; to tell a story that was not true, and thereby to invent the difference between truth and falsehood. For this distinction opened up the possibility both of imaginative invention and of critical discussion.

The idea of truth and falsehood—which I think is of the greatest importance for mankind—is the result of the discovery of the lie. We owe much to the man who first told a lie in order, perhaps, to escape from the unpleasant consequences of something he had to say. For without the idea of falsehood we could not have the idea of truth and all that this distinction has subsequently meant to human development. Bees, of course, have a language too; one which, we believe, has some descriptive powers. But bees cannot lie, I suppose.

What I really want to stress is the special importance of *human* language which seems to be, strangely enough, the only inherited exosomatic tool of mankind. Many people place special emphasis on the use by man of tools such as a stick or a stone or, say, an axe. Perhaps one of these was man's first tool, but man has no genetically inherited exosomatic tools except human language. It is our one great inherited tool, and it makes possible the richness of our other tools, for it makes it possible to change them and improve them by means of criticism.

ECCLES :

But I want to come in now; language is not inherited, only the potentiality for language.

POPPER :

Of course.

ECCLES:

But then the potentialities to carve and to sculpt and to paint are inherited in the same way.

POPPER:

But while many healthy men do not carve or paint, all healthy men do speak some language, although, of course, only the potentialities are inherited. Newborn babies do not talk, and we do not all speak the same language. I cannot speak any Dutch except *"kan niet verstaan"*, so I am well aware that language is not inherited in *that* sense. But it is inherited as a disposition, as a need that has to be satisfied if frustration and dehumanization are to be avoided.

There is, in man, an incredibly strong need to learn a language, as we see, for example, from the autobiography of Helen Keller. She was blind and deaf and could not speak. She had no means of formulating words until, one day, her teacher gave her a tactile signal for water while her hand was placed in running water. And then, suddenly, she had the idea : this signal, this tapping signal, means "water". This idea suddenly occurred to her, and it turned her into a human being : she subsequently described herself as having been a kind of animal before this happened. Language made her a human being.

In my opinion, this shows that she had a disposition to learn a language. But it is more than just a disposition; it is a need which must be fulfilled in order to become fully human.

ECCLES:

Yes.

ELDERS:

Perhaps I could now suggest that we move to the last part of our discussion, that is to say to questions about social theories. I must say, Sir Karl, that I am not quite sure myself if social questions are in your first, second or third Worlds :

I think in fact that they must be in all three. But one of the most puzzling problems about your ideas for many people is the big difference between the revolutionary character of your scientific and intellectual ideas and, on the other hand, the more gradualistic doctrines of piecemeal reform and piecemeal engineering of your social theories. Some people even get the impression that what you say about intellectual theories and social theories is actually inconsistent.

POPPER:

Perhaps I could formulate your question like this. On the one hand, I believe that science, like any product of the human intellect, evolves by revolutionary steps. Theories are falsified and overthrown. On the other hand, I am highly critical of attempts at violent social revolution, and I have suggested that we should make reforms in a piecemeal manner. I have been judged by some people to be inconsistent because I am a revolutionary in the intellectual field, but not in the social field.

In fact, not only is there no inconsistency, but my social views can be looked upon as being a consequence of my views on intellectual revolutions. I have already, earlier in this discussion, said something about World 3 which I regard as crucial. For in my opinion, where mankind differs from the animals is that our evolution takes place outside ourselves, exosomatically, by means of the growth of our theories in World 3. One difference that this makes between ourselves and other animals is particularly important. For while animals, for instance an amoeba, will die if they are the carriers of false or inappropriate theories, man can let his theories die in his stead. While animals will die with their false theories—theories which are incorporated into their sense-organs, or which they hold in the form of expectations about the world—men can criticise their theories and eliminate them without having to eliminate those who produce them or advocate them.

Now, in the sphere of social ideas there are two things particularly worth noting. First of all, as man is fallible, his ideas about society and social action are likely to be false, and in need of criticism. Social actions, typically, have unintended consequences. It seems reasonable to submit our social theories to criticism—and thus to a process of elimination or improvement—rather than to commit ourselves to them uncritically; not least because in the social sphere it is not just we who may die if we fail to weed out our mistaken theories, but also many other people.

Now the theory of piecemeal social engineering that I have suggested we should adopt in social policy has one main rationale. It is simply that we should do things in society in such a way as to enable us to criticise and improve our theories when we find that they are leading us to undesirable consequences which we had not anticipated. Piecemeal social engineering does *not* restrict us to minor changes. What it does do is to suggest that we should make changes in such a way that, when undesirable consequences arise, we can detect what is responsible for things going wrong.

However, this critical attitude seems to me incompatible with violent revolution; or, more precisely, with all attempts to overthrow a democracy by violence.

I think you will see from this that my opposition to so-called social revolution is not inconsistent with my views on intellectual revolutions. Rather, it is closely related to them. I might sum this up by saying: you may have your revolutions; but have them within World 3.

ELDERS:
But, Sir Karl, isn't your idea of rationality as a substitute for and improvement on violence perhaps a kind of translation of the Darwinist or Skinnerian theory of the survival of the fittest? Aren't you just saying with your theories what Darwin did when he spoke of the struggle for life ...?

POPPER:
No, there is a real difference. Darwin's theory is a theory of killing. Darwin's theory consists in the main of a theory of

elimination in the struggle for life, and that means killing. My social theory is not an evolutionary theory in this sense, but an application of Darwin's theory to the products of human thought: kill your thought, kill your false thought, criticize your false thought; in this way you may make progress; not by killing each other, but by killing the products of your thought.

ELDERS:

That's true. But can you give a foundation, empirical or otherwise, for your strong belief in rationality? Is it just an ethical postulate or desire, or is it also something more that you use in your theories?

POPPER:

If you ask me whether I believe that all men are rational, my answer is no, I do not think we are rational. If you ask me whether we *ought* to be rational and ought to try to be as rational as possible—and by rational I mean self-critical—then my answer is yes. Very few people are really self-critical, but everyone should try to be self-critical. That, in brief, is my answer to your question.

Rationality consists in the main of criticism. There is nothing more rational than a critical discussion.

ELDERS:

Sir John, if you think of the American Negroes in the slums, do you think that Sir Karl's answer would be quite satisfying for them?

ECCLES:

I don't know if I want to answer that question. In the first place, how many of you here know about this problem from your own personal experience? How many of you understand the problem in America today? Imagine what your position might be like in Holland if you had these racial problems with you. I think that the problem requires a great deal more understanding, a great deal more putting yourself in the position of other people.

What I will say is that violence provides no solution; I deplore all violence. I think this angry violence destroys everybody, you get less good on all sides, and that is what I fear in America today. It's only a fringe of people who *are* violent, but that fringe is becoming so popularised and advertised, that you think it is all that way. This is not at all true, and I think that in Holland you would probably have a quite inadequate understanding of this intense problem in America. I'm not an American, you understand, I'm an observer as you are, but I do live in Buffalo.

ELDERS:

But let us then put it in a more general way, Sir John. If the people in power are not using your high intellectual and moral standards, how can you defend yourself against this kind of power? Can you defend yourself with your mind only, without resorting to your fists?

ECCLES:

I believe in this. I can do nothing politically, but I could do quite a lot philosophically, if people will only read what I write! I have written a book called *Facing Reality*, which has just been published; it has hardly yet been reviewed in America at all, but it has been reviewed in England, and it has been published in Germany. This is the way I *can* help. I'm trying to get people to understand what life is, what an individual person is; to see the mystery and wonder of existence of each individual being; how they come to be, and their conditions of existence throughout life. I want to see everybody with a maximum of opportunity for what I call self-fulfilment; so that people go through life thinking their life has been good, and that they've made the most of their opportunities. They can then become happy and creative people and will be able to continue with the growth of civilisation, which is, I think, what we all want.

We want the refinements and the developments of this World 3 as defined by Sir Karl, the world of culture and civilisation. If you belong to one of those fringe groups that want to destroy our civilisation and say our society is evil, science is evil, have no more science; technology pollutes, have no more technology : well, I would say to them, go back and *live* in a Stone Age country. I can tell you where to go. Go to the highlands of New Guinea. I've been there, I've seen Stone Age people living. You do not know what it is like to live without culture and all the advantages of civilisation. I'm not saying that all is good in our society, but I'm saying that we should appreciate it. And we should then try to see that every person gets the best possible opportunities.

Further I would say that for the most part neither the blacks nor the whites in America would want to have forcible desegregation of schools, if there were a good alternative. I can suggest a good alternative, namely to make the schools where the minorities go better than the others, by giving them better teachers, giving teachers more salary to teach there, giving them better conditions, better opportunities. I believe that everybody born in a rich country deserves to have the maximum opportunities to develop with all his potentialities.

This is one of my messages.

I want always to tell people, that we are *not* like Skinner would have us. You know, there is a book that has just been written by Skinner called *Beyond Freedom and Dignity*. He is I think one of the really dangerous men today. He claims that he now understands the springs of human action, because he has worked on rats and pigeons and conditioned them by what is termed operant conditioning. He is proposing in his book that *he* knows enough that, given the complete domination of a country, he could arrange for all the babies when born to be conditioned in special Skinner boxes that the babies would like. They would be so conditioned that gradually they would grow up to do what the leaders of the country wanted. Everyone will be perfectly conditioned to be a useful cog in society, in the big machine of society. And he even decides that it is not cruel, because they would be conditioned to be happy doing this. He thinks this is the only way society can go on; in this kind of dehumanised, animal situation.

This is power, ruthless power; the complete reverse of the ideal system I would propose. Like Sir Karl, I want people, every human being, to be treated as a special person, like you know yourself to be.

My aim would be to make people appreciate that everybody else is like themselves, with their own inner experiences and desires and memories and hopes, and I want to give the new generation hope and meaning in life. I want to tell them that they're not just the offspring of an evolutionary process, and that their behaviour isn't entirely the result of their conditioning, but that they are immensely mysterious beings, which I think they are. Scientifically, as a brain-scientist, I can say that how we come to be and how we are what we are, is beyond any understanding. Therefore, I think that every person should be regarded, if you like, as infinitely valuable. If we could get *these* concepts across in our handling of social problems, it would transform the problems of the world.

We should visualise this world of ours as a little speck in cosmic space, this beautiful and salubrious little world of ours. Nowhere else in the cosmos are there likely to be any living beings like us, conscious living beings. I think that the chances are so remote, that you can safely say: nowhere else.

This is one little green isle—the earth—with its vegetation and its animal life and us in the immensity of the cosmos, in this otherwise meaningless cosmos. We are the only beings searching for meaning and for ideas and understanding, so creating the World 3 that Sir Karl has so impressed upon us. Let us think of this world of ours in the immensity of space, and of the wonder of the conscious life that we participate in.

ELDERS:

Sir Karl, do you want to react to this?

POPPER:

Yes ... I feel it is time to conclude and I would say, in brief, that freedom is more valuable even than happiness.

ECCLES:

Yes, I agree with you.

POPPER:

Happiness is very valuable, but freedom is more valuable. And if I may conclude with another sentence: what we need very urgently as intellectuals, and also from intellectuals, is more intellectual honesty, more intellectual modesty, and more intellectual humility.

ECCLES:

That is a good note to finish on. I think if the academics could only be *humble* for a bit, the general public might start to believe in them again. But so many are arrogant and want power. They want power to frighten people and so to gain power over them. For example, to give you a specific instance, many computer technologists would like us to think that with computer technology they will soon have machines that are cleverer than man and that are more powerful than man. Hence they would have us believe that eventually these machines will take us over, so that we are going to be relegated to the role of a species on the way to extinction because the computers will do everything so much better and more effectively. This is science-fiction. It is absolute nonsense because computers only do what they're programmed to do. Yet this threat is developed by some who work with computers because they want power over people. And power is just as evil a temptation for academics as it is for everybody else.

ELDERS:

Sir Karl, Sir John, I would like to thank you very much for your inspiring discussion, and also to thank you on behalf of the audience here and at home. Thank you both.

Are there any questions? If someone wants to ask a question, please go ahead.

QUESTION:

Sir Karl, you have used the terms World 1, World 2 and World 3. I was wondering what you meant by the word "world", because I might imagine that there are people present in this audience who may think that only World 2 exists, and that World 1 and World 3 only exist as a result of World 2. There is a German mystic, Meister Eckhart, who said: "Without *me* God could not exist". I would therefore be very pleased to hear what you have to say, as a philosopher, about your term "world".

POPPER:

I shall be glad to answer this question as well as I can when I have understood it. Unfortunately, I couldn't hear what you said. Perhaps one of the people here could explain it to me.

ECCLES:

I can start if you like, to answer; I heard it perfectly. Sir Karl will come in as soon as he hears me. [*Laughter.*] Now we differ about this; *I* believe with you, in the first place, that World 2 is the world of primary reality, this is what we know directly. This is the world of experience and memory and imagination and emotion and theory.

And because of what is given to us by our sense organs, through the whole of life, as we go on exploring and learning, we gradually come to know more and more in detail about an external world, the World 1. That's the second reality; I believe in that too, but it is not immediately given. World 2, the world of all conscious experience, is immediately given; the other world is derivative by analysis of our sensory impressions—and we can be fooled by them, as occurs when we have illusions produced by mirrors for example, or when we suffer from hallucinations. This World 1 I believe is real, it is but a world of secondary reality.

And World 3 is again a world that we know of, because we sense it; we sense art forms and objects and books and so on. When reading a book, you have the book and you see the printed letters, and this, if you know the language, is coded and can be made into sense. In that way the World 3 ideas in the book come to be transmuted into World 2 happenings so that you can know them.

POPPER:

Was that the answer or was that the question? [*Laughter.*]

ECCLES:

That was the answer. The question was simply this: you only know World 2, how do you know Worlds 1 and 3? And I'm trying to tell him.

ELDERS:

Well, Sir Karl, Sir John made your second world into his first world.

POPPER:

My answer to this is different from Sir John's. It is that in all philosophical questions we have to start from common sense. And common sense tells us, first of all, about the existence of World 1. Thus, my answer is that the world of primary reality—or whatever you call it—is the physical world, World 1.

We learn, I suggest, first about the physical world. It is only later on that we become aware that we have something like consciousness, and that our psychological World 2 plays a role in our reactions to the physical World 1. I therefore believe that the numbering 1, 2, 3, corresponds to the development of the commonsense view of reality. Of course, I think we should criticise common sense, and I do not think that it can be appealed to as an authority or as a source of certain knowledge; but I do think that we cannot avoid it as a starting point—a fallible starting point.

However, I do not think that this difference between Sir John and myself is a very important one. What I think *is* important, and on this we are in agreement, is to recognise that all three worlds exist; World 1, World 2 and World 3.

ECCLES :

I agree; except that you said "common sense tells us". Now this is putting *us*, as World 2, first. You've started off by implying : this something in the external world tells us.

POPPER :

I think that the point about these worlds is not that we can cut them cleanly and easily into three. It is, rather, a matter of emphasis. If we lay emphasis on the *logical content* of what I am saying then our emphasis is on World 3. If we lay emphasis on my *feelings or intentions* when I am speaking, then our emphasis is on World 2. If we lay emphasis on the noises I make with my tongue while speaking, or on my brain processes, or on the movements of my muscles, then our emphasis is on World 1.

ECCLES :

Yes, I agree with you.

QUESTION :

I have two small questions, one for Sir Karl : you said that freedom is the most important thing for man. Do you think that violence has a role in defending freedom ?

POPPER :

I did not actually say that. I said that freedom is more important *even* than happiness. I do not know what is the most important thing for me ... that depends on the situation.

QUESTION:

You think freedom is very important?

POPPER:

Yes.

QUESTION:

But do you think that violence has any role in the defence of freedom?

POPPER:

In its defence, yes.

QUESTION:

My question to Sir John is this: you pointed to the fact that the world is very small, especially when compared to the universe. But isn't that only one side of the problem, one side of things? The world is perhaps physically very small, but on the other hand it is nevertheless divided into more than one hundred and thirty groups of people each living under their own government. On a global level there is total anarchy. Isn't that just as much a view of reality as your saying that the world is small?

POPPER:

I would like to say a little more on the question that was addressed to me. I am an enemy of violence, and I believe that violence cannot resolve our difficulties. Our problem is: what can we do to reduce violence as much as possible. And my answer is: only through reasonableness. The only way in which we can reduce violence is through reasonableness, not by means of violence.

ELDERS:

Sir Karl, can we go on with this question: would you accept the use of violence in certain circumstances?

POPPER :

That is a very abstract and difficult question. It reminds me of the famous problem of Carneades. Carneades was a Greek philosopher who discovered a problem he thought was insoluble. If he is in a shipwreck, and on the ship are his mother-in-law and his grandmother and he can only save one of the two, whom should he save, his mother-in-law or his grandmother ? In my opinion, general questions like the one you have asked me are more like riddles than questions that can be seriously discussed. In a certain definite situation I think it is conceivable that the use of violence may be necessary. But when our Chairman once asked me what I would do if he wanted to kill me; say, to shoot me, I said that I would let him kill me. I know I have to die in any case, and I would rather be killed by our Chairman than kill our Chairman to prevent it.

So sometimes these questions are very simply answered, sometimes they are very difficult to answer. But I do not think that the question as such is particularly fruitful. What *is* fruitful and important is to fight violence by non-violent means, as far as this is at all possible.

But I admit that there is a difference between an attack upon freedom and the defence of freedom; and if freedom is being violently attacked, the use of violence in its defence may be justified.

This is, I think, the only answer which I can give to the question.

ECCLES :

Now I come to your question. Our world is a very tiny speck in this immense cosmos, beyond imagining. Big as it looks, it is like a little spaceship, and we are on this spaceship as passengers, if you like. We don't know how we got there, that is the mystery, we woke up on this spaceship, nowhere else. We find we have many other passengers coming and going from this ship. How should we look at it ?

I think that we *must* eventually come to the idea that all

men are brothers; that is the only sensible way to live in this unique and wonderful world of ours.

I admit that there are immense difficulties, because there are great totalitarian states, who are committed to their imperialism at all costs. But here in Western Europe you are trying to lead a reasonable life of getting on with people, with your European Economic Community, which I hope grows. I see all these efforts of mankind. We *have somehow* to come to terms with the nationalistic ambitions of countries. How this can be done I don't know, but I always feel that we have to try to get a philosophy of reasonableness, a philosophy of understanding.

I worked with the World Health Organisation for some years, on the Scientific Advisory Council. I have great respect for the members of the WHO. They are attacking the health problems of all the developing countries with devotion and intelligence. This is a good model for future international action.

More and more I hope that this will happen, but I must say, that at the present time it looks as if a quarrelsome lot of passengers have got on to this ship! We ought all the time to appreciate the extraordinary problems of existing here with one another, and to try to see them in their right perspectives.

This world is small in the cosmos. And although there are all these different countries, a hundred and thirty that you mentioned, this is part of the power problem. I believe that the lust for power is the most evil thing in the world today. We have to try to reduce it as much as we can, and get people to be humble and more friendly to each other, more understanding, more appreciating, more human.

ELDERS:
Another question.

QUESTION:
I have a question for Sir Karl. Mr. Elders mentioned four

reasons why you are famous. But I think that the most important one, a fifth one, has been forgotten. It is that you are at this moment the best-known opponent of the so-called Frankfurt School, the proponents of a dialectical or critical theory of society. It is certainly too much to ask you to give here, in a nutshell, an explanation of why you are an opponent of that critical theory. But perhaps I can whittle my question down to this, and ask you what you think of dialectical thinking and dialectical concepts? That is to say, on what level do you think that dialectics makes a certain sense and on what level do you think it is pure nonsense?

POPPER:

Thank you for your question. First of all, about dialectic. It is a topic that I have written about, but it is not one that I can easily talk about in a situation like this, as dialectic is a technical term which has been used in different ways by different people. In one of its senses, for instance in Plato, it is more or less equivalent to critical discussion, and of this I am all in favour. The Hegelian view of dialectic makes it primarily a description of the development of the history of ideas; however, I think that Hegel's view is, ultimately, highly misleading. The simple view that we progress intellectually by problem solving and by trial and error succeeds, I believe, in capturing at least some of the good points of Hegel's view, while being free of its pernicious consequences. As to the Marxist dialectic, here again my feelings are mixed. While I have the greatest respect for Marx and Engels as independent and critical thinkers, and believe that we can learn a lot from their work, I also believe that their views are open to serious objections. Having said this, I must say that, in their work, the dialectic seems to me one of the weakest elements. Engels' use of the materialist dialectic as a philosophy of nature can hardly be taken seriously. And the theory of history to which Marx and Engels were led by their use of dialectics seems to me untenable.

As for the Frankfurt School, it is true that I am known as

an opponent of the Frankfurt School, but I have never discussed their work in any detail. I have, of course, written
about dialectic and about Marx and Hegel; and some of the
criticisms that I have made in the course of these writings
may well apply to the Frankfurt School. But I have never
written anything about the Frankfurt School along these
lines. While I know of the work of the Frankfurt School, I
do not have a very high opinion of it; and until fairly recently
I did not know that it was so influential.

The way in which I became involved in a clash with the
Frankfurt School was a little strange. It so happened that
I was invited to open a discussion on the logic of the social
sciences at a congress of sociologists at Tübingen. I was asked
by the conveners of the congress to give my talk in the form
of several definite theses, and actually to number these
theses, so that people could refer to them more easily in the
discussion. I had not been asked to discuss the Frankfurt
School, and my paper did not specially discuss them. But
a member of the Frankfurt School happened to reply to my
paper.

Subsequently a book was published. It consists, first of all,
of two long introductions by the member of the Frankfurt
School who had replied to my paper. He had become dissatisfied with his reply, and had therefore written these introductions to the book. Then follows my brief paper, and I
cannot say that I think it particularly good. Next comes the
original reply to my paper, and then comes a further reply,
written by Professor Habermas, another member of the
Frankfurt School, who was dissatisfied with things as they
stood. He was then answered by Professor Albert, who came
to my defence; and so the discussion went on. As a result,
my opening paper, which was the starting point of the whole
affair, is squeezed in among hundreds of pages by or about
the Frankfurt School. But no explanation is given in the book
of how the book came about. Moreover, in the course of the
discussion, none of my critics discussed any one of my
numbered theses. Consequently, nobody reading the book can

understand what my paper is doing there, or why it takes the strange form of numbered theses.

I might perhaps add a word on the great influence of the Frankfurt School. When considering their influence one must bear in mind, I think, that after the breakdown of Hitler's regime many people in Germany felt the need for a new sort of leadership, and a new sort of philosophy. Unfortunately the Frankfurt School was there to meet the need.

ELDERS:

Perhaps, Sir Karl, I may add that in your *Reason or Revolution* you state that the substantial issue between the Frankfurt School and yourself is revolution versus piecemeal reform.

POPPER:

Yes, we do disagree on this issue. But there is another disagreement which is, perhaps, even more important. It is about intellectual standards, and concerns the way in which we should speak, and write, and state our arguments. It is my view that we should speak and write simply and clearly, so that anyone who is interested can understand what we are trying to say. But the view exemplified by the Frankfurt School is very different. They are an example of a tradition in German philosophy which I think is quite pernicious. It is a tradition which accepts that something is profound when it cannot readily be understood, and that the sign of the man who has had a university education is that he can write and speak in a manner which is both impressive and incomprehensible.

This is quite an important point. For while argument and critical discussion are possible between men who disagree, say, about revolution and piecemeal reform, rationality itself is destroyed by a tradition which encourages incomprehensibility, and which thus makes critical discussion difficult or even impossible.

ELDERS :

Well, are there any more questions?

QUESTION :

Sir Karl said that a statement is true when it corresponds to the facts. My question is : how can you be certain that a correspondence between a statement and the facts is true?

POPPER :

My answer to your question is very simple : you *cannot* be sure that a statement corresponds to the facts.

But perhaps I ought to say a little more about the correspondence theory of truth, and the rehabilitation of this theory which, I think, can be attributed to Alfred Tarski. Tarski's view contained the following idea, which I think was decisive. If I wish to speak about the correspondence between a statement and a fact, then I have to have at my disposal a language in which I can speak about *both*—statements *and* facts. Tarski's great discovery was that we have to talk about the correspondence between statements and facts in a language different from the one in which the statements themselves are formed. He called such a language a semantical metalanguage. In a semantical metalanguage you can (1) *speak about statements*; for instance, by naming statements, describing statements or analysing statements. And you also can (2) *speak about facts*; for example about the fact that the glass in front of me contains some apple juice.

Now if you have such a language, in which you can speak both about statements *and* about facts, then it is almost trivial that you can say how a statement corresponds to the facts. The statement "This glass contains apple juice" will correspond to the facts if and only if this glass contains apple juice. Here I have spoken in a metalanguage about a statement, namely the statement "This glass contains apple juice", and also about a fact, namely *the fact that* this glass contains apple juice. This seems very trivial, but a theory of truth has to be trivial, for we all know what we mean by truth. If a judge says to a witness "Swear to speak the truth, the whole truth and nothing but the truth", then he does not combine this with a lecture about the meaning of truth; rather, he assumes that the witness knows what is meant.

The theory of truth is difficult in one sense, as Tarski discovered, in so far as we have to speak in a semantical metalanguage, a language in which we can speak about language, and, at the same time, about facts; but in another sense it is almost trivial.

ELDERS:

Now, are there any more questions?

QUESTION:

I suppose it doesn't matter if we jump from one subject to another, but my question is this: Mr. Elders put a question to you about a supposed inconsistency in your writings; on one hand you are in favour of revolutionary new ideas in science, as a general methodologist, while in the logic of social sciences you advocate piecemeal social engineering.

Now I think your answer was very elegant, but I was very much disappointed by it. I suppose everybody remembers what you said about killing ideas and not killing people, but your answer implies that any social revolution, which you are explicitly against, must be violent and must involve killing; whereas, of course, this is not necessarily the case at all. There are many revolutionary social ideas, for instance well-known anarchist ideals which suggest that there shouldn't be any states at all, that we shouldn't be organised in a state, which are advocated by people who do not propound violence at all. They are very peaceful people.

Of course, there are examples of revolutions which are very bloody; the history of world revolution is, unfortunately, drenched in blood; but I think this should not be necessarily so.

POPPER :

One can quarrel about words for ever. For instance, about whether or not a revolution which is not violent is really a revolution. It is this sort of verbal issue which I think we should avoid. Let me deal with your question rather differently.

First of all, my alleged inconsistency. What are my views on the theory of knowledge and on social philosophy which have sometimes been taken to be inconsistent ? In the theory of knowledge my view is that we should discuss theories and overthrow them by means of criticism. In social philosophy my view is that we should discuss theories and, so far as is possible, foresee the unintended consequences of our actions by means of our theories before we act. This is particularly important for actions which are revolutionary in the sense that they are violent. If you undertake violent actions, particularly on a large scale, then very often the result will be not the outcome that you desired, but something very different.

ELDERS :

Sir Karl, I believe that you have misunderstood the question ...

POPPER :

No, I do not think so. The question was as to what my attitude is towards anarchist ideas of non-violent revolution.

Now I am, in a sense, an anarchist. I do not love governments any more than does an anarchist. I too dream of a world without government. Yet I know only too well that it is a dream. To my mind, government is an evil, but a necessary evil.

As to bringing about a world without government by non-violent means, I must say that this seems to me impossible. There is a very simple argument for its impossibility. It is just that there are many people who would resort to violence to defend the governments in question. And they would, if necessary, defend governments with weapons; perhaps even with hydrogen bombs. For this reason it is, in my opinion, a sheer dream to think that we could bring about a world without government by non-violent means and thus achieve anarchy.

QUESTION :

Would you be prepared to work with anarchists, by means of piecemeal social engineering towards an anarchist state?

POPPER :

I have made it quite clear in my writings that one of the main tasks of social engineering should be to tame the power of the state, and particularly to check the ability of rulers to exercise arbitrary personal power. It is my view that the power of governments is everywhere far too great; particularly in totalitarian states, but also in democracies. Let me give you an example. I am an Englishman by naturalisation and there is very much that I admire in England. But the power of the English Prime Minister is, in my opinion, much too great. His position enables him to do much more harm than he should be able to do. I am not saying that he *does* harm, only that he *could* do a lot of harm. Thus I have written that the art of good government consists in establishing a state of affairs, or a constitution, that prevents rulers from doing too much harm; which curbs the power of rulers to do harm.

Yet I also have reasons for believing that anarchy is impracticable, and that we cannot do without government. One has only to look at the anarchy of the international scene. Thus it would be nice if we could do without government, but I believe that we cannot. However, I do also believe that we could do with much less government.

QUESTION :

I think, then, that we agree on this, that you are misinterpreted when people say that this way of solving social problems by slow reform implies that you are a conservative. You are quite open to new and revolutionary ideals.

POPPER :

The question is not whether we are to solve social problems by means of slow reform or fast revolution. It is rather whether we should or should not think out before we act what the consequences of our action will be. This question —about foreseeing the unintended consequences of our actions—applies to all projected changes, both large and small.

Again, let me give you an example. Consider the British system of medical socialisation, the National Health Service. I do not wish to deny that many people's lives have been saved, or that many people have been relieved from the financial worries of paying heavy expenses for serious operations. But there have been many bad consequences. Patients are, in many cases, treated very badly; hospitals do not have enough money spent on them and they are badly under-staffed. And doctors and nurses are badly overworked and badly paid. The organisation was, in fact, not well thought out from the start; there was no attempt to profit from the experiences with health services in other countries. And I think that much more could in fact be done, perhaps even for the same money, in a better-organised system.

In New Zealand and Australia there existed better forms of organisation before the British system was set up than now exist in Britain. And I may mention that more recently Medicare in the United States, though perhaps too expensive for the government, has produced some really wonderful results for its patients.

There is also another thing. Young people, understandably enough, are often appalled by the bad things in our society, and frequently think that if very radical action is taken, all our problems could be solved at a stroke. What they tend to forget is that society consists of many many millions of people, and that any solution to a social problem is likely to have its repercussions upon the activities of all of them. We have in my opinion too many people on this earth to allow any easy solution of social problems; and if we do not think carefully before we act, many of these people are likely to get hurt, or even to be killed.

QUESTION:

Part of my question has already been answered by the last part of what you said to the previous questioner. What I was going to ask you was this: you say that most problems can be solved just by thinking. For example, we can achieve a state without a government just by thinking. On the other hand you say: no, this is not possible, because there are always people who will destroy this attempt, and that is the reason why you should have a government.

So do you in fact think that this is the best solution now and forever, with governments as they are now? Is there to be no changing of society?

POPPER:

I am sorry, but I could not hear your question.

ELDERS:

Well, I think that I understood the question. Are you saying that Sir Karl is in fact defending the political *status quo*?

QUESTION:

Yes; does he in fact think that it is the best thing?

POPPER:

You have to start from the political *status quo*. But this does not mean that the *status quo* is unalterable, and it does not mean that we cannot improve the *status quo*. But a man who does not accept the *status quo* as a starting point just breaks the world into pieces.

I do not know whether this is an answer to your question.

QUESTION :

Not really; you say we just have to go on by means of reasonable reason, by thinking and finding out; but you have stated that in some situations you have to use violence. So I can see that in fact you are saying that in some situations it is good that there should be a revolution.

ELDERS :

Perhaps I may try to extrapolate your question in this way : he is saying, Sir Karl, if I understand him correctly, that on the one hand you are much like Kant, defending an abstract rationality or morality. But on the other hand, if you speak about the political *status quo*, then you relate your values primarily to the facts, to the existing power structure.

POPPER :

I think that we always have to start from the *status quo*. This indeed may at first sound strange, but if you think about it, you will see that there is really no other sensible way to approach things. For it is the *status quo* that poses our problems for us, and it is to the *status quo* that we have to relate our actions when trying to do things better.

The only alternative is to pretend that we are in the position of Adam and Eve and that we can start everything afresh. But this is sheer folly. Is it really likely that if we ignore the way things are—what the power-situation is, who lives where, what their feelings about things are—that we will be able to solve any of our problems ? It seems to me to be clear enough that to act in a way that ignores how things are is to act in a way that is, at best, foolish, and, if it involves the welfare of others, little short of criminal.

One reason that this may sound strange is due to a muddle that has been created for us by, among others, the Frankfurt School. For they have managed to confuse at least some of you here in the following way. You seem to have the impression that there is a conflict between taking a realistic view of the *status quo* and being critical of it. This is simply a muddle, and a dangerous and silly muddle. Our preferences, our views of what ought to be, are not in conflict with our acceptance of a *description* of the way things actually are.

My view is, briefly, that we ought to face the facts squarely and that we should then stand up for our moral ideas, and, more particularly, for reasons I have explained in my writings, stand against those facts, those states of affairs, which we regard as evil.

ELDERS :

Do I understand you correctly, Sir Karl, to be saying that one accepts the political *status quo* as a minor evil in relation to a greater evil?

POPPER :

No, that is not my view. My view is, rather, that we have to start from the *status quo* even if we wish to criticise it. I do not agree with the present *status quo*, although I do think it includes some wonderful achievements. Let me give one example. It is, at the moment, possible for millions of students who could never before have gone to university to have the benefit of a university education. This is one thing which is part of the present *status quo*, and I think it is a wonderful thing, and a great improvement on how things were before.

But, of course, things could be better. For universities are examination-ridden. I think that things could be much improved by a very radical reform of examinations. And I also think that universities are beset by other evils.

In some cases, however, and these will probably be typical, we will be faced by a choice of evils, and will wish to choose the lesser evil.

ELDERS :

Well, I think it is already very late, so I propose, Sir Karl, Sir John, that we will now really finish. Thank you very much.

NOAM CHOMSKY
and
MICHEL FOUCAULT

Human Nature:
Justice versus Power

HUMAN NATURE: Justice versus Power

ELDERS:

Ladies and gentlemen, welcome to the third debate of the International Philosophers' Project. Tonight's debaters are Mr. Michel Foucault, of the Collège de France, and Mr. Noam Chomsky, of the Massachusetts Institute of Technology. Both philosophers have points in common and points of difference. Perhaps the best way to compare both philosophers would be to see them as tunnellers through a mountain working at opposite sides of the same mountain with different tools, without even knowing if they are working in each other's direction.

But both are doing their jobs with quite new ideas, digging as profoundly as possible with an equal commitment in philosophy as in politics: enough reasons, it seems to me, for us to expect a fascinating debate about philosophy and about politics.

I intend, therefore, not to lose any time and to start off with a central, perennial question: the question of human nature.

All studies of man, from history to linguistics and psychology, are faced with the question of whether, in the last instance, we are the product of all kinds of external factors, or if, in spite of our differences, we have something we could call a common human nature, by which we can recognise each other as human beings.

So my first question is to you Mr. Chomsky, because you often employ the concept of human nature, in which connection you even use terms like "innate ideas" and "innate structures". Which arguments can you derive from linguistics to give such a central position to this concept of human nature?

CHOMSKY:

Well, let me begin in a slightly technical way.

A person who is interested in studying languages is faced with a very definite empirical problem. He's faced with an organism, a mature, let's say adult, speaker, who has somehow acquired an amazing range of abilities, which enable him in particular to say what he means, to understand what people say to him, to do this in a fashion that I think is proper to call highly creative ... that is, much of what a person says in his normal intercourse with others is novel, much of what you hear is new, it doesn't bear any close resemblance to anything in your experience; it's not random novel behaviour, clearly, it's behaviour which is in some sense which is very hard to characterise, appropriate to situations. And in fact it has many of the characteristics of what I think might very well be called creativity.

Now, the person who has acquired this intricate and highly articulated and organised collection of abilities—the collection of abilities that we call knowing a language—has been exposed to a certain experience; he has been presented in the course of his lifetime with a certain amount of data, of direct experience with a language.

We can investigate the data that's available to this person; having done so, in principle, we're faced with a reasonably clear and well-delineated scientific problem, namely that of accounting for the gap between the really quite small quantity of data, small and rather degenerate in quality, that's presented to the child, and the very highly articulated, highly systematic, profoundly organised resulting knowledge that he somehow derives from these data.

Furthermore we notice that varying individuals with very varied experience in a particular language nevertheless arrive at systems which are very much congruent to one another. The systems that two speakers of English arrive at on the basis of their very different experiences are congruent in the sense that, over an overwhelming range, what one of them says, the other can understand.

Furthermore, even more remarkable, we notice that in a wide range of languages, in fact all that have been studied seriously, there are remarkable limitations on the kind of systems that emerge from the very different kinds of experiences to which people are exposed.

There is only one possible explanation, which I have to give in a rather schematic fashion, for this remarkable phenomenon, namely the assumption that the individual himself contributes a good deal, an overwhelming part in fact, of the general schematic structure and perhaps even of the specific content of the knowledge that he ultimately derives from this very scattered and limited experience.

A person who knows a language has acquired that knowledge because he approached the learning experience with a very explicit and detailed schematism that tells him what kind of language it is that he is being exposed to. That is, to put it rather loosely: the child must begin with the knowledge, certainly not with the knowledge that he's hearing English or Dutch or French or something else, but he *does* start with the knowledge that he's hearing a human language of a very narrow and explicit type, that permits a very small range of variation. And it is because he begins with that highly organised and very restrictive schematism, that he is able to make the huge leap from scattered and degenerate data to highly organised knowledge. And furthermore I should add that we can go a certain distance, I think a rather long distance, towards presenting the properties of this system of knowledge, that I would call innate language or instinctive knowledge, that the child brings to language learning; and also we can go a long way towards describing the system that is mentally represented when he has acquired this knowledge.

I would claim then that this instinctive knowledge, if you like, this schematism that makes it possible to derive complex and intricate knowledge on the basis of very partial data, is one fundamental constituent of human nature. In this case I think a fundamental constituent because of the role that language plays, not merely in communication, but also in expression of thought and interaction between persons; and I assume that in other domains of human intelligence, in other domains of human cognition and behaviour, something of the same sort must be true.

Well, this collection, this mass of schematisms, innate organising principles, which guides our social and intellectual and individual behaviour, that's what I mean to refer to by the concept of human nature.

ELDERS:

Well, Mr. Foucault, when I think of your books like *The History of Madness* and *Words and Objects*, I get the impression that you are working on a completely different level and with a totally opposite aim and goal; when I think of the word schematism in relation to human nature, I suppose you are trying to elaborate several periods with several schematisms. What do you say to this?

FOUCAULT:

Well, if you don't mind I will answer in French, because my English is so poor that I would be ashamed of answering in English.

It is true that I mistrust the notion of human nature a little, and for the following reason: I believe that of the concepts or notions which a science can use, not all have the same degree of elaboration, and that in general they have neither the same function nor the same type of possible use in scientific discourse. Let's take the example of biology. You will find concepts with a classifying function, concepts with a differentiating function, and concepts with an analytical function: some of them enable us to characterise objects, for example that of "tissue"; others to isolate elements, like that of "hereditary feature"; others to fix relations, such as that of "reflex". There are at the same time elements which play a role in the discourse and in the internal rules of the reasoning practice. But there also exist "peripheral" notions, those by which scientific practice designates itself, differentiates itself in relation to other practices, delimits its domain of objects, and designates what it considers to be the totality of its future tasks. The notion of life played this role to some extent in biology during a certain period.

In the seventeenth and eighteenth centuries, the notion of life was hardly used in studying nature: one classified natural beings, whether living or non-living, in a vast hierarchical tableau which went from minerals to man; the break between the minerals and the plants or animals was relatively undecided; epistemologically it was only important to fix their positions once and for all in an indisputable way.

At the end of the eighteenth century, the description and analysis of these natural beings showed, through the use of more highly perfected instruments and the latest techniques, an entire domain of objects, an entire field of relations and processes which have enabled us to define the specificity of biology in the knowledge of nature. Can one say that research into life has finally constituted itself in biological science? Has the concept of life been responsible for the organisation of biological knowledge? I don't think so. It seems to me more likely that the transformations of biological knowledge at the end of the eighteenth century, were demonstrated on one hand by a whole series of new concepts for use in scientific discourse and on the other hand gave rise to a notion like that of life which has enabled us to designate, to delimit and to situate a certain type of scientific discourse, among other things. I would say that the notion of life is not a *scientific concept*; it has been an *epistemological indicator* of which the classifying, delimiting and other functions had an effect on scientific discussions, and not on what they were talking about.

Well, it seems to me that the notion of human nature is of the same type. It was not by studying human nature that linguists discovered the laws of consonant mutation, or

Freud the principles of the analysis of dreams, or cultural anthropologists the structure of myths. In the history of knowledge, the notion of human nature seems to me mainly to have played the role of an epistemological indicator to designate certain types of discourse in relation to or in opposition to theology or biology or history. I would find it difficult to see in this a scientific concept.

CHOMSKY:

Well, in the first place, if we were able to specify in terms of, let's say, neural networks the properties of human cognitive structure that make it possible for the child to acquire these complicated systems, then I at least would have no hesitation in describing those properties as being a constituent element of human nature. That is, there is something biologically given, unchangeable, a foundation for whatever it is that we do with our mental capacities in this case.

But I would like to pursue a little further the line of development that you outlined, with which in fact I entirely agree, about the concept of life as an organising concept in the biological sciences.

It seems to me that one might speculate a bit further—speculate in this case, since we're talking about the future, not the past—and ask whether the concept of human nature or of innate organising mechanisms or of intrinsic mental schematism or whatever we want to call it, I don't see much difference between them, but let's call it human nature for shorthand, might not provide for biology the next peak to try to scale, after having—at least in the minds of the biologists, though one might perhaps question this—already answered to the satisfaction of some the question of what is life.

In other words, to be precise, is it possible to give a biological explanation or a physical explanation ... is it possible to characterise, in terms of the physical concepts presently available to us, the ability of the child to acquire complex systems of knowledge; and furthermore, critically, having acquired such systems of knowledge, to make use of this knowledge in the free and creative and remarkably varied ways in which he does?

Can we explain in biological terms, ultimately in physical terms, these properties of both acquiring knowledge in the first place and making use of it in the second? I really see no reason to believe that we can; that is, it's an article of faith on the part of scientists that since science has explained many other things it will also explain this.

In a sense one might say that this is a variant of the body–mind problem. But if we look back at the way in which science has scaled various peaks, and at the way in which the concept of life was finally acquired by science after having been beyond its vision for a long period, then I think we notice at many points in history—and in fact the seventeenth and eighteenth centuries are particularly clear examples—that scientific advances were possible precisely because the domain of physical science was itself enlarged. Classic cases are Newton's gravitational forces. To the Cartesians, action at a distance was a mystical concept, and in fact to Newton himself it was an occult quality, a mystical entity, which didn't belong within science. To the common sense of a later generation, action at a distance has been incorporated within science.

What happened was that the notion of body, the notion of the physical had changed. To a Cartesian, a strict Cartesian, if such a person appeared today, it would appear that there is no explanation for the behaviour of the heavenly bodies. Certainly there is no explanation for the phenomena that are explained in terms of electro-magnetic force, let's say. But by the extension of physical science to incorporate hitherto unavailable concepts, entirely new ideas, it became possible to successively build more and more complicated structures that incorporated a larger range of phenomena.

For example, it's certainly not true that the physics of the Cartesians is able to explain, let's say, the behaviour of elementary particles in physics, just as it's unable to explain the concepts of life.

Similarly, I think, one might ask the question whether physical science as known today, including biology, incorporates within itself the principles and the concepts that will enable it to give an account of innate human intellectual capacities and, even more profoundly, of the ability to make use of those capacities under conditions of freedom in the way which humans do. I see no particular reason to believe that biology or physics now contain those concepts, and it may be that to scale the next peak, to make the next step, they will have to focus on this organising concept, and may very well have to broaden their scope in order to come to grips with it.

FOUCAULT:
Yes.

ELDERS:
Perhaps I may try to ask one more specific question leading out of both your answers, because I'm afraid otherwise the debate will become too technical. I have the impression that one of the main differences between you both has its origin in a difference in approach. You, Mr. Foucault, are especially interested in the way science or scientists function in a certain period, whereas Mr. Chomsky is more interested in the so-called "what-questions": why we possess language—not just how language functions, but what's the *reason* for our having language. We can try to elucidate this in a more general way: you, Mr. Foucault, are delimiting eighteenth-century rationalism, whereas you, Mr. Chomsky, are combining eighteenth-century rationalism with notions like freedom and creativity.

Perhaps we could illustrate this in a more general way with examples from the seventeenth and eighteenth centuries.

CHOMSKY:

Well, first I should say that I approach classical rationalism not really as a historian of science or a historian of philosophy, but from the rather different point of view of someone who has a certain range of scientific notions and is interested in seeing how at an earlier stage people may have been groping towards these notions, possibly without even realising what they were groping towards.

So one might say that I'm looking at history not as an antiquarian, who is interested in finding out and giving a precisely accurate account of what the thinking of the seventeenth century was—I don't mean to demean that activity, it's just not mine—but rather from the point of view of, let's say, an art lover, who wants to look at the seventeenth century to find in it things that are of particular value, and that obtain part of their value in part because of the perspective with which he approaches them.

And I think that, without objecting to the other approach, my approach is legitimate; that is, I think it is perfectly possible to go back to earlier stages of scientific thinking on the basis of our present understanding, and to perceive how great thinkers were, within the limitations of their time, groping towards concepts and ideas and insights that they themselves could not be clearly aware of.

For example, I think that anyone can do this about his own thought. Without trying to compare oneself to the great thinkers of the past, anyone can ...

ELDERS:

Why not?

CHOMSKY:

... look at ...

ELDERS:

Why not?

CHOMSKY:

> All right [*laughs*], anyone can consider what he now knows
> and can ask what he knew twenty years ago, and can see that
> in some unclear fashion he was striving towards something
> which he can only now understand ... if he is fortunate.
>
> Similarly I think it's possible to look at the past, without
> distorting your view, and it is in these terms that I want to
> look at the seventeenth century. Now, when I look back at
> the seventeenth and eighteenth centuries, what strikes me
> particularly is the way in which, for example, Descartes and
> his followers were led to postulate mind as a thinking sub-
> stance independent of the body. If you look at their reasons
> for postulating this second substance, mind, thinking entity,
> they were that Descartes was able to convince himself,
> rightly or wrongly, it doesn't matter at the moment, that
> events in the physical world and even much of the be-
> havioural and psychological world, for example a good deal
> of sensation, were explicable in terms of what he considered
> to be physics—wrongly, as we now believe—that is, in terms
> of things bumping into each other and turning and moving
> and so on.
>
> He thought that in those terms, in terms of the mechanical
> principle, he could explain a certain domain of phenomena;
> and then he observed that there was a range of phenomena
> that he argued could not be explained in those terms. And
> he therefore postulated a creative principle to account for
> that domain of phenomena, the principle of mind with its
> own properties. And then later followers, many who didn't
> regard themselves as Cartesians, for example many who
> regarded themselves as strongly anti-rationalistic, developed
> the concept of creation within a system of rule.
>
> I won't bother with the details, but my own research into
> the subject led me ultimately to Wilhelm von Humboldt,
> who certainly didn't consider himself a Cartesian, but never-
> theless in a rather different framework and within a different
> historical period and with different insight, in a remarkable
> and ingenious way, which, I think, is of lasting importance,

also developed the concept of internalised form—fundamentally the concept of free creation within a system of rule—in an effort to come to grips with some of the same difficulties and problems that the Cartesians faced in their terms.

Now I believe, and here I would differ from a lot of my colleagues, that the move of Descartes to the postulation of a second substance was a very scientific move; it was not a metaphysical or an anti-scientific move. In fact, in many ways it was very much like Newton's intellectual move when he postulated action at a distance; he was moving into the domain of the occult, if you like. He was moving into the domain of something that went beyond well-established science, and was trying to integrate it with well-established science by developing a theory in which these notions could be properly clarified and explained.

Now Descartes, I think, made a similar intellectual move in postulating a second substance. Of course he failed where Newton succeeded; that is, he was unable to lay the groundworks for a mathematical theory of mind, as achieved by Newton and his followers, which laid the groundwork for a mathematical theory of physical entities that incorporated such occult notions as action at a distance and later electromagnetic forces and so on.

But then that poses for us, I think, the task of carrying on and developing this, if you like, mathematical theory of mind; by that I simply mean a precisely articulated, clearly formulated, abstract theory which will have empirical consequences, which will let us know whether the theory is right or wrong, or on the wrong track or the right track, and at the same time will have the properties of mathematical science, that is, the properties of rigour and precision and a structure that makes it possible for us to deduce conclusions from assumptions and so on.

Now it's from that point of view that I try to look back at the seventeenth and eighteenth centuries and to pick out points, which I think are really there, even though I certainly recognise, and in fact would want to insist, that the individuals in question may not have seen it this way.

ELDERS:

Mr. Foucault, I suppose you will have a severe criticism of this?

FOUCAULT:

No ... there are just one or two little historical points. I cannot object to the account which you have given in your historical analysis of their reasons and of their modality. But there is one thing one could nevertheless add: when you speak of creativity as conceived by Descartes, I wonder if you don't transpose to Descartes an idea which is to be found among his successors or even certain of his contemporaries. According to Descartes, the mind was not so very creative. It saw, it perceived, it was illuminated by the evidence.

Moreover, the problem which Descartes never resolved nor entirely mastered, was that of understanding how one could pass from one of these clear and distinct ideas, one of these intuitions, to another, and what status should be given to the evidence of the passage between them. I can't see exactly either the creation in the moment where the mind grasped the truth for Descartes, or even the real creation in the passage from one truth to another.

On the contrary, you can find, I think, at the same time in Pascal and Leibniz, something which is much closer to what you are looking for: in other words in Pascal and in the whole Augustinian stream of Christian thought, you find this idea of a mind in profundity; of a mind folded back in the intimacy of itself which is touched by a sort of unconsciousness, and which can develop its potentialities by the deepening of the self. And that is why the grammar of Port-Royal, to which you refer, is, I think, much more Augustinian than Cartesian.

And furthermore you will find in Leibniz something which you will certainly like: the idea that in the profundity of the mind is incorporated a whole web of logical rela-

tions which constitutes, in a certain sense, the rational
unconscious of the consciousness, the not yet clarified and
visible form of the reason itself, which the monad or the
individual develops little by little, and with which he understands the whole world.

That's where I would make a very small criticism.

ELDERS:

Mr. Chomsky, one moment please.

I don't think it's a question of making a historical criticism, but of formulating your own opinions on these quite
fundamental concepts....

FOUCAULT:

But one's fundamental opinions can be demonstrated in precise analyses such as these.

ELDERS:

Yes, all right. But I remember some passages in your *History
of Madness*, which give a description of the seventeenth and
eighteenth centuries in terms of repression, suppression and
exclusion, while for Mr. Chomsky this period is full of
creativity and individuality.

Why do we have at that period, for the first time, closed
psychiatric or insane asylums? I think this is a very fundamental question....

FOUCAULT:

... on creativity, yes!

But I don't know, perhaps Mr. Chomsky would like to
speak about it ...

ELDERS:

No, no, no, please go on. Continue.

FOUCAULT:

No, I would like to say this: in the historical studies that

I have been able to make, or have tried to make, I have without any doubt given very little room to what you might call the creativity of individuals, to their capacity for creation, to their aptitude for inventing by themselves, for originating concepts, theories or scientific truths by themselves.

But I believe that my problem is different to that of Mr. Chomsky. Mr. Chomsky has been fighting against linguistic behaviourism, which attributed almost nothing to the creativity of the speaking subject; the speaking subject was a kind of surface on which information came together little by little, which he afterwards combined.

In the field of the history of science or, more generally, the history of thought, the problem was completely different.

The history of knowledge has tried for a long time to obey two claims. One is the claim of *attribution* : each discovery should not only be situated and dated, but should also be attributed to someone; it should have an inventor and someone responsible for it. General or collective phenomena on the other hand, those which by definition can't be "attributed", are normally devalued : they are still traditionally described through words like "tradition', "mentality", "modes"; and one lets them play the negative role of a brake in relation to the "originality" of the inventor. In brief, this has to do with the principle of the sovereignty of the subject applied to the history of knowledge. The other claim is that which no longer allows us to save the subject, but the truth : so that it won't be compromised by history, it is necessary not that the truth constitutes itself in history, but only that it reveals itself in it; hidden to men's eyes, provisionally inaccessible, sitting in the shadows, it will wait to be unveiled. The history of truth would be essentially its delay, its fall or the disappearance of the obstacles which have impeded it until now from coming to light. The historical dimension of knowledge is always negative in relation to the truth. It isn't difficult to see how these two claims were adjusted, one to the other : the phenomena of collective order, the "common thought", the "prejudices" of the "myths" of a period, constituted the obstacles which the subject of knowledge had to surmount or to outlive in order to have access finally to the truth; he had to be in an "eccentric" position in order to "discover". At one level this seems to be invoking a certain "romanticism" about the history of science: the solitude of the man of truth, the originality which reopened itself onto the original through history and despite it. I think that, more fundamentally, it's a matter of superimposing the theory of knowledge and the subject of knowledge on the history of knowledge.

And what if understanding the relation of the subject to the truth, were just an effect of knowledge? What if understanding were a complex, multiple, non-individual formation, not "subjected to the subject", which produced effects of truth? One should then put forward positively this entire dimension which the history of science has negativised; analyse the productive capacity of knowledge as a collective practice; and consequently replace individuals and their "knowledge" in the development of a knowledge which at a given moment functions according to certain rules which one can register and describe.

You will say to me that all the Marxist historians of science have been doing this for a long time. But when one sees how they work with these facts and especially what use they make of the notions of consciousness, of ideology as opposed to science, one realises that they are for the main part more or less detached from the theory of knowledge.

In any case, what I am anxious about is substituting transformations of the understanding for the history of the discoveries of knowledge. Therefore I have, in appearance at least, a completely different attitude to Mr. Chomsky apropos creativity, because for me it is a matter of effacing the dilemma of the knowing subject, while for him it is a matter of allowing the dilemma of the speaking subject to reappear.

But if he has made it reappear, if he has described it, it is because he can do so. The linguists have for a long time now analysed language as a system with a collective value. The understanding as a collective totality of rules allowing such and such a knowledge to be produced in a certain period, has hardly been studied until now. Nevertheless, it presents some fairly positive characteristics to the observer. Take for example medicine at the end of the eighteenth century: read twenty medical works, it doesn't matter which, of the years 1770 to 1780, then twenty others from the years 1820 to 1830, and I would say, quite at random, that in forty or fifty years everything had changed; what one talked about, the way one talked about it, not just the remedies, of course, not just the maladies and their classifications, but the outlook itself. Who was responsible for that? Who was the author of it? It is artificial, I think, to say Bichat, or even to expand a little and to say the first anatomical clinicians. It's a matter of a collective and complex transformation of medical understanding in its practice and its rules. And this transformation is far from a negative phenomenon: it is the suppression of a negativity, the effacement of an obstacle, the disappearance of prejudices, the abandonment of old myths, the retreat of irrational beliefs, and access finally freed to experience and to reason; it represents the application of an entirely new *grille*, with its choices and exclusions; a new play with its own rules, decisions and limitations, with its own inner logic, its parameters and its blind alleys, all of which lead to the modification of the point of origin. And it is in this functioning that the understanding itself exists. So, if one studies the history of knowledge, one sees that there are two broad directions of analysis: according to one, one has to show how, under what conditions and for what reasons, the understanding modifies itself in its formative rules, without passing through an original "inventor" discovering the "truth"; and according to the other, one has to show how the working of the rules of an understanding can produce in an individual new and unpublished knowledge. Here my aim rejoins, with imperfect methods and in a quite inferior mode, Mr. Chomsky's project: accounting for the fact that with a few rules or definite elements, unknown totalities, never even produced, can be brought to light by individuals. To resolve this problem, Mr. Chomsky has to reintroduce the dilemma of the subject in the field of grammatical analysis. To resolve an analogous problem in the field of history with which I am involved, one has to do the opposite, in a way: to introduce the point of view of understanding, of its rules, of its systems, of its transformations of totalities in the game of individual knowledge. Here and there the problem of creativity cannot be resolved in the same way, or rather, it can't be formulated in the same terms, given the state of disciplines inside which it is put.

CHOMSKY:

I think in part we're slightly talking at cross purposes, because of a different use of the term creativity. In fact, I should say that my use of the term creativity is a little bit idiosyncratic and therefore the onus falls on me in this case, not on you. But when I speak of creativity, I'm not attributing to the concept the notion of value that is normal when we speak of creativity. That is, when you speak of scientific creativity, you're speaking, properly, of the achievements of a Newton. But in the context in which I have been speaking about creativity, it's a normal human act.

I'm speaking of the kind of creativity that any child demonstrates when he's able to come to grips with a new situation: to describe it properly, react to it properly, tell one something about it, think about it in a new fashion for him and so on. I think it's appropriate to call those acts creative, but of course without thinking of those acts as being the acts of a Newton.

In fact it may very well be *true* that creativity in the arts or the sciences, that which goes beyond the normal, may really involve properties of, well, I would also say of human nature, which may not exist fully developed in the mass of mankind, and may not constitute part of the normal creativity of everyday life.

Now my belief is that science can look forward to the problem of normal creativity as a topic that it can perhaps incorporate within itself. But I don't believe, and I suspect you will agree, that science can look forward, at least in the reasonable future, to coming to grips with true creativity, the achievements of the great artist and the great scientist. It has no hope of accommodating these unique phenomena within its grasp. It's the lower levels of creativity that I've been speaking of.

Now, as far as what you say about the history of science is concerned, I think that's correct and illuminating and particularly relevant in fact to the kinds of enterprise that I see lying before us in psychology and linguistics and the philosophy of the mind.

That is, I think there are certain topics that have been repressed or put aside during the scientific advances of the past few centuries.

For example, this concern with low level creativity that I'm referring to was really present in Descartes also. For example, when he speaks of the difference between a parrot, who can mimic what is said, and a human, who can say new things that are appropriate to the situation, and when he specifies that as being the distinctive property that designates the limits of physics and carries us into the science of the mind, to use modern terms, I think he really is referring to the kind of creativity that I have in mind; and I quite agree with your comments about the other sources of such notions.

Well, these concepts, even in fact the whole notion of the organisation of sentence structure, were put aside during the period of great advances that followed from Sir William Jones and others and the development of comparative philology as a whole.

But now, I think, we can go beyond that period when it

was necessary to forget and to pretend that these phenomena did not exist and to turn to something else. In this
period of comparative philology and also, in my view, struc-
tural linguistics, and much of behavioural psychology, and
in fact much of what grows out of the empiricist tradition
in the study of mind and behaviour, it is possible to put aside
those limitations and bring into our consideration just those
topics that animated a good deal of the thinking and speculation of the seventeenth and eighteenth centuries, and to
incorporate them within a much broader and I think deeper
science of man that will give a fuller role—though it is
certainly not expected to give a complete understanding—
to such notions as innovation and creativity and freedom
and the production of new entities, new elements of thought
and behaviour within some system of rule and schematism.
Those are concepts that I think we can come to grips with.

ELDERS:
Well, may I first of all ask you not to make your answers so
lengthy. [*Foucault laughs.*]
When you discuss creativity and freedom, I think that one
of the misunderstandings, if any misunderstandings have
arisen, has to do with the fact that Mr. Chomsky is starting
from a limited number of rules with infinite possibilities of
application, whereas you, Mr. Foucault, are stressing the
inevitability of the "grille" of our historical and psychological determinisms, which also applies to the way in which
we discover new ideas.
Perhaps we can sort this out, not by analysing the
scientific process, but just by analysing our own thought
process.
When you discover a new fundamental idea, Mr. Foucault, do you believe, that as far as your own personal
creativity is concerned something is happening that makes
you feel that you are being liberated; that something new
has been developed? Perhaps afterwards you discover that it
was not so new. But do you yourself believe that, within

your own personality, creativity and freedom are working together, or not?

FOUCAULT:

Oh, you know, I don't believe that the problem of personal experience is so very important ...

ELDERS:

Why not?

FOUCAULT:

... in a question like this. No, I believe that there is in reality quite a strong similarity between what Mr. Chomsky said and what I tried to show: in other words there exist in fact only possible creations, possible innovations. One can only, in terms of language or of knowledge, produce something new by putting into play a certain number of rules which will define the acceptability or the grammaticality of these statements, or which will define, in the case of knowledge, the scientific character of the statements.

Thus, we can roughly say that linguists before Mr. Chomsky mainly insisted on the rules of construction of statements and less on the innovation represented by every new statement, or the hearing of a new statement. And in the history of science or in the history of thought, we placed more emphasis on individual creation, and we had kept aside and left in the shadows these communal, general rules, which obscurely manifest themselves through every scientific discovery, every scientific invention, and even every philosophical innovation.

And to that degree, when I no doubt wrongly believe that I am saying something new, I am nevertheless conscious of the fact that in my statement there are rules at work, not only linguistic rules, but also epistemological rules, and those rules characterise contemporary knowledge.

CHOMSKY:

Well, perhaps I can try to react to those comments within

my own framework in a way which will maybe shed some light on this.

Let's think again of a human child, who has in his mind some schematism that determines the kind of language he can learn. Okay. And then, given experience, he very quickly knows the language, of which this experience is a part, or in which it is included.

Now this is a normal act; that is, it's an act of normal intelligence, but it's a highly creative act.

If a Martian were to look at this process of acquiring this vast and complicated and intricate system of knowledge on the basis of this ridiculously small quantity of data, he would think of it as an immense act of invention and creation. In fact, a Martian would, I think, consider it as much of an achievement as the invention of, let's say, any aspect of a physical theory on the basis of the data that was presented to the physicist.

However, if this hypothetical Martian were then to observe that every normal human child immediately carries out this creative act and they all do it in the same way and without any difficulty, whereas it takes centuries of genius to slowly carry out the creative act of going from evidence to a scientific theory, then this Martian would, if he were rational, conclude that the structure of the knowledge that is acquired in the case of language is basically internal to the human mind; whereas the structure of physics is not, in so direct a way, internal to the human mind. Our minds are not constructed so that when we look at the phenomena of the world theoretical physics comes forth, and we write it down and produce it; that's not the way our minds are constructed.

Nevertheless, I think there is a possible point of connection and it might be useful to elaborate it: that is, how is it that we are able to construct any kind of scientific theory at all? How is it that, given a small amount of data, it's possible for various scientists, for various geniuses even, over a long period of time, to arrive at some kind of a theory, at least in some cases, that is more or less profound and more or less empirically adequate.

This is a remarkable fact.

And, in fact, if it were not the case that these scientists, including the geniuses, were beginning with a very narrow limitation on the class of possible scientific theories, if they didn't have built into their minds somehow an obviously unconscious specification of what is a possible scientific theory, then this inductive leap would certainly be quite impossible: just as if each child did not have built into his mind the concept of human language in a very restricted way, then the inductive leap from data to knowledge of a language would be impossible.

So even though the process of, let's say, deriving knowledge of physics from data is far more complex, far more difficult for an organism such as ours, far more drawn out in time, requiring intervention of genius and so on and so forth, nevertheless in a certain sense the achievement of discovering physical science or biology or whatever you like, is based on something rather similar to the achievement of the normal child in discovering the structure of his language: that is, it *must* be achieved on the basis of an initial limitation, an initial restriction on the class of possible theories. If you didn't begin by knowing that only certain things are possible theories, then no induction would be possible at all. You could go from data anywhere, in any direction. And the fact that science converges and progresses itself shows us that such initial limitations and structures exist.

If we really want to develop a theory of scientific creation, or for that matter artistic creation, I think we have to focus attention precisely on that set of conditions that, on the one hand, delimits and restricts the scope of our possible knowledge, while at the same time permitting the inductive leap to complicated systems of knowledge on the basis of a small amount of data. That, it seems to me, would be the way to progress towards a theory of scientific creativity, or in fact towards any question of epistemology.

ELDERS:

Well, I think if we take this point of the initial limitation with all its creative possibilities, I have the impression that for Mr. Chomsky rules and freedom are not opposed to each other, but more or less imply each other. Whereas I get the impression that it is just the reverse for you, Mr. Foucault. What are your reasons for putting it the opposite way, for this really is a very fundamental point in the debate, and I hope we can elaborate it.

To formulate the same problem in other terms: can you think of universal knowledge without any form of repression?

FOUCAULT:

Well, in what Mr. Chomsky has just said there is something which seems to me to create a little difficulty; perhaps I understood it badly.

I believe that you have been talking about a limited number of possibilities in the order of a scientific theory. That is true if you limit yourself to a fairly short period of time, whatever it may be. But if you consider a longer period, it seems to me that what is striking is the proliferation of possibilities by divergences.

For a long time the idea has existed that the sciences, knowledge, followed a certain line of "progress", obeying the principle of "growth", and the principle of the convergence of all these kinds of knowledge. And yet when one sees how the European understanding, which turned out to be a world-wide and universal understanding in a historical and geographical sense, developed, can one say that there has been growth? I, myself, would say that it has been much more a matter of transformation.

Take, as an example, animal and plant classifications. How often have they not been rewritten since the Middle Ages according to completely different rules: by symbolism, by natural history, by comparative anatomy, by the theory of evolution. Each time this rewriting makes the knowledge completely different in its functions, in its economy, in its internal relations. You have there a principle of divergence, much more than one of growth. I would much rather say that there are many different ways of making possible simultaneously a few types of knowledge. There is, therefore, from a certain point of view, always an excess of *data* in relation to possible systems in a given period, which causes them to be experienced within their boundaries, even in their deficiency, which means that one fails to realise their creativity; and from another point of view, that of the historian, there is an excess, a proliferation of systems for a small amount of *data*, from which originates the widespread idea that it is the discovery of new facts which determines movement in the history of science.

CHOMSKY:

Here perhaps again, let me try to synthesise a bit. I agree with your conception of scientific progress; that is, I don't think that scientific progress is simply a matter of the accumulated addition of new knowledge and the absorption of new theories and so on. Rather I think that it has this sort of jagged pattern that you describe, forgetting certain problems and leaping to new theories ...

FOUCAULT:

And transforming the same knowledge.

CHOMSKY:

Right. But I think that one can perhaps hazard an explanation for that. Oversimplifying grossly, I really don't mean what I'm going to say now literally, one might suppose that the following general lines of an explanation are accurate: it is as if, as human beings of a particular biologically given organisation, we have in our heads, to start with, a certain set of possible intellectual structures, possible sciences. Okay?

Now, in the lucky event that some aspect of reality happens to have the character of one of these structures in our mind, then we have a science: that is to say that, fortunately, the structure of our mind and the structure of some aspect of reality coincide sufficiently so that we develop an intelligible science.

It is precisely this initial limitation in our minds to a certain kind of possible science which provides the tremendous richness and creativity of scientific knowledge. It is important to stress—and this has to do with your point about limitation and freedom—that were it not for these limitations, we would not have the creative act of going from a little bit of knowledge, a little bit of experience, to a rich and highly articulated and complicated array of knowledge. Because if anything could be possible, then nothing would be possible.

But it is precisely because of this property of our minds, which in detail we don't understand, but which, I think, in a general way we can begin to perceive, which presents us with certain possible intelligible structures, and which in the course of history and insight and experience begin to come into focus or fall out of focus and so on; it is precisely because of this property of our minds that the progress of science, I think, has this erratic and jagged character that you describe.

That doesn't mean that everything is ultimately going to fall within the domain of science. Personally I believe that many of the things we would like to understand, and maybe the things we would *most* like to understand, such as the nature of man, or the nature of a decent society, or lots of other things, might really fall outside the scope of possible human science.

ELDERS:
Well, I think that we are confronted again with the question of the inner relation between limitation and freedom. Do

you agree, Mr. Foucault, with the statement about the combination of limitation, fundamental limitation ...

FOUCAULT:

It is not a matter of combination. Only creativity is possible in putting into play of a system of rules; it is not a mixture of order and freedom.

Where perhaps I don't completely agree with Mr. Chomsky, is when he places the principle of these regularities, in a way, in the interior of the mind or of human nature.

If it is a matter of whether these rules are effectively put to work by the human mind, all right; all right, too, if it is a question of whether the historian and the linguist can think it in their turn; it is all right also to say that these rules should allow us to realise what is said or thought by these individuals. But to say that these regularities are connected, as conditions of existence, to the human mind or its nature, is difficult for me to accept: it seems to me that one must, before reaching that point—and in any case I am talking only about the understanding—replace it in the field of other human practices, such as economics, technology, politics, sociology, which can serve them as conditions of formation, of models, of place, of apparition, etc. I would like to know whether one cannot discover the system of regularity, of constraint, which makes science possible, somewhere else, even outside the human mind, in social forms, in the relations of production, in the class struggles, etc.

For example, the fact that at a certain time madness became an object for scientific study, and an object of knowledge in the West, seems to me to be linked to a particular economic and social situation.

Perhaps the point of difference between Mr. Chomsky and myself is that when he speaks of science he probably thinks of the formal organisation of knowledge, whereas I am speaking of knowledge itself, that is to say, I think of the content of various knowledges which is dispersed into a particular society, permeates through that society, and as-

1. Sir Alfred Ayer (left) and Arne Naess (right) debate 'The Glass is on the Table — an empiricist versus a total view', at the International School of Philosophy, Amersfoort. Fons Elders is in the Chair.
Photographs: Nederlandse Omroep Stichting

2. Sir John Eccles (left) and Sir Karl Popper (right) consider
'Falsifiability and Freedom' at the Binnenhof, The Hague.
Photographs: Nederlandse Omroep Stichting

3. Noam Chomsky (left) and Michel Foucault (right) discuss 'Human
Nature: Justice versus Power' at the Technical High School,
Eindhoven.
Photographs: Nederlandse Omroep Stichting

4. Henri Lefebvre (left) and Leszek Kolakowski (right) debate
'Evolution or Revolution' in the Lutheran Church, Amsterdam.
Photographs: Nederlandse Omroep Stichting

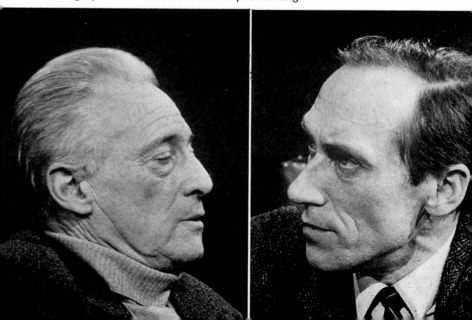

serts itself as the foundation for education, for theories, for practices, etc.

ELDERS:

But what does this theory of knowledge mean for your theme of the death of man or the end of the period of the nineteenth-twentieth centuries?

FOUCAULT:

But this doesn't have any relation to what we are talking about.

ELDERS:

I don't know, because I was trying to apply what you have said to your anthropological notion. You have already refused to speak about your own creativity and freedom, haven't you? Well, I'm wondering what are the psychological reasons for this ...

FOUCAULT:

[*Protesting*.] Well, you can wonder about it, but I can't help that.

ELDERS:

Ah, well.

FOUCAULT:

I am not wondering about it.

ELDERS:

But what are the objective reasons, in relation to your conception of understanding, of knowledge, of science, for refusing to answer these personal questions?

When there is a problem for you to answer, what are your reasons for making a problem out of a personal question?

FOUCAULT:

No, I'm not making a problem out of a personal question, I make of a personal question an absence of a problem.

Let me take a very simple example, which I will not analyse, but which is this: How was it possible that men began, at the end of the eighteenth century, for the first time in the history of Western thought and of Western knowledge, to open up the corpses of people in order to know what was the source, the origin, the anatomical needle, of the particular malady which was responsible for their deaths?

The idea seems simple enough. Well, four or five thousand years of medicine in the West were needed before we had the idea of looking for the cause of the malady in the lesion of a corpse.

If you tried to explain this by the personality of Bichat, I believe that would be without interest. If, on the contrary, you tried to establish the place of disease and of death in society at the end of the eighteenth century, and what interest industrial society effectively had in quadrupling the entire population in order to expand and develop itself, as a result of which medical surveys of society were made, big hospitals were opened, etc.; if you tried to find out how medical knowledge became institutionalised in that period, how its relations with other kinds of knowledge were ordered, well, then you could see how the relationship between disease, the hospitalised, ill person, the corpse, and pathological anatomy were made possible.

Here is, I believe, a form of analysis which I don't say is new, but which in any case has been much too neglected; and personal events have almost nothing to do with it.

ELDERS:

Yes, but nevertheless it would have been very interesting for us to know a little bit more about your arguments to refute this.

Could you, Mr. Chomsky—and as far as I'm concerned,

it's my last question about this philosophical part of the debate—give your ideas about, for example, the way the social sciences are working? I'm thinking here especially about your severe attacks on behaviourism. And perhaps you could even explain a little the way Mr. Foucault is now working in a more or less behaviouristic way. [*Both philosophers laugh.*]

CHOMSKY:

I would like to depart from your injunction very briefly, just to make one comment about what Mr. Foucault just said.

I think that illustrates very nicely the way in which we're digging into the mountain from opposite directions, to use your original image. That is, I think that an act of scientific creation depends on two facts: one, some intrinsic property of the mind, another, some set of social and intellectual conditions that exist. And it is not a question, as I see it, of which of these we should study; rather we will understand scientific discovery, and similarly any other kind of discovery, when we know what these factors are and can therefore explain how they interact in a particular fashion.

My particular interest, in this connection at least, is with the intrinsic capacities of the mind; yours, as you say, is in the particular arrangement of social and economic and other conditions.

FOUCAULT:

But I don't believe that difference is connected to our characters—because at this moment it would make Mr. Elders right, and he must not be right.

CHOMSKY:

No, I agree, and ...

FOUCAULT:

It's connected to the state of knowledge, of knowing, in which we are working. The linguistics with which you have

been familiar, and which you have succeeded in transforming, excluded the importance of the creative subject, of the
creative speaking subject; while the history of science such
as it existed when people of my generation were starting to
work, on the contrary, exalted individual creativity ...

CHOMSKY:
Yes.

FOUCAULT:
... and put aside these collective rules.

CHOMSKY:
Yes, yes.

QUESTION:
Ah ...

ELDERS:
Yes, please go on.

QUESTION:
It goes a bit back in your discussion, but what I should like
to know, Mr. Chomsky, is this: you suppose a basic system
of what must be in a way elementary limitations that are
present in what you call human nature; to what extent do
you think these are subject to historical change? Do you
think, for instance, that they have changed substantially
since, let's say, the seventeenth century? In that case, you
could perhaps connect this with the ideas of Mr. Foucault?

CHOMSKY:
Well, I think that as a matter of biological and anthropological fact, the nature of human intelligence certainly has not
changed in any substantial way, at least since the seventeenth century, or probably since Cro-Magnon man. That
is, I think that the fundamental properties of our intelli-

gence, those that are within the domain of what we are discussing tonight, are certainly very ancient; and that if you took a man from five thousand or maybe twenty thousand years ago, and placed him as a child within today's society, he would learn what everyone else learns, and he would be a genius or a fool or something else, but he wouldn't be fundamentally different.

But, of course, the level of acquired knowledge changes, social conditions change—those conditions that permit a person to think freely and break through the bonds of, let's say, superstitious constraint. And as those conditions change, a given human intelligence will progress to new forms of creation. In fact this relates very closely to the last question that Mr. Elders put, if I can perhaps say a word about that.

Take behavioural science, and think of it in these contexts. It seems to me that the fundamental property of behaviourism, which is in a way suggested by the odd term behavioural science, is that it is a negation of the possibility of developing a scientific theory. That is, what defines behaviourism is the very curious and self-destructive assumption that you are *not* permitted to create an interesting theory.

If physics, for example, had made the assumption that you have to keep to phenomena and their arrangement and such things, we would be doing Babylonian astronomy today. Fortunately physicists never made this ridiculous, extraneous assumption, which has its own historical reasons and had to do with all sorts of curious facts about the historical context in which behaviourism evolved.

But looking at it purely intellectually, behaviourism is the arbitrary insistence that one must not create a scientific theory of human behaviour; rather one must deal directly with phenomena and their interrelation, and no more—something which is totally impossible in any other domain, and I assume impossible in the domain of human intelligence or human behaviour as well. So in this sense I don't think that behaviourism is a science. Here is a case in point of just the kind of thing that you mentioned and that Mr. Foucault is discussing: under certain historical circumstances, for example those in which experimental psychology developed, it was—for some reason which I won't go into—interesting and maybe important to impose some very strange limitations on the kind of scientific theory construction that was permitted, and those very strange limitations are known as behaviourism. Well, it has long since run its course, I think. Whatever value it may have had in 1880, it has no function today except constraining and limiting scientific inquiry and should therefore simply be dispensed with, in the same way one would dispense with a physicist who said: you're not allowed to develop a general physical theory, you're only allowed to plot the motions of the planets and make up more epicycles and so on and so forth. One forgets about that and puts it aside. Similarly one should put aside the very curious restrictions that define behaviourism; restrictions which are, as I said before, very much suggested by the term behavioural science itself.

We can agree, perhaps, that behaviour in some broad sense constitutes the data for the science of man. But to define a science by its data, would be to define physics as the theory of meter-readings. And if a physicist were to say: yes, I'm involved in meter-reading science, we could be pretty sure that he was not going to get very far. They might talk about meter-readings and correlations between them and such things, but they wouldn't ever create physical theory.

And so the term itself is symptomatic of the disease in this case. We should understand the historical context in which these curious limitations developed, and having understood them, I believe, discard them and proceed in the science of man as we would in any other domain, that is by discarding entirely behaviourism and in fact, in my view, the entire empiricist tradition from which it evolved.

QUESTION:

So you are not willing to link your theory about innate limitations, with Mr. Foucault's theory of the "grille". There might be a certain connection. You see, Mr. Foucault says that an upsurge of creativity in a certain direction automatically removes knowledge in another direction, by a system of "grilles". Well, if you had a changing system of limitations, this might be connected.

CHOMSKY:

Well, the reason for what he describes, I think, is different. Again, I'm oversimplifying. We have more possible sciences available intellectually. When we try out those intellectual constructions in a changing world of fact, we will not find cumulative growth. What we will find are strange leaps: here is a domain of phenomena, a certain science applies very nicely; now slightly broaden the range of phenomena, then another science, which is very different, happens to apply very beautifully, perhaps leaving out some of these other phenomena. Okay, that's scientific progress and that leads to the omission or forgetting of certain domains. But I think the reason for this is precisely this set of principles, which unfortunately, we don't know, which makes the whole discussion rather abstract, which defines for us what is a possible intellectual structure, a possible deep-science, if you like.

ELDERS:

Well, let's move over now to the second part of the discussion, to politics. First of all I would like to ask Mr. Foucault why he is so interested in politics, because he told me that in fact he likes politics much more than philosophy.

FOUCAULT:

I've never concerned myself, in any case, with philosophy. But that is not a problem. [*He laughs.*]

Your question is: why am I so interested in politics? But

if I were to answer you very simply, I would say this: *why shouldn't I be interested?* That is to say, what blindness, what deafness, what density of ideology would have to weigh me down to prevent me from being interested in what is probably the most crucial subject to our existence, that is to say the society in which we live, the economic relations within which it functions, and the system of power which defines the regular forms and the regular permissions and prohibitions of our conduct. The essence of our life consists, after all, of the political functioning of the society in which we find ourselves.

So I can't answer the question of why I should be interested; I could only answer it by asking why shouldn't I be interested?

ELDERS:
You are obliged to be interested, isn't that so?

FOUCAULT:
Yes, at least, there isn't anything odd here which is worth question or answer. Not to be interested in politics, that's what constitutes a problem. So instead of asking me, you should ask someone who is not interested in politics and then your question would be well-founded, and you would have the right to say "Why, damn it, are you not interested?" [*They laugh and the audience laughs.*]

ELDERS:
Well, yes, perhaps. Mr. Chomsky, we are all very interested to know your political objectives, especially in relation to your well-known anarcho-syndicalism or, as you formulated it, libertarian socialism. What are the most important goals of your libertarian socialism?

CHOMSKY:
I'll overcome the urge to answer the earlier very interesting question that you asked me and turn to this one.

Let me begin by referring to something that we have already discussed, that is, *if* it is correct, as I believe it is, that a fundamental element of human nature is the need for creative work, for creative inquiry, for free creation without the arbitrary limiting effect of coercive institutions, then, of course, it will follow that a decent society should maximise the possibilities for this fundamental human characteristic to be realised. That means trying to overcome the elements of repression and oppression and destruction and coercion that exist in any existing society, ours for example, as a historical residue.

Now any form of coercion or repression, any form of autocratic control of some domain of existence, let's say, private ownership of capital or state control of some aspects of human life, any such autocratic restriction on some area of human endeavour, can be justified, *if at all, only* in terms of the need for subsistence, or the need for survival, or the need for defence against some horrible fate or something of that sort. It cannot be justified intrinsically. Rather it must be overcome and eliminated.

And I think that, at least in the technologically advanced societies of the West we are now certainly in a position where meaningless drudgery can very largely be eliminated, and to the marginal extent that it's necessary, can be shared among the population; where centralised autocratic control of, in the first place, economic institutions, by which I mean either private capitalism or state totalitarianism or the various mixed forms of state capitalism that exist here and there, has become a destructive vestige of history.

They are all vestiges that have to be overthrown, eliminated in favour of direct participation in the form of workers' councils or other free associations that individuals will constitute themselves for the purpose of their social existence and their productive labour.

Now a federated, decentralised system of free associations, incorporating economic as well as other social institutions, would be what I refer to as anarcho-syndicalism; and it seems to me that this is the appropriate form of social organisation for an advanced technological society, in which human beings do *not* have to be forced into the position of tools, of cogs in the machine. There is no longer any social necessity for human beings to be treated as mechanical elements in the productive process; that can be overcome and we must overcome it by a society of freedom and free association, in which the creative urge that I consider intrinsic to human nature, will in fact be able to realise itself in whatever way it will.

And again, like Mr. Foucault, I don't see how any human being can fail to be interested in this question. [*Foucault laughs.*]

ELDERS :

Do you believe, Mr. Foucault, that we can call our societies in anyway democratic, after listening to this statement from Mr. Chomsky ?

FOUCAULT :

No, I don't have the least belief that one could consider our our society democratic. [*Laughs.*]

If one understands by democracy the effective exercise of power by a population which is neither divided nor hierarchically ordered in classes, it is quite clear that we are very far from democracy. It is only too clear that we are living under a regime of a dictatorship of class, of a power of class which imposes itself by violence, even when the instruments of this violence are institutional and constitutional; and to that degree, there isn't any question of democracy for us.

Well. When you asked me why I was interested in politics, I refused to answer because it seemed evident to me, but perhaps your question was How am I interested in it ?

And had you asked me that question, and in a certain sense I could say you have, I would say to you that I am much less advanced in my way, I go much less far than Mr. Chomsky. That is to say that I admit to not being able to

define, nor for even stronger reasons to propose, an ideal
social model for the functioning of our scientific or technological society.

On the other hand, one of the tasks that seems immediate
and urgent to me, over and above anything else, is this:
that we should indicate and show up, even where they are
hidden, all the relationships of political power which actually control the social body and oppress or repress it.

What I want to say is this: it is the custom, at least in
European society, to consider that power is localised in the
hands of the government and that it is exercised through a
certain number of particular institutions, such as the administration, the police, the army, and the apparatus of the state.
One knows that all these institutions are made to elaborate
and to transmit a certain number of decisions, in the name of
the nation or of the state, to have them applied and to
punish those who don't obey. But I believe that political
power also exercises itself through the mediation of a certain
number of institutions which look as if they have nothing in
common with the political power, and as if they are independent of it, while they are not.

One knows this in relation to the family; and one knows
that the university, and in a general way, all teaching
systems, which appear simply to disseminate knowledge,
are made to maintain a certain social class in power; and to
exclude the instruments of power of another social class.
Institutions of knowledge, of foresight and care, such as
medicine, also help to support the political power. It's also
obvious, even to the point of scandal, in certain cases related
to psychiatry.

It seems to me that the real political task in a society such
as ours is to criticise the workings of institutions, which appear to be both neutral and independent; to criticise and
attack them in such a manner that the political violence
which has always exercised itself obscurely through them
will be unmasked, so that one can fight against them.

This critique and this fight seem essential to me for different reasons: firstly, because political power goes much deeper than one suspects; there are centres and invisible, little-known points of support; its true resistance, its true solidity is perhaps where one doesn't expect it. Probably it's insufficient to say that behind the governments, behind the apparatus of the State, there is the dominant class; one must locate the point of activity, the places and forms in which its domination is exercised. And because this domination is not simply the expression in political terms of economic exploitation, it is its instrument and, to a large extent, the condition which makes it possible; the suppression of the one is achieved through the exhaustive discernment of the other. Well, if one fails to recognise these points of support of class power, one risks allowing them to continue to exist; and to see this class power reconstitute itself even after an apparent revolutionary process.

CHOMSKY:

Yes, I would certainly agree with that, not only in theory but also in action. That is, there are two intellectual tasks: one, and the one that I was discussing, is to try to create the vision of a future just society; that is to create, if you like, a humanistic social theory that is based, if possible, on some firm and humane concept of the human essence or human nature. That's one task.

Another task is to understand very clearly the nature of power and oppression and terror and destruction in our own society. And that certainly includes the institutions you mentioned, as well as the central institutions of any industrial society, namely the economic, commercial and financial institutions and in particular, in the coming period, the great multi-national corporations, which are not very far from us physically tonight [i.e. Philips at Eindhoven].

Those are the basic institutions of oppression and coercion and autocratic rule that appear to be neutral despite everything they say: well, we're subject to the democracy of the market place, and that must be understood precisely in terms of their autocratic power, including the particular form of autocratic control that comes from the domination of market forces in an inegalitarian society.

Surely we must understand these facts, and not only understand them but combat them. And in fact, as far as one's own political involvements are concerned, in which one spends the majority of one's energy and effort, it seems to me that they must certainly be in that area. I don't want to get personal about it, but my own certainly are in that area, and I assume everyone's are.

Still, I think it would be a great shame to put aside entirely the somewhat more abstract and philosophical task of trying to draw the connections between a concept of human nature that gives full scope to freedom and dignity and creativity and other fundamental human characteristics, and to relate that to some notion of social structure in which those properties could be realised and in which meaningful human life could take place.

And in fact, if we are thinking of social transformation or social revolution, though it would be absurd, of course, to try to sketch out in detail the goal that we are hoping to reach, still we should know something about where we think we are going, and such a theory may tell it to us.

FOUCAULT:

Yes, but then isn't there a danger here? If you say that a certain human nature exists, that this human nature has not been given in actual society the rights and the possibilities which allow it to realise itself ... that's really what you have said, I believe.

CHOMSKY:

Yes.

FOUCAULT:

And if one admits that, doesn't one risk defining this human nature—which is at the same time ideal and real, and has been hidden and repressed until now—in terms borrowed from our society, from our civilisation, from our culture?

I will take an example by greatly simplifying it. The socialism of a certain period, at the end of the nineteenth century, and the beginning of the twentieth century, admitted in effect that in capitalist societies man hadn't realised the full potential for his development and self-realisation; that human nature was effectively alienated in the capitalist system. And it dreamed of an ultimately liberated human nature.

What model did it use to conceive, project, and eventually realise that human nature? It was in fact the bourgeois model.

It considered that an alienated society was a society which, for example, gave pride of place to the benefit of all, to a sexuality of a bourgeois type, to a family of a bourgeois type, to an aesthetic of a bourgeois type. And it is moreover very true that this has happened in the Soviet Union and in the popular democracies: a kind of society has been reconstituted which has been transposed from the bourgeois society of the nineteenth century. The universalisation of the model of the bourgeois has been the utopia which has animated the constitution of Soviet society.

The result is that you too realised, I think, that it is difficult to say exactly what human nature is.

Isn't there a risk that we will be led into error? Mao Tse-Tung spoke of bourgeois human nature and proletarian human nature, and he considers that they are not the same thing.

CHOMSKY:

Well, you see, I think that in the intellectual domain of political action, that is the domain of trying to construct a vision of a just and free society on the basis of some notion of human nature, we face the very same problem that we face in immediate political action, namely, that of being impelled to do something, because the problems are so great, and yet knowing that whatever we do is on the basis of a very partial understanding of the social realities, and the human realities in this case.

For example, to be quite concrete, a lot of my own activity really has to do with the Vietnam war, and some of my own energy goes into civil disobedience. Well, civil disobedience in the U.S. is an action undertaken in the face of considerable uncertainties about its effects. For example, it threatens the social order in ways which might, one might argue, bring about fascism; and that would be a very bad thing for America, for Vietnam, for Holland and for everyone else. You know, if a great Leviathan like the United States were really to become fascist, a lot of problems would result; so that is one danger in undertaking this concrete act.

On the other hand there is a great danger in not undertaking it, namely, if you don't undertake it, the society of Indo-China will be torn to shreds by American power. In the face of these uncertainties one has to choose a course of action.

Well, similarly in the intellectual domain, one is faced with the uncertainties that you correctly pose. Our concept of human nature is certainly limited; it's partially socially conditioned, constrained by our own character defects and the limitations of the intellectual culture in which we exist. Yet at the same time it is of critical importance that we know what impossible goals we're trying to achieve, if we hope to achieve some of the possible goals. And that means that we have to be bold enough to speculate and create social theories on the basis of partial knowledge, while remaining very open to the strong possibility, and in fact overwhelming probability, that at least in some respects we're very far off the mark.

ELDERS:
Well, perhaps it would be interesting to delve a little deeper into this problem of strategy. I suppose that what you call

civil disobedience is probably the same as what we call extra-parliamentary action?

CHOMSKY:

No, I think it goes beyond that.

Extra-parliamentary action would include, let's say, a mass legal demonstration, but civil disobedience is narrower than all extra-parliamentary action, in that it means direct defiance of what is alleged, incorrectly in my view, by the state to be law.

ELDERS:

So, for example, in the case of Holland, we had something like a population census. One was obliged to answer questions on official forms. You would call it civil disobedience if one refused to fill in the forms?

CHOMSKY:

Right. I would be a little bit careful about that, because, going back to a very important point that Mr. Foucault made, one does not necessarily allow the state to define what is legal. Now the state has the power to enforce a certain concept of what is legal, but power doesn't imply justice or even correctness; so that the state may define something as civil disobedience and may be wrong in doing so.

For example, in the United States the state defines it as civil disobedience to, let's say, derail an ammunition train that's going to Vietnam; and the state is *wrong* in defining that as civil disobedience, because it's legal and proper and should be done. It's proper to carry out actions that will prevent the criminal acts of the state, just as it is proper to violate a traffic ordinance in order to prevent a murder.

If I had stopped my car in front of a traffic light which was red, and then I drove through the red traffic light to prevent somebody from, let's say, machine-gunning a group of people, of course that's not an illegal act, it's an appropriate and proper action; no sane judge would convict you for such an action.

Similarly, a good deal of what the state authorities define as civil disobedience is not really civil disobedience: in fact, it's legal, obligatory behaviour in violation of the commands of the state, which may or may not be legal commands.

So one has to be rather careful about calling things illegal, I think.

FOUCAULT:

Yes, but I would like to ask you a question. When, in the United States, you commit an illegal act, do you justify it in terms of justice or of a superior legality, or do you justify it by the necessity of the class struggle, which is at the present time essential for the proletariat in their struggle against the ruling class?

CHOMSKY:

Well, here I would like to take the point of view which is taken by the American Supreme Court and probably other courts in such circumstances; that is, to try to settle the issue on the narrowest possible grounds. I would think that ultimately it would make very good sense, in many cases, to act against the legal institutions of a given society, if in so doing you're striking at the sources of power and oppression in that society.

However, to a very large extent existing law represents certain human values, which are decent human values; and existing law, correctly interpreted, permits much of what the state commands you not to do. And I think it's important to exploit the fact ...

FOUCAULT:

Yeah.

CHOMSKY:

... it's important to exploit the areas of law which are

properly formulated and then perhaps to act directly against those areas of law which simply ratify some system of power.

FOUCAULT:
But, but, I, I ...

CHOMSKY:
Let me get ...

FOUCAULT:
My question, my question was this: when you commit a clearly illegal act ...

CHOMSKY:
... which *I* regard as illegal, not just the state.

FOUCAULT:
No, no, well, the state's ...

CHOMSKY:
... that the state regards as illegal ...

FOUCAULT:
... that the state considers as illegal.

CHOMSKY:
Yeah.

FOUCAULT:
Are you committing this act in virtue of an ideal justice, or because the class struggle makes it useful and necessary? Do you refer to ideal justice, that's my problem.

CHOMSKY:
Again, very often when I do something which the state re-

gards as illegal, I regard it as legal : that is, I regard the state as criminal. But in some instances that's not true. Let me be quite concrete about it and move from the area of class war to imperialist war, where the situation is somewhat clearer and easier.

Take international law, a very weak instrument as we know, but nevertheless one that incorporates some very interesting principles. Well, international law is, in many respects, the instrument of the powerful : it is a creation of states and their representatives. In developing the presently existing body of international law, there was no participation by mass movements of peasants.

The structure of international law reflects that fact; that is, international law permits much too wide a range of forceful intervention in support of existing power structures that define themselves as states against the interests of masses of people who happen to be organised in opposition to states.

Now that's a fundamental defect of international law and I think one is justified in opposing that aspect of international law as having no validity, as having no more validity than the divine right of kings. It's simply an instrument of the powerful to retain their power.

But, in fact, international law is not *solely* of that kind. And in fact there are interesting elements of international law, for example, embedded in the Nuremberg principles and the United Nations Charter, which permit, in fact, I believe, *require* the citizen to act against his own state in ways which the state will falsely regard as criminal. Nevertheless, he's acting legally, because international law also happens to prohibit the threat or use of force in international affairs, except under some very narrow circumstances, of which, for example, the war in Vietnam is not one. This means that in the particular case of the Vietnam war, which interests me most, the American state is acting in a criminal capacity. And the people have the right to stop criminals from committing murder. Just because the criminal happens to call your action illegal when you try to stop him, it doesn't mean it *is* illegal.

A perfectly clear case of that is the present case of the Pentagon Papers in the United States, which, I suppose, you know about.

Reduced to its essentials and forgetting legalisms, what is happening is that the state is trying to prosecute people for exposing its crimes. That's what it amounts to.

Now, obviously that's absurd, and one must pay no attention whatsoever to that distortion of any reasonable judicial process. Furthermore, I think that the existing system of law even explains *why* it is absurd. But if it didn't, we would then have to oppose that system of law.

FOUCAULT:

So it is in the name of a purer justice that you criticise the functioning of justice?

There is an important question for us here. It is true that in all social struggles, there is a question of "justice". To put it more precisely, the fight against class justice, against its injustice, is always part of the social struggle: to dismiss the judges, to change the tribunals, to amnesty the condemned, to open the prisons, has always been part of social transformations as soon as they become slightly violent. At the present time in France the function of justice and the police is the target of many attacks from those whom we call the "gauchistes". But if justice is at stake in a struggle, then it is as an instrument of power; it is not in the hope that finally one day, in this or another society, people will be rewarded according to their merits, or punished according to their faults. Rather than thinking of the social struggle in terms of "justice", one has to emphasise justice in terms of the social struggle.

CHOMSKY:

Yeah, but surely you believe that your role in the war is a just role, that you are fighting a just war, to bring in a concept from another domain. And that, I think, is important. If you thought that you were fighting an unjust war, you couldn't follow that line of reasoning.

I would like to slightly reformulate what you said. It seems to me that the difference isn't between legality and ideal justice; it's rather between legality and better justice.

I would agree that we are certainly in no position to create a system of ideal justice, just as we are in no position to create an ideal society in our minds. We don't know enough and we're too limited and too biased and all sorts of other things. But we are in a position—and we must act as sensitive and responsible human beings in that position—to imagine and move towards the creation of a better society and also a better system of justice. Now this better system will certainly have its defects. But if one compares the better system with the existing system, without being confused into thinking that our better system is the ideal system, we can then argue, I think, as follows:

The concept of legality and the concept of justice are not identical; they're not entirely distinct either. Insofar as legality incorporates justice in this sense of better justice, referring to a better society, then we should follow and obey the law, and force the state to obey the law and force the great corporations to obey the law, and force the police to obey the law, if we have the power to do so.

Of course, in those areas where the legal system happens to represent not better justice, but rather the techniques of oppression that have been codified in a particular autocratic system, well, then a reasonable human being should disregard and oppose them, at least in principle; he may not, for some reason, do it in fact.

FOUCAULT:
But I would merely like to reply to your first sentence, in which you said that if you didn't consider the war you make against the police to be just, you wouldn't make it.

I would like to reply to you in terms of Spinoza and

say that the proletariat doesn't wage war against the ruling class because it considers such a war to be just. The proletariat makes war with the ruling class because, for the first time in history, it wants to take power. And because it will overthrow the power of the ruling class it considers such a war to be just.

CHOMSKY:
Yeah, I don't agree.

FOUCAULT:
One makes war to win, not because it is just.

CHOMSKY:
I don't, personally, agree with that.

For example, if I could convince myself that attainment of power by the proletariat would lead to a terrorist police state, in which freedom and dignity and decent human relations would be destroyed, then I wouldn't want the proletariat to take power. In fact the only reason for wanting any such thing, I believe, is because one thinks, rightly or wrongly, that some fundamental human values will be achieved by that transfer of power.

FOUCAULT:
When the proletariat takes power, it may be quite possible that the proletariat will exert towards the classes over which it has just triumphed, a violent, dictatorial and even bloody power. I can't see what objection one could make to this.

But if you ask me what would be the case if the proletariat exerted bloody, tyrannical and unjust power towards itself, then I would say that this could only occur if the proletariat hadn't really taken power, but that a class outside the proletariat, a group of people inside the proletariat, a bureaucracy or petit bourgeois elements had taken power.

CHOMSKY:
Well, I'm not at all satisfied with that theory of revolution

for a lot of reasons, historical and others. But even if one were to accept it for the sake of argument, still that theory maintains that it is proper for the proletariat to take power and exercise it in a violent and bloody and unjust fashion, because it is claimed, and in my opinion falsely, that that will lead to a more just society, in which the state will wither away, in which the proletariat will be a universal class and so on and so forth. If it weren't for that future justification, the concept of a violent and bloody dictatorship of the proletariat would certainly be unjust. Now this is another issue, but I'm very sceptical about the idea of a violent and bloody dictatorship of the proletariat, especially when expressed by self-appointed representatives of a vanguard party, who, we have enough historical experience to know and might have predicted in advance, will simply be the new rulers over this society.

FOUCAULT:
Yes, but I haven't been talking about the power of the proletariat, which in itself would be an unjust power; you are right in saying that this would obviously be too easy. I would like to say that the power of the proletariat could, in a certain period, imply violence and a prolonged war against a social class over which its triumph or victory was not yet totally assured.

CHOMSKY:
Well, look, I'm not saying there is an absolute.... For example, I am not a committed pacifist. I would not hold that it is under all imaginable circumstances wrong to use violence, even though use of violence is in some sense unjust. I believe that one has to estimate relative justices.

But the use of violence and the creation of some degree of injustice can only be justified on the basis of the claim and the assessment—which always ought to be undertaken very, very seriously and with a good deal of scepticism—that this violence is being exercised because a more just result is going to be achieved. If it does not have such a grounding, it is really totally immoral, in my opinion.

FOUCAULT:

I don't think that as far as the aim which the proletariat proposes for itself in leading a class struggle is concerned, it would be sufficient to say that it is in itself a greater justice. What the proletariat will achieve by expelling the class which is at present in power and by taking over power itself, is precisely the suppression of the power of class in general.

CHOMSKY:

Okay, but that's the further justification.

FOUCAULT:

That is the justification, but one doesn't speak in terms of justice but in terms of power.

CHOMSKY:

But it *is* in terms of justice; it's because the end that will be achieved is claimed as a just one.

No Leninist or whatever you like would dare to say "We, the proletariat, have a right to take power, and then throw everyone else into crematoria." If that were the consequence of the proletariat taking power, of course it would not be appropriate.

The idea is—and for the reasons I mentioned I'm sceptical about it—that a period of violent dictatorship, or perhaps violent and bloody dictatorship, is justified because it will mean the submergence and termination of class oppression, a proper end to achieve in human life; it is because of that final qualification that the whole enterprise might be justified. Whether it is or not is another issue.

FOUCAULT:

If you like, I will be a little bit Nietzschean about this; in other words, it seems to me that the idea of justice in itself is an idea which in effect has been invented and put to work in different types of societies as an instrument of a certain political and economic power or as a weapon against that power. But it seems to me that, in any case, the notion of justice itself functions within a society of classes as a claim made by the oppressed class and as justification for it.

CHOMSKY:

I don't agree with that.

FOUCAULT:

And in a classless society, I am not sure that we would still use this notion of justice.

CHOMSKY:

Well, here I really disagree. I think there is some sort of an absolute basis—if you press me too hard I'll be in trouble, because I can't sketch it out—ultimately residing in fundamental human qualities, in terms of which a "real" notion of justice is grounded.

I think it's too hasty to characterise our existing systems of justice as merely systems of class oppression; I don't think that they are that. I think that they embody systems of class oppression and elements of other kinds of oppression, but they also embody a kind of groping towards the true humanly, valuable concepts of justice and decency and love and kindness and sympathy, which I think are real.

And I think that in any future society, which will, of course, never be the perfect society, we'll have such concepts again, which we hope, will come closer to incorporating a defence of fundamental human needs, including such needs as those for solidarity and sympathy and whatever, but will probably still reflect in some manner the inequities and the elements of oppression of the existing society.

However, I think what you're describing only holds for a very different kind of situation.

For example, let's take a case of national conflict. Here are two societies, each trying to destroy the other. No question of justice arises. The only question that arises is Which side are you on? Are you going to defend your own society and destroy the other?

I mean, in a certain sense, abstracting away from a lot of historical problems, that's what faced the soldiers who were massacring each other in the trenches in the First World War. They were fighting for nothing. They were fighting for the right to destroy each other. And in that kind of circumstance no questions of justice arise.

And of course there were rational people, most of them in jail, like Karl Liebknecht, for example, who pointed that out and were in jail because they did so, or Bertrand Russell, to take another example on the other side. There were people who understood that there was no point to that mutual massacre in terms of any sort of justice and that they ought to just call it off.

Now those people were regarded as madmen or lunatics and criminals or whatever, but of course they were the only sane people around.

And in such a circumstance, the kind that you describe, where there is no question of justice, just the question of who's going to win a struggle to the death, then I think the proper human reaction is: call it off, don't win either way, try to stop it—and of course if you say that, you'll immediately be thrown in jail or killed or something of that sort, the fate of a lot of rational people.

But I don't think that's the typical situation in human affairs, and I don't think that's the situation in the case of class-conflict or social revolution. There I think that one can and *must* give an argument, if you can't give an argument you should extract yourself from the struggle. Give an argument that the social revolution that you're trying to achieve *is* in the ends of justice, *is* in the ends of realising fundamental human needs, not merely in the ends of putting some other group into power, because they want it.

FOUCAULT:

Well, do I have time to answer?

ELDERS:

Yes.

FOUCAULT:

How much? Because ...

ELDERS:

Two minutes. [*Foucault laughs.*]

FOUCAULT:

But I would say that that is unjust. [*Everybody laughs.*]

CHOMSKY:

Absolutely, yes.

FOUCAULT:

No, but I don't want to answer in so little time. I would simply say this, that finally this problem of human nature, when put simply in theoretical terms, hasn't led to an argument between us; ultimately we understand each other very well on these theoretical problems.

On the other hand, when we discussed the problem of human nature and political problems, then differences arose between us. And contrary to what you think, you can't prevent me from believing that these notions of human nature, of justice, of the realisation of the essence of human beings, are all notions and concepts which have been formed within our civilisation, within our type of knowledge and our form of philosophy, and that as a result form part of our class system; and one can't, however regrettable it may be, put forward these notions to describe or justify a fight which should—and shall in principle—overthrow the very fundaments of our society. This is an extrapolation for which I can't find the historical justification. That's the point ...

CHOMSKY:
It's clear.

ELDERS:
Mr. Foucault, if you were obliged to describe our actual society in pathological terms, which of its kinds of madness would most impress you?

FOUCAULT:
In our contemporary society?

ELDERS:
Yes.

FOUCAULT:
If I were to say with which malady contemporary society is most afflicted?

ELDERS:
Yes.

FOUCAULT:
The definition of disease and of the insane, and the classification of the insane has been made in such a way as to exclude from our society a certain number of people. If our society characterised itself as insane, it would exclude itself. It pretends to do so for reasons of internal reform. Nobody is more conservative than those people who tell you that the modern world is afflicted by nervous anxiety or schizophrenia. It is in fact a cunning way of excluding certain people or certain patterns of behaviour.

So I don't think that one can, except as a metaphor or a game, validly say that our society is schizophrenic or paranoid, unless one gives these words a non-psychiatric meaning. But if you were to push me to an extreme, I would say that our society has been afflicted by a disease, a very curious, a very paradoxical disease, for which we haven't yet found a name; and this mental disease has a very curious symptom, which is that the symptom itself brought the mental disease into being. There you have it.

ELDERS:

Great. Well, I think we can immediately start the discussion.

QUESTION:

Mr. Chomsky, I would like to ask you one question. In your discussion you used the term "proletariat"; what do you mean by "proletariat" in a highly developed technological society? I think this is a Marxist notion, which doesn't represent the exact sociological state of affairs.

CHOMSKY:

Yes, I think you are right, and that is one of the reasons why I kept hedging on that issue and saying I'm very sceptical about the whole idea, because I think the notion of a proletariat, if we want to use it, has to be given a new interpretation fitting to our present social conditions. Really, I'd even like to drop the word, since it's so loaded with specific historical connotations, and think instead of the people who do the productive work of the society, manual and intellectual work. I think those people should be in a position to organise the conditions of their work, and to determine the ends of their work and the uses to which it's put; and, because of my concept of human nature, I really think of that as partially including everyone. Because I think that any human being who is not physically or mentally deformed—and here I again must disagree with Monsieur Foucault and express my belief that the concept of mental illness probably *does* have an absolute character, to some extent at least—is not only capable of, but is insistent upon doing productive, creative work, if given the opportunity to do so.

I've never seen a child who didn't want to build something out of blocks, or learn something new, or try the next task. And the only reason why adults aren't like that is, I suppose, that they have been sent to school and other oppressive institutions, which have driven that out of them.

Now if that's the case, then the proletariat, or whatever you want to call it, can really be universal, that is, it can be all those human beings who are impelled by what I believe to be the fundamental human need to be yourself, which means to be creative, to be exploratory, to be inquisitive ...

QUESTION:
May I interrupt?

CHOMSKY:
... to do useful things, you know.

QUESTION:
If you use such a category, which has another meaning in Marxist ...

CHOMSKY:
That's why I say maybe we ought to drop the concept.

QUESTION:
Wouldn't you do better to use another term? In this situation I would like to ask another question: which groups, do you think, will make the revolution?

CHOMSKY:
Yes, that's a different question.

QUESTION:
It's an irony of history that at this moment young intellectuals, coming from the middle and upper classes, call themselves proletarians and say we must join the proletarians. But I don't see any class-conscious proletarians. And that's the great dilemma.

CHOMSKY:

Okay. Now I think you're asking a concrete and specific question, and a very reasonable one.

It is not true in our given society that all people are doing useful, productive work, or self-satisfying work—obviously that's very far from true—or that, if they were to do the kind of work they're doing under conditions of freedom, it would thereby become productive and satisfying.

Rather there are a very large number of people who are involved in other kinds of work. For example, the people who are involved in the management of exploitation, or the people who are involved in the creation of artificial consumption, or the people who are involved in the creation of mechanisms of destruction and oppression, or the people who are simply not given any place in a stagnating industrial economy. Lots of people are excluded from the possibility of productive labour.

And I think that the revolution, if you like, should be in the *name* of all human beings; but it will have to be conducted by certain categories of human beings, and those will be, I think, the human beings who really *are* involved in the productive work of society. Now *what* this is will differ, depending upon the society. In our society it includes, I think, intellectual workers; it includes a spectrum of people that runs from manual labourers to skilled workers, to engineers, to scientists, to a very large class of professionals, to many people in the so-called service occupations, which really do constitute the overwhelming mass of the population, at least in the United States, and I suppose probably here too, and will become the mass of the population in the future.

And so I think that the student-revolutionaries, if you like, have a point, a partial point: that is to say, it's a very important thing in a modern advanced industrial society how the trained intelligentsia identifies itself. It's very important to ask whether they are going to identify themselves as social managers, whether they are going to be technocrats, or servants of either the state or private power, or, alternatively, whether they are going to identify themselves as part of the work force, who happen to be doing intellectual labour.

If the latter, then they can and should play a decent role in a progressive social revolution. If the former, then they're part of the class of oppressors.

QUESTION:

Thank you.

ELDERS:

Yes, go on please.

QUESTION:

I was struck, Mr. Chomsky, by what you said about the intellectual necessity of creating new models of society. One of the problems we have in doing this with student groups in Utrecht is that we are looking for consistency of values. One of the values you more or less mentioned is the necessity of decentralisation of power. People on the spot should partici-pate in decision-making.

That's the value of decentralisation and participation: but on the other hand we're living in a society that makes it more and more necessary—or seems to make it more and more necessary—that decisions are made on a world-wide scale. And in order to have, for example, a more equal distribution of welfare, etc., it might be necessary to have more centralisation. These problems should be solved on a higher level. Well, that's one of the inconsistencies we found in creating your models of society, and we should like to hear some of your ideas on it.

I've one small additional question—or rather a remark—to make to you. That is: how can you, with your very courageous attitude towards the war in Vietnam, survive in an institution like MIT, which is known here as one of the great war contractors and intellectual makers of this war?

CHOMSKY:

Well, let me answer the second question first, hoping that I don't forget the first one. Oh, no, I'll try the first question first; and then remind me if I forget the second.

In general, I am in favour of decentralisation. I wouldn't want to make it an absolute principle, but the reason I would be in favour of it, even though there certainly is, I think, a wide margin of speculation here, is because I would imagine that in general a system of centralised power will operate very efficiently in the interest of the most powerful elements *within it*.

Now a system of decentralised power and free association will of course face the problem, the specific problem that you mention, of inequity—one region is richer than the other, etc. But my own guess is that we're safer in trusting to what I hope are the fundamental human emotions of sympathy and the search for justice, which may arise within a system of free association.

I think we're safer in hoping for progress on the basis of those human instincts than on the basis of the institutions of centralised power, which, I believe, will almost inevitably act in the interest of their most powerful components.

Now that's a little abstract and too general, and I wouldn't want to claim that it's a rule for all occasions, but I think it's a principle that's effective in a lot of occasions.

So, for example, I think that a democratic socialist libertarian United States would be more likely to give substantial aid to East Pakistani refugees than a system of centralised power which is basically operating in the interest of multinational corporations. And, you know, I think the same is true in a lot of other cases. But it seems to me that that principle, at least, deserves some thought.

As to the idea, which was perhaps lurking in your question anyway—it's an idea that's often expressed—that there is some technical imperative, some property of advanced technological society that requires centralised power and decision-making—and a lot of people say that, from Robert McNamara on down—as far as I can see it's perfect nonsense, I've never seen any argument in favour of it.

It seems to me that modern technology, like the technology of data-processing, or communication and so on, has precisely the opposite implications. It implies that relevant information and relevant understanding can be brought to everyone quickly. It doesn't have to be concentrated in the hands of a small group of managers who control all knowledge, all information and all decision-making. So technology, I think, can be liberating, it has the property of being possibly liberating; it's converted, like everything else, like the system of justice, into an instrument of oppression because of the fact that power is badly distributed. I don't think there is anything in modern technology or modern technological society that leads away from decentralisation of power, quite the contrary.

About the second point, there are two aspects to that : one is the quesion how MIT tolerates me, and the other question is how I tolerate MIT. [*Laughter.*]

Well, as to how MIT tolerates me, here again, I think, one shouldn't be overly schematic. It's true that MIT is a major institution of war-research. But it's also true that it embodies very important libertarian values, which are, I think, quite deeply embedded in American society, fortunately for the world. They're not deeply embedded enough to save the Vietnamese, but they are deeply embedded enough to prevent far worse disasters.

And here, I think, one has to qualify a bit. There is imperial terror and aggression, there is exploitation, there is racism, lots of things like that. But there is also a real concern, coexisting with it, for individual rights of a sort which, for example, are embodied in the Bill of Rights, which is by no means simply an expression of class oppression. It is also an expression of the necessity to defend the individual against state power.

Now these things coexist. It's not that simple, it's not just all bad or all good. And it's the particular balance in which they coexist that makes an institute that produces weapons of war be willing to tolerate, in fact, in many ways even encourage, a person who is involved in civil disobedience against the war.

Now as to how I tolerate MIT, that raises another question.

There are people who argue, and I have never understood the logic of this, that a radical ought to dissociate himself from oppressive institutions. The logic of that argument is that Karl Marx shouldn't have studied in the British Museum which, if anything, was the symbol of the most vicious imperialism in the world, the place where all the treasures an empire had gathered from the rape of the colonies, were brought together.

But I think Karl Marx was quite right in studying in the British Museum. He was right in using the resources and in fact the liberal values of the civilisation that he was trying to overcome, against it. And I think the same applies in this case.

QUESTION:
But aren't you afraid that your presence at MIT gives them a clean conscience?

CHOMSKY:
I don't see how, really. I mean, I think my presence at MIT serves marginally to help, I don't know how much, to increase student activism against a lot of the things that MIT as an institution does. At least I *hope* that's what it does.

ELDERS:
Is there another question?

QUESTION:
I would like to get back to the question of centralisation. You said that technology does not contradict decentralisation. But the problem is, can technology criticise itself, its influences, and so forth? Don't you think that it might be necessary to have a central organisation that could criticise the influence of technology on the whole universe? And I

don't see how that could be incorporated in a small technological institution.

CHOMSKY:

Well, I have nothing against the interaction of federated free
associations; and in that sense centralisation, interaction,
communication, argument, debate, can take place, and so
on and so forth, and criticism, if you like. What I am talking
about is the centralisation of power.

QUESTION:

But of course power is needed, for instance to forbid some
technological institutions from doing work that will only
benefit the corporation.

CHOMSKY:

Yeah, but what I'm arguing is this: if we have the choice
between trusting in centralised power to make the right decision in that matter, or trusting in free associations of
libertarian communities to make that decision, I would rather
trust the latter. And the reason is that I think that they
can serve to maximise decent human instincts, whereas a
system of centralised power will tend in a general way to
maximise one of the worst of human instincts, namely the
instinct of rapaciousness, of destructiveness, of accumulat-
ing power to oneself and destroying others. It's a kind of
instinct which does arise and functions in certain historical
circumstances, and I think we want to create the kind of
society where it is likely to be repressed and replaced by
other and more healthy instincts.

QUESTION:

I hope you are right.

ELDERS:

Well, ladies and gentlemen, I think this must be the end of
the debate. Mr. Chomsky, Mr. Foucault, I thank you very

much for your far-reaching discussion over the philosophical and theoretical, as well as the political questions of the debate, both for myself and also on behalf of the audience, here and at home.

LESZEK KOLAKOWSKI
and
HENRI LEFÈBVRE

Evolution or Revolution

Evolution or Revolution

ELDERS:

Ladies and gentlemen, during this series of debates on philosophy and on society, we have encountered a fundamental
difficulty because many people are not used to thinking in
philosophical terms. These same people think, and I believe
they are right, that what the philosophers say remains
abstract, in other words it has no relation to their own ways
of expressing themselves.

Mr. Lefèbvre, Mr. Kolakowski, are you, yourselves, nevertheless convinced that we can attract the attention of the
audience, here and at home, not because of these monumental chairs in which we are sitting, not because of the religious and intellectual aura associated with this church where
we are meeting, but because of the importance of your
ideas? Mr. Kolakowski....

KOLAKOWSKI:

Well, you answer this question!

LEFÈBVRE:

I'm willing to answer first. The classic philosophical ideas are
obscure because of their terminology. Nevertheless, in contemporary thinking, we have succeeded in presenting a certain number of ideas which can be directly understood by
any individual of average culture or merely some experience
of social life.

I will give an example: the notion of the consumer society. I believe myself to be the author of that term, but
people have attributed the idea to different sources: some
attribute it to Galbraith and I don't know whom, but that's
not important. It's the success itself of the idea which has

made its origin of little relevance. One can't attribute it today to a definite system, to a dated philosophical way of thinking. This idea has made its way; it has helped to awaken the conscience of modern society, the critical conscience.

ELDERS:

Excuse me, Mr. Lefèbvre, but you are deviating a little from the question, because it's a rather personal question, and not a question about philosophy itself.

LEFÈBVRE:

I think I will in any case answer your question by saying that philosophy has today gone beyond the stage of initiation, at which it was something reserved only for a minority. Perhaps it is no longer exactly a matter of philosophy, but of concepts of philosophical importance, on the way to philosophy, which are capable of penetrating that consciousness which one might call the cultivated consciousness. I have quoted the concept of the consumer society; alternatively we could take the concept of alienation, a concept which has been absorbed to an extremely large extent, although it's of philosophical origin.

ELDERS:

Do you still call yourself a philosopher?

LEFÈBVRE:

No, I consider myself a meta-philosopher, that is to say I don't build a system. I aim to take from philosophy those ideas which are capable of arousing the critical consciousness, ideas that are destined for a higher and at the same time more profound consciousness of the world in which we live.

ELDERS:

Mr. Kolakowski, do you agree with this idea of meta-philosophy?

KOLAKOWSKI:

First, I don't understand what it means exactly. Meta-philosophy, that is to say, reflections on philosophy.... It's certainly a legitimate reflection. But when I force myself to reflect on the question which you just asked, the first thing which comes to mind is that philosophy, such as I understand it, is not a science. It's not a scientific activity to make philosophy. I don't think that philosophy, in the technical sense of the word, is of capital importance. But I think that what philosophers do is quite simply to articulate the daily experiences of a certain community in a slightly complicated language.

ELDERS:

You say that philosophy is not a science, yet we have presented you as a Marxist. Isn't that a little troublesome?

KOLAKOWSKI:

What is troublesome?

ELDERS:

Are you still a Marxist, in your own opinion?

KOLAKOWSKI:

Well, frankly, that doesn't interest me: that is to say, I am completely indifferent whether someone wants to call me a Marxist or not.

ELDERS:

And if I called you a Catholic? Would it be the same if I called you a Catholic?

KOLAKOWSKI:

No, I am not a Catholic, certainly, because I was not baptised in a Catholic church; and that is the definition of a Catholic. And there is no baptism in Marxism, only belonging to the party. Well, I was baptised in that sense, but I'm not any more. So really, I am indifferent about it. I don't deny that I am, as are many others under the influence of Marx, of the Marxist thought in general. But I don't know any definition applicable to our period which can determine who is or who is not a Marxist, because there are at least a dozen different Marxisms which oppose each other. And there is really not very much sense in trying to define exactly who is or isn't a Marxist.

LEFÈBVRE:

I willingly accept this idea that there are many different and even contradictory Marxisms which can claim the same tradition, for finally—and this always happens in the so-called history of philosophy—the philosophy, the stream of thought, divides itself into currents and opposing tendencies.

ELDERS:

Yes, but for many people this vagueness of Marxism implies *a priori* its condemnation.

But in relation to this, there is another question: Mr. Lefèbvre, is the Marxist manner of thinking the only one which can lead to a complete understanding of a society as far as you are concerned?

LEFÈBVRE:

Wait, there are different questions here. We should follow up with what was said at the beginning. I would like to return to the idea of meta-philosophy.

Firstly, Marx has said that the revolution, the way he thinks of it, conceives it, and projects it, is not a philosophy, but the realisation of that philosophy. In the course of its history, philosophy creates a certain idea of the human being, and the revolution realises this idea, but not without modifying and transforming it. Meta-philosophy is the idea that philosophy leads towards an idea or a projection of a human being, which the revolution realises. That's the first point.

KOLAKOWSKI :

You don't think that he might have had a false consciousness on this point ?

LEFÈBVRE :

Surely, and if one only reproduces his arguments, without
confronting it with what has happened since, one can engage
oneself in false consciousness. But in this Marx is only a
means of getting through to our time. I think that the
understanding of our time has to begin with the thought of
Marx and that it even has to begin with attempts to restitute
it as an integral whole.

Thereafter one tries to understand what has happened,
because the great works of Marx are now a century old
and many things have happened since. In my opinion, and
I can't see how you could refute this idea, the analysis of
what has happened over the century can only be made by
starting with Marx, even if this only amounts to an analysis
of the deception or of the errors or the illusions that originated with the thought of Marx.

KOLAKOWSKI :

Yes, okay.

LEFÈBVRE :

I think that one has to start with the thought of Marx to
understand our time. This is the unavoidable, necessary, but
insufficient starting point.

KOLAKOWSKI :

Yes, everybody would agree with this.

LEFÈBVRE :

Yes, but all the better if everybody did agree, for that would
mean that the people who don't attach any importance to
Marxist ideas would consider them nevertheless as an historical phenomenon of indisputable importance. I believe that,

basically, there are two parts to Marx. There is a scientific part, which one can discuss, and then a part which consists of preoccupations with the end of the modern world. The two parts don't exactly coincide: for example, the notion of alienation doesn't exactly go along with what was scientifically elaborated.

ELDERS:

We will come back to this notion of alienation.

LEFÈBVRE:

Yes, but you can't put it between parentheses, can you?

ELDERS:

Okay, but as we don't agree on a clear enough definition of Marxism in general, I would like to ask you to indicate the objectives of your personal Marxism, because it is not very clear yet. At this time, I still don't know if you are a Marxist or not. But if you're going to say what are the objectives of your Marxism, according to your own definition, then we will know.

KOLAKOWSKI:

It's necessary that I should come back to the problem which Henri has posed, that is to say, to that coincidence between the scientific and the philosophical or ideological sides of Marxism.

I am not of the opinion that there is such a divergence in Marx himself. I believe, on the contrary, that *Capital* is a direct continuation of more or less normative ideas which he developed in the forties: especially that the very notion of the exchange value is an elaboration of the notion of alienation. Basically it is the same thing. First of all, I believe that the notion of alienation is a normative notion, because alienation means man in a situation in which he has been deprived of his humanity. Thus the notion itself presupposes a concept of man such as he should be, such as he would be if his empirical existence conformed to the claims of his nature. Well, I think that the notion of exchange value is the direct prolongation of this same concept, because, as we know it, exchange value, as defined in *Capital*, is not a quantitative notion. One cannot measure its value. It's precisely man, made into an object in his products, who is not able to dominate, and whose products are subjected to the laws of the market.

ELDERS:

Will you explain to the audience this notion of exchange value, because I don't think that most people are familiar with it.

KOLAKOWSKI:

Well, it's the key notion of *Capital*. The value of merchandise defines itself by the socially necessary time of work in the given technological conditions. Marx starts his theoretical work with an explanation of this notion, but he is very conscious of the fact that exchange value itself can't explain the movement of prices. This is not a quantitative notion. On the contrary, it is a notion the ideological function of which is to present human work as the unique source of exchange value, as opposed to the value of usage, that is to say the physical qualities of things which make them useful.

ELDERS:

So work is not quantitative?

KOLAKOWSKI:

It is not quantitative. It becomes quantitative only through money.

ELDERS:

Oh, but that is another thing, precisely because prices are not values. Prices are determined by other factors.

LEFÈBVRE:

But also by values....

KOLAKOWSKI:

Also, yes, among others. Among other factors, prices are determined by value, of course, but we aren't able to separate the influence of the different factors in such a way as to be able to distil, so to speak, the value in the products, independently of prices. There is no method at all of doing this.

ELDERS:

But maybe everything you have said is rather technical ...

KOLAKOWSKI:

That's a fact.

ELDERS:

... and the problem remains that we still don't know the objectives of your Marxism. Will you respond, Mr. Lefèbvre?

LEFÈBVRE:

With a certain stubbornness, I continue what we have already said. I don't think that there is a divergence between the philosophy and the science in Marx. I don't think that there is a separation, a split between on the one hand the theory of alienation, a philosophical theory taken from Hegel, extracted from Hegelianism, and restated in quite a different way, and on the other the theory of economic science and, finally, the critique of political economy in *Capital*. But the destinies of these two inseparable aspects of the work of Marx have been different. On one side we have a political economy which is derived from it, namely the socialist planned economy; and the theory of—or the attempts at—a planned or semi-planned economy in the capitalist countries. That is the destiny of the economic part of the work of Marx.

As for the philosophy, alienation has produced something like a transformation of consciousness, much more profound than the economic theory, for one has become conscious of alienation in different domains; alienation of youth, alienation of adolescents, alienation of women, alienation of the worker, alienation of the colonised, and so on. The course of the notion of alienation has been very different from that of Marxist science.

ELDERS:

Yet, Mr. Lefèbvre, you have been invited here not because of Marx, but because of yourself. So, once again, what are the objectives of your Marxism? So far you have been talking as a professor of philosophy, isn't that so? But we invited you as a philosopher in your own right.

LEFÈBVRE:

I talk as someone who, years ago, drew the notion of alienation out of the obscurity in which it had been buried and gave support to its striking trajectory across the world in such a way that, having been a yeast and a ferment in Europe, it has today reached America, where it has become a banality. But by becoming a banality itself, it becomes efficient, and efficient in depth. Marxism has become a social and political force in two ways: through the theory of alienation and through political economy and the critique of political economy. And there is a consciousness of alienation, which has seized the entire world, were it not that political alienation in all those countries where the state is powerful and vigorous imposes constraint and repression. This consciousness of political alienation is an important phenomenon today, and even a political phenomenon.

ELDERS:

But you are excluded from the French communist party because of a certain alienation on your side, according to the official party?

LEFÈBVRE:
I left the French communist party for political reasons.

ELDERS:
But you were excluded.

LEFÈBVRE:
Excluded? What does that mean? I have left it.

ELDERS:
You literally used this word in your autobiography, *La Somme et le Reste*.

LEFÈBVRE:
This was ironically ...

ELDERS:
No, it was true!

LEFÈBVRE:
It was ironically.

ELDERS:
Where are the books, where are the books?

KOLAKOWSKI:
Well, let's call it self-expulsion.

LEFÈBVRE:
If you please, the immediate reason for my departure from the French communist party was that the French communist party wasn't supporting the case of the Algerians enough.

ELDERS:
Ah, well.

LEFÈBVRE:
There was an immediate political reason. In 1956, '57, '58,

the Algerian revolution had begun and the French communist party didn't support Algeria; that was the political
reason. Now there is a theoretical and ideological reason,
which is that I have affirmed that there is an alienation in
relation to the State, a political alienation, and that the
State as the State is a power of oppression and repression,
which creates a particular alienation which retains society
within its existing limits in relation to the possibilities which
it contains in itself; and that is political alienation. The definition of alienation which I use, which comes from Marx,
but which has to be inferred, is the following : there is alienation when an individual or social being can't realise the
potential which he carries in himself, because his potential is
blocked by pressure or repression. That is the definition of
alienation.

KOLAKOWSKI :
But in any case, it is not exact.

LEFÈBVRE :
But it is mine.

KOLAKOWSKI :
Ah, it is yours ?

LEFÈBVRE :
Yes, yes, Elders asks for the definition of alienation according
to a good Marxist. Well, I reply.

KOLAKOWSKI :
Excuse me, what I wanted to say is simply that it doesn't
correspond exactly to the concept of alienation as used by
Marx, because in Marx alienation means precisely a situation
in which man and the society are incapable of controlling
their own products. There are, of course, political institutions, but they are derivative : the principal source of
alienation is the alienation of merchandise itself, that is to

say the existence of the market which functions according to its own laws, the existence of exchange value, of money. All other forms of alienation are derived from this, as is the existence of the bureaucracy of the State, which has transformed itself into an autonomous force, an autonomous power. And even the existence of religious internationalisation is all derived from it. The principal point is that society is not able to control the material products which it produces.

LEFÈBVRE:
But if you please, there is already the idea in Marx that ...

ELDERS:
No, but Marx is dead now, right?

LEFÈBVRE:
Not completely.

ELDERS:
Yes.

LEFÈBVRE:
But you kill him! You want to kill him! Not so fast!

ELDERS:
No, the other Marxists!

LEFÈBVRE:
May I answer you briefly?
In Marx there is still the idea that the conditions, the premisses of a different society, of a new society, have already been realised and that only a certain number of social and political conditions in relation to production prevent this realisation; the revolution consists of breaking these obstacles which stand in the way of a new, already possible society. This is in all the works of Marx. And I know that

what you say is not false, but as far as I am concerned, I have inferred a meaning which is not exactly the one you give and which seems to me correct also, according to the thought of Marx. That's really dialectical, isn't it?

KOLAKOWSKI:
Well.

ELDERS:
Will you explain this word? For example, you are also an alienated person from the point of view of your party, or from the old Polish party, isn't that so?

KOLAKOWSKI:
The Polish party is dead. But I really prefer to keep away from this word alienation. Now really everyone talks about alienation on any occasion.

LEFÈBVRE:
That's true, that's true. We can't talk about it any more. When a young girl of fourteen loses her boyfriend she says she is alienated. Well then, we can't talk about it any more. But that doesn't prevent the concept from progressing quietly along.

KOLAKOWSKI:
Yes.

ELDERS:
No, but to come back to this question of your expulsion, can one compare the conflict of loyalty that you have had with that of many Catholic priests at the present time?

KOLAKOWSKI:
Catholic priests?

ELDERS:
Yes. They often have a conflict of loyalty with their chur-

ches, from the point of view of the orthodoxy. The official party in Poland, the French communist party and the Soviet Union still have a fairly Stalinist Marxism: so you are both expelled and you are both alienated from their points of view. You are both lost sons, right?

KOLAKOWSKI:

No, we think they are politically alienated.

LEFÈBVRE:

Yes, but there is quite a difference between the father and the son, isn't there?

ELDERS:

But do you think there is a certain parallel with the conflict of loyalty of many Catholic priests?

KOLAKOWSKI:

That depends. The Catholic priests either leave the Church or are expelled from the Church for different reasons. One reason is disobedience and another is heresy. There are two reasons which one has to distinguish clearly.

ELDERS:

And you belong to the category of "heresy"?

KOLAKOWSKI:

To both!

ELDERS:

To both?

KOLAKOWSKI:

Yes. You can be disobedient without being heretical.

ELDERS:

Yes, but if you are heretical, you are disobedient.

KOLAKOWSKI:
Yes.

ELDERS:
So what?

KOLAKOWSKI:
Yes.

ELDERS:
You have talked about yourself already in relation to this notion of alienation. Perhaps we could try to formulate this notion in other terms. You are quite well-versed in the history of theology. Does Marxism wait for the Christian heaven on earth? You have written that there are certain parallels. Do you believe that the Marxist waits for heaven on earth?

KOLAKOWSKI:
I don't like these parallels very much, for a simple reason. There are, of course, parallels and similarities which are evident, between the political mechanisms in the functioning of the apparatus of socialist states or communist parties and those of the ecclesiastical apparatus. But the analogies are limited, quite simply because religion is still an attempt to transcend not only the immediate, but also the temporary condition, temporality itself.

ELDERS:
Yes, but there are, I think, some Christian elements in Marxism. For example, although the notion of historicity can be exaggerated, it can imply the notion of a social paradise, a paradise of heaven on earth, a society without classes.

KOLAKOWSKI:
The idea of salvation?

ELDERS:
Yes.

KOLAKOWSKI:

If one uses the idea of salvation in such a general sense that it also embraces earthly salvation, well then, yes, there are analogies. The idea of salvation is the idea of the return of man to his source, and hope in the identification of the empirical existence of man with his essence. One can also ask why so many people try to demonstrate the common inspiration in Marxism and religious thinking.

ELDERS:

It is striking. Well, there must be something between the two?

KOLAKOWSKI:

I can only repeat what Maritain has said: that all idea of earthly happiness, of earthly paradise, can only be considered by a Christian as a relative goal, while for a Marxist, it's always the absolute goal. Seeing that any idea of the perfect society can, in the eyes of a Christian, only be a relative idea, all possible comparisons and also any collaboration between the two ideas are limited. What Maritain realised, and what many contemporary theologians don't seem to notice is that Christianity transcends the earthly condition, that will not say that it can't collaborate with all those who want to ameliorate social conditions in the limits of the temporal. It seems even obvious and banal at first sight, but I believe that Maritain was right, and that these are two completely different views: one either considers earthly goals or a perfect imaginary society as a goal in itself, or one relativises them in relation to really absolute goals.

LEFÈBVRE:

But I don't know what you are trying to say; do you perhaps want to say that Christianity is a heresy of Judaism, and that Marxism is a heresy of Christianity, and that now, in relation to Marxism, we will see some heresies flowering? It's possible, but as a heresy according to Christianity, Marxism has introduced and proposed objectives, bringing a completely different sense of time. The idea is that the human being realises himself by work and by struggle. He realises himself not in the name of a transcendental existence, but through his history and in his work, work that develops and is amplified and deepens itself as a creative force, mobilising nature and making possible all the struggles of history, including the struggle between classes. This idea of the realisation of man by himself, through his efforts, is something quite different from the Christian religion, it seems to me. And what always differs and is itself united in this is the question of giving a meaning to historical time, though this meaning is not always the same. It's not the idea of a realisation arranged by a divine providence, it's the idea of a being which realises itself through its struggles and its action.

ELDERS:
But Christianity also knows the notion of linear time; Calvinism is familiar with this notion of work and salvation by work. So now everything you've said affirms the problem, I think.

KOLAKOWSKI:
It's true, of course, that Christianity accepts linear time, but that is only to say that there aren't historical cycles, there is no eternal return of things, etc. Linear time says that human history is divided by certain irreversible events such as the Creation, the Resurrection of Christ, and the Second Coming. The coming of Christ is the cause, essentially, because we are saved; this is irreversible. This doesn't necessarily imply, nor does it exclude, an idea of progress, of course.

ELDERS:
Do you agree?

LEFÈBVRE:
I will ask you, because I'm hardly a theologian.

ELDERS:

No, but he says that Marxism, if I have really understood him, doesn't recognise this notion of progress.

KOLAKOWSKI:

I don't want to say that it doesn't recognise this notion. I want to say that the Christian philosophy of history doesn't imply this notion. I am willing to admit that a Christian can accept this notion without contradiction to his faith, of course. But religious history doesn't necessarily imply the notion of progress, except for the actual coming of Christ on earth. For the Marxists, the essential thing is the belief that history marches necessarily towards a determined goal, to the collective salvation, while there is no social salvation in the Christian idea; there is individual salvation, but society is not immortal.

LEFÈBVRE:

Unless you propose at this moment a new heresy which consists of thinking that there will be a salvation for society. A new heresy in Christianity would be interesting.

KOLAKOWSKI:

If it could still be called Christianity.

LEFÈBVRE:

You think not? Why not?

KOLAKOWSKI:

I don't see how one could insert the concept of social salvation into Christianity.

LEFÈBVRE:

No, I can't either.

ELDERS:

But you have written a book of eight hundred pages: *Les Chrétiens sans Église.*

KOLAKOWSKI:
Yes.

ELDERS:
And many of the mystics were full of social enthusiasm for a new order : for religious, but also social, right? I don't quite understand when you now say that this notion is completely strange to Christianity. Why then this book of eight hundred pages?

KOLAKOWSKI:
It was not my book ...

ELDERS:
It was not your book?

KOLAKOWSKI:
Yes, but it wasn't a book on the idea of social salvation. On the contrary, it was a book essentially on the idea of personal salvation, either by mystics, or by virtue, or by the Church. But not by the amelioration or by the reconstruction of society.

LEFÈBVRE:
I would like to add two things. First, the dates of history are not quite the same in Marxist and theological thinking. The great dates of history, for Marxist thought, are the passages from one society to another, let's say from ancient society to feudal society, from feudal society to capitalism, and from capitalism to socialism, to another society which would be the socialist society. On the other hand, I think that Marx never excluded the idea that history might fail. He never said that he was absolutely certain that all the struggles and all the transformations of society would end up in the blossoming of a new society. In my opinion, this millennium is not in the thought of Marx. How many times has Marx not insisted on the fact that ancient society failed, and that

it had been transformed only after an interminable deca-
dence. And I think this idea is important, the idea that Marx
never announced the birth of a new society as necessary and
inevitable. He said that this new society would be the result
of real struggles under specific conditions; if it so happened
that these conditions were not favourable, our period would
therefore culminate in gigantic failure. And I don't at all
think of abandoning Marxism for that. I think that it is
a very important idea: there is no accomplishment, no
inevitable salvation, there is no redemption of the human
species.

KOLAKOWSKI:

I'm willing to admit that the thought of Marx is a little
equivocal on this point, but I would like to quote an actual
phrase of Marx's: "Although the working class may under-
go temporary failures, the great laws of history will necessarily bring them victory". This is an exact quotation from
an article he wrote in the *New York Tribune*.

LEFÈBVRE:

At a certain determined date ...

KOLAKOWSKI:

Yes, in the fifties.

LEFÈBVRE:

Yes, yes, it's the period of great expectations. *The Critique
of the Gotha Programme* of 1875 was altogether different
in what it had to say: as you know, Marx then warned the
political leaders of the working class who seemed to him to
be moving in the wrong direction, that of state socialism—
solemn warnings which end with these terrible words, "I
have said and I have saved my soul". In Latin: *dixi et salvavi
animam meam.*

KOLAKOWSKI:

Yes, that's true.

ELDERS:

You are talking too much about Marx, I think.

LEFÈBVRE:

Well, you said that he is dead ... we have made him live again.

ELDERS:

You have made a fortune from Marx, I think.

No, let's return to this difficult notion of alienation, Mr. Kolakowski. A large part of philosophy and of contemporary science has been strongly influenced by positivism: in other words, people want to base their ideas firmly on facts. You have called this alienation.

KOLAKOWSKI:

Oh, no, not at all! My American editor gave if that title. I didn't know anything about it, I wasn't responsible.

ELDERS:

No?

KOLAKOWSKI:

No, no.

ELDERS:

Not at all?

KOLAKOWSKI:

No, no, I refused the title.

ELDERS:

And the content of the book?

KOLAKOWSKI:

No, not the content of the book, although it had been horribly translated. Not the content, but the title.

ELDERS:

But the title means something, perhaps not much, but nevertheless ... you don't agree with the title. Perhaps we can return to the question. As we can't define the notion of alienation, we could take the contrary concept, couldn't we, namely that of familiarity. Well then, from what familiarity in the order of ideas are we alienated?

KOLAKOWSKI:

I'm sorry, I don't understand the question.

ELDERS:

Haven't you attacked positivism?

KOLAKOWSKI:

Yes, partially.

ELDERS:

Ah yes, partially. So which part of positivism do you not agree with?

KOLAKOWSKI:

Well, mainly I would say that I don't agree with a certain number of interdictions which positivism imposes on human thought, and in particular with those interdictions on posing questions which don't allow formulation in such a way that one can obtain answers conformable to the claims of science. Briefly, what I attack is scientism. I think that we will always ask ourselves questions which can't be inferred in terms of analytical reason, and that we are so to speak, culturally obliged to reflect, to respond to these questions, knowing all the time that we cannot give answers which would be valid from the point of view of science.

ELDERS:

Is this scientism linked up, for you, with the antinomy of human liberty?

KOLAKOWSKI :
    In which sense ?

ELDERS :
    You have written on the antinomy of human liberty, that
    we are finite in one way, and completely unique in another
    way. There is something absolute in the human order, but
    at the same time something definitely finite, and this you
    have called an antinomy in the human order. I would like
    to know if this notion of the tension between the absolute
    order and the finite order in ourselves, in the human species,
    is the base of your critique of positivism.

KOLAKOWSKI :
    I think that it is rational technology which produces the cri-
    teria of scientific thought and which therefore allows us to
    think rationally about our environment and to control it
    technologically. But at the same time we live in the mythical
    world from which we are not able to liberate ourselves.
    Myth is necessarily part of our consciousness, and there are
    always conflicts between these two layers of our conscious-
    ness.

ELDERS :
    You agree that we shouldn't transcend the order of myths ?

LEFÈBVRE :
    Oh no, but my objection against positivism would agree or
    converge with that of Leszek, although still in quite a
    different way. I reproach positivism for eliminating the nega-
    tive, for eliminating the critique or the critical aspect, for
    eliminating critical concepts and critical theories under the
    façade of positivity. I reproach it for eliminating the tragic
    by eliminating the critical and the negative. And finally, I
    reproach it for eliminating struggle along with the tragic. In
    other words, the critique which I would make of positivism
    converges with that of Leszek Kolakowski, but it is very

different in its orientation. The important thing for me is to restitute the rights of critical thought and the action which is inspired by critical thought against positivism.

KOLAKOWSKI :

I can't see how positivism must fight the idea of negativity in this way.

LEFÈBVRE :

Oh well, firstly it has always tended to the liquidation of critical thought even more than to the liquidation of the negative.

KOLAKOWSKI :

One has to clarify the notion, because positivism was very militant against precisely what it calls prejudices, mytho-logical thought, metaphysics. So I can't see in which sense it is against the critique. What does this mean ?

LEFÈBVRE :

Well, by conferring privileges on what is established, on the fact, on that which describes itself and establishes itself.

KOLAKOWSKI :

Well, I don't agree with that. What you have just said is exactly the critique which Marcuse makes in his book on Hegel, *Reason and Revolution*. But I don't agree. I don't see how confidence in facts can logically coincide or result logically in the defence of the *status quo*. There is really no logical relationship.

LEFÈBVRE :

There is no logical relationship, but the very method which attributes an exclusive value to the fact and to what is established leads very quickly to an ideology which accepts the established order by right of the fact and by right of what is established.

KOLAKOWSKI:

You think therefore that there is a psychological rather than a logical relationship?

LEFÈBVRE:

There is a practical relationship.

KOLAKOWSKI:

I'm not sure about that. Ultimately it was positivist thought which gave birth to the modern bourgeois world with its ideas of freedom and egality. The idea of stabilisation is not included in positivist philosophy itself.

ELDERS:

But I think that there is a certain misunderstanding between you both; your criterion, Mr. Kolakowski, is a logical criterion, while you, Mr. Lefèbvre, use instead a sociological and historical criterion. What strikes me, Mr. Kolakowski, is that you say we can't transcend the order of myths. This implies a positivist notion, doesn't it, because we can't describe the order of human values in exact terms. Well, how can you defend this order of myths? You defend it, but with a certain scepticism which is very close to the position of the positivists.

KOLAKOWSKI:

To the degree that I refuse to believe the world of values can justify itself in the same way as the world of facts, yes, in this sense I accept the positivist critique.

ELDERS:

And how would you defend your notion of the plurality of values?

KOLAKOWSKI:

No, I can't defend it with scientific means. I believe there is a decision here which is finally rooted in the will. I'd say socially rooted, of course, but a decision doesn't justify **itself** in the way that one can justify a scientific theory.

ELDERS :

It's a theoretical position which bases itself on existentialism, isn't it? On experiences?

KOLAKOWSKI :

Why?

ELDERS :

Because it is based on the will, on a decision.

KOLAKOWSKI :

This is not specifically existential. But at the least, I would even accept this notion in the sense of Jaspers, yes.

LEFÈBVRE :

Values are also facts as social facts. Values are present in a society in which one can discern certain characteristics.

KOLAKOWSKI :

Therefore one can investigate values as social, psychological facts, but they can't be justified by this sort of investigation.

ELDERS :

Yes, perhaps it would be a good idea if you explained the difference between value as a fact and value in itself, because I don't think it will be a clear enough distinction for most people. Will you explain this difference?

LEFÈBVRE :

I don't think there are values in themselves at all. I think all values are attached to facts in themselves, they are embodied in the society.

ELDERS :

Yes, naturally.

LEFÈBVRE:

And because of this quality values wear themselves out, they live and die. I don't think one can eternalise whatever value it may be. And when a value is worn out, it is dead.

ELDERS:

Very well, but what you now say is almost complete relativism. You attack what you have called bureaucratic or consumer society on the basis of certain values. When you now say that all these values are like facts that will die, well then, everybody can defend all values, even the war in Vietnam.

LEFÈBVRE:

Oh, not at all.

ELDERS:

Oh yes!

LEFÈBVRE:

But how is one to attack a society? What does it mean to criticise society! To criticise a society is to show a contradiction between the way society exists and functions in reality, and the way it appears and justifies itself. In other words, there is a contrast and even a contradiction between the values it claims to represent and its reality. If I criticise the consumer society, I show that it talks about happiness, whereas it achieves malaise and dissatisfaction. One criticises society by contrasting the actual symptoms of its malaise and its dissatisfaction everywhere, with its ideological or value-making justification, which is happiness.

ELDERS:

Oh yes, that's true.

LEFÈBVRE:

And then I show the contrast and even the conflict between the two. The critique is internal to this particular society.

KOLAKOWSKI:
Yes, but in this case it is a critique of institutional hypocrisy.

LEFÈBVRE:
No, not only of hypocrisy, of deception.

KOLAKOWSKI:
Maybe it is the contrast between what society is in reality and what it appears to be, or between the totality of values through which it presents itself and those values it actually practices. But you agree that if such a critique is to have some efficacy, it's only due to the fact that people not only believe that there is this contrast, but that there are also genuine values.

ELDERS:
When I say I will kill—assuming I am not a hypocrite—how would you react according to your values?

LEFÈBVRE:
What?!

ELDERS:
When I say that after this debate I will kill you ...

LEFÈBVRE:
Do you want to kill me?

ELDERS:
Yes.

LEFÈBVRE:
But I'll kill you! I'll kill you first!

ELDERS:
But on the base of which value are you going to do this?

LEFÈBVRE:

Oh no, it's you who has taken the initiative of wanting to kill me, you said it!

KOLAKOWSKI:

It's very difficult in many circumstances to determine who was first. It's a very bad field for discussion. Who was first? Who will begin? It's like children who throw the responsibility back on us ...

LEFÈBVRE:

He started it!

KOLAKOWSKI:

No, but he asks how one can, in the case of a conflict on a verbal level, rather than on the level of acts, determine who is wrong and who is right. And whether it is possible to determine it or not.

ELDERS:

Then one has to defend your values against yourself, I believe.

LEFÈBVRE:

I don't think you intend to kill me at all, nor I kill you, because there is no class struggle between us.

KOLAKOWSKI:

Ah, you believe people kill each other only in a class struggle?

LEFÈBVRE:

No, no, I haven't said that!

KOLAKOWSKI:

Yes, but that's an implication of your idea.

ELDERS:

You use the concept of happiness in contrast with our managed consumer society not only because of hypocrisy, but surely also because of another concept of happiness in your philosophy, or meta-philosophy. And this concept is not completely relativist for you.

LEFÈBVRE:

No, the critique has significance only because the people to whom it's addressed and who receive it, feel that something else is possible. It is not the notion of value that is crucial for me, it's the notion of the possible. I have just defined it.

ELDERS:

Is it a fact or a value?

LEFÈBVRE:

It's a perception. One perceives the possible.

KOLAKOWSKI:

Let's suppose that it is so. Why should I choose such a possibility and not another? There are still different possibilities. But if there were only one, it wouldn't be a sufficient reason for choosing it, because it's conceivable that there is only one possibility for me—to know that the world has to perish in an atomic war. It's not a good reason for precipitating this disaster.

LEFÈBVRE:

I don't understand your argument.

KOLAKOWSKI:

The notion of the possible doesn't help us.

LEFÈBVRE:

Yes, it does!

KOLAKOWSKI:

Because if there are different possibilities included in reality,

I have to choose, and I need a basis from which to choose. If there is only one possibility, it is not a sufficient reason for choosing it.

LEFÈBVRE:
But if there is a possibility of atomic war and of nuclear destruction of the earth, one has to try to eliminate just such a possibility.

KOLAKOWSKI:
Why?

LEFÈBVRE:
Why? Oh, there's no absolute reason, that is true.

ELDERS:
Ah, but that's something, isn't it?

KOLAKOWSKI:
Well, if against you, I supported the idea of an atomic war which was going to destroy the world, we would be in the same position.

LEFÈBVRE:
No, not at all. Why?

KOLAKOWSKI:
That is to say, we are equally justified!

LEFÈBVRE:
No, no, it is because we are not trying to reflect on the possible, that all the possibilities are indifferent to and equivalent with each other.

ELDERS:
But why not?

LEFÈBVRE :

Why not, indeed? From the point of view of the absolute, you could say, it makes absolutely no difference whether there is or isn't an atomic war. You can say this: you are making philosophy in the most classical sense of the term.

I will explain my position, because I've been brought to reflect on possibilities. It's not a philosophical reflection in the classical sense. I'll give an example of this reflection on possibilities; today, in the second half of the twentieth century, the automation of production is possible. That is to say, the really up-to-date thing in terms of the economic analysis of the productive forces is, I repeat, the complete automation of the process of production, in other words, non-work: in the future, on the horizon of our society, non-work is a possibility. Yet bourgeois society, our actual society within the framework of capitalism, is not concerned with the automation of production, but with the automation of administration. In other words, it tends to maintain and to keep up work, because non-work would mean the end of exploitation, which would mark the passage from scarcity to abundance. We are in a period when the possibility of a fundamental transformation, caused by technical progress, has been blocked and replaced by an inverse possibility. And this is a deep cause of revolutionary will. It is not a question of values, and it's not a question of an option, of an alternative in the philosophical sense, it's a question of the possible and the impossible.

KOLAKOWSKI :

Ah, but no, because there is nevertheless an option.

LEFÈBVRE :

Is there an option?

KOLAKOWSKI :

Yes, there is. If there are two contradictory possibilities, you have to choose one of them.

LEFÈBVRE :
Yes, you choose, so you choose, the bourgeois order, for example.

KOLAKOWSKI :
Ah yes.

LEFÈBVRE :
Well, choose the bourgeois order, say it clearly.

KOLAKOWSKI :
But if I do choose it, why not?

LEFÈBVRE :
Well, nothing is stopping you. You can even lead your struggle, which will be a class struggle to maintain the bourgeois order.

KOLAKOWSKI :
Yes.

LEFÈBVRE :
Nothing is stopping you.

KOLAKOWSKI :
Suppose I do it.

LEFÈBVRE :
Well, what do you want me to say?

KOLAKOWSKI :
Ah, precisely....

LEFÈBVRE :
But nothing, on the speculative level. You have chosen, that's all. And I have chosen the other side. Perfect.... But it isn't true. You haven't done it.

KOLAKOWSKI:
It isn't true.

LEFÈBVRE:
It isn't true. It's a philosophical fiction between us.

KOLAKOWSKI:
Yes, it isn't true, but what isn't true? If I were to choose, I would be aware that I had chosen on the basis of certain values which I admit to.

LEFÈBVRE:
I am afraid this produces something more compatible with the bourgeois and capitalist order than with a transformation of society which, moreover, is not that which has taken place until now under the heading of socialism. The so-called socialist societies are also preparing to automate management and not production.

KOLAKOWSKI:
Yes, surely.

LEFÈBVRE:
And to keep up work, to make the workers work.

KOLAKOWSKI:
Yes, okay. I will simply say, more or less consciously, and usually less than more, that one chooses a certain perspective as being more compatible with an ideology, with a totality of values which one is not obliged to articulate clearly or to put in a philosophical system, but which we still admit, more or less unconsciously, because of the education, the ideological influences, etc. which we have undergone. But they are values which you can't justify absolutely.

ELDERS:
Mr. Kolakowski, I don't agree when you say you are justified

in not establishing your values. If you don't do so as a philosopher, will you leave it then, to the politicians, or to the theologians? Then everything ultimately becomes arbitrary.

KOLAKOWSKI:

Yes, ultimately, it becomes arbitrary.

ELDERS:

So, are you a philosopher?

KOLAKOWSKI:

I don't say that ...

ELDERS:

... an obscurity?

KOLAKOWSKI:

No, I don't say that I am happy about it. I say that's the way it is.

ELDERS:

It's true, but that goes for all the people here, too.

KOLAKOWSKI:

Yes.

ELDERS:

Well, then?

KOLAKOWSKI:

For anyone.

ELDERS:

What have you to tell the people here? Because if you cannot establish the basis of your values better, what are we doing here?

KOLAKOWSKI:

I'll have to use rhetoric, but one shouldn't confuse rhetoric with argumentation. I am all for propaganda and rhetoric, but I don't want to confuse them with argumentation.

ELDERS:

You made a distinction between possibilities which are not in the realm of logic, but in the realm of choice, which is not of a logical order. For example, you can buy a red or a blue car. That is not a logical question. But perhaps there is a contradiction involved if you say that your values exist, but not from the point of view of "human values". You will say that your values exist, that they are good values as far as you are concerned, but at the same time they aren't good at all for others.

KOLAKOWSKI:

Yes.

ELDERS:

Perhaps even very bad.

KOLAKOWSKI:

Yes.

ELDERS:

Is there a contradiction?

KOLAKOWSKI:

In this sense only, that there is a conflict between the scientific perspective and the mythological perspective. I am unable to make a synthesis: I admit it, and very willingly. I don't even think that such a synthesis is possible. If someone proves to me that it is possible, I would be very happy.

ELDERS:

But wait a moment. In my opinion, you have already passed

through three phases: the Marxist phase, the existentialist phase, and now the positivist phase. Again you make this distinction between the scientific order, the so-called order of facts, and, on the other hand, the order of myth.

KOLAKOWSKI:

Yes...

ELDERS:

It is a positivist distinction, isn't it?

KOLAKOWSKI:

Yes, it is a positivist distinction.

ELDERS:

You agree now?

KOLAKOWSKI:

Okay, with this important addition, which is not positivist, that I admit we aren't able to free ourselves from the mythological options. That is to say I don't admit rationalism in the sense which has perhaps been best defined by Locke and which consists of this: the degree of conviction with which we admit any ideas must correspond exactly to the degree of their justification. I don't admit this restriction, because I think it's impossible.

ELDERS:

Yes, but you still talk about myth, and you say that we can't free ourselves of myth. How do you know this? You say it, but how do you know it? It implies that you have a certain limitation, in relation to the "human order", and by this, you nevertheless speak about the human order. So you establish an idea of a limitation on yourself, on your own philosophy.

KOLAKOWSKI:

Yes...

ELDERS:

But why? Is that a choice? A theoretical choice or a practical choice?

KOLAKOWSKI:

Oh, I believe that it is a very well established choice, both in the order of values and in the order of our reflection on the absolute, but that one hasn't found absolutely any means of getting there which could be integrated within the order of science, that's all. Perhaps someone could propose a better solution. I can't see any.

LEFÈBVRE:

I would like to continue my earlier argument, recalling some small points. I think I am completely faithful to the analysis of Marx, but Marx hasn't said everything; but he isn't dead, for all that. There is something new in the productive forces, in the capacities of production. And today, if we aren't very careful and extremely watchful, we can know what is going to happen tomorrow. And that isn't a matter of a philosophical option. When the complete life of each individual is to be indexed on perforated cards, and when the administrators are responsible for the entire management of society —and I must emphasise the management, and not the production, because this is fundamental—and when they also control the entire management of production, then we will have a society in which the individual won't exist any more. The individual will be a juridical and moral fiction.

KOLAKOWSKI:

And why should the individual exist?

LEFÈBVRE:

Ah, indeed. There is no reason whatsoever, from the point of view of the absolute, everything becomes the same, everything becomes equal, and it's not important whether the world exists, if there is atomic destruction. This is nihilism, this is nihilism!

KOLAKOWSKI:

Yes, it is.

ELDERS:

But, are you also a nihilist at the level of values?

LEFÈBVRE:

No, not at all. Absolutely not. Through the analysis of what is happening in contemporary society, I try to see what the alternative can be, if you like: the alternative between extinction or destruction, and what can develop out of it— what is possible.

ELDERS:

Yes, but will you make this notion of the possible more concrete in relation to your utopian conception?

LEFÈBVRE:

Well, first, I believe the potentials, the possibilities contained in this period of industrialisation are changing profoundly. A new society is being sketched out, and it could miscarry: its complete failure could ultimately lead to our complete destruction, the destruction of nature and of the planet. I call the society which is being outlined the "urban society", because its characteristic is that it will be a society of the town, or rather of the extension of the town. It will no longer be based on enterprise: the society which bases itself on enterprise, on industrial production, is at the end of the road, and all schemes of thought which have been inspired by it are now exhausted, as are its values. Once again, another society is constituting itself, which can fail, particularly if one gives a free hand to the big enterprises, which aim to stifle the seeds of a new society by its programming, its use of administrators for management, and will even go so far as to affect the individual. I note that these problems aren't philosophical problems. A little while ago, UNESCO held a session during which the dangers of indexing on perforated cards the total life of individuals and of groups was spelt out, with all the possibilities that this will give to the power of the state and of the police. That would be the end, that would be death. The other possibility is to surmount this obstacle, or these obstacles, and to develop this new urban society, which will be characterised by being founded not on the administration of production, but on the administration of space—in other words, what the town and its extentions are concerned with. I think that industrial society is living its last days in terrible convulsions, to make room either for death, or for a new society, which will be, if you like, the society announced by Marx, though Marx hadn't seen it in this way. Marx envisaged a society founded on the administration of production, whereas I believe it will be a society based on the administration of space, which is very different in its principle and its applications. For the time being, given all the difficulties, this perspective has a utopian side. And that is what I call the concrete utopia.

ELDERS:

And which group forms the principle element in this transformation from modern society to the utopian society you describe?

LEFÈBVRE:

The struggle of a class, of the working class has been through its old objectives, which are quantitative, concerning salaries and hours. Without it being realised this class struggle, shifts little by little towards new objectives, those of the administration of space. And outside the working class, there are other social and political forces, which gradually come on stage on a world scale, both in the under-developed countries and in the developed countries. But in my opinion, the working class remains the kernel of this transformation.

ELDERS:

Yes, but at the same time you say the working class has to represent the utopian consciousness ...

LEFÈBVRE :

Ah no, I haven't said that it represents the utopian consciousness. The utopian consciousness is a theoretical consciousness, a consciousness which comes from theory, from
theoretical thought.

ELDERS :

But in the thinking of Marx, to quote him in my turn, the
working class was a carrier of a certain utopian consciousness.

LEFÈBVRE :

One could say so, but only as far as there are in the working
class, for Marx, aspirations to a new society, to a socialist
society. It happens, moreover, that socialism based on industrialisation, on the administration of industrial production,
on the planned and programmed economy, is going bank-
rupt. One has to reconsider the ideas of humanism, of socialism, of the new society, and to put them in the context of
what has happened over half a century.

ELDERS :

But as far as these ideas of changing life completely are concerned, do you think, Mr. Kolakowski, that the Left, the
ideology of the Left, can help in this process?

KOLAKOWSKI :

Well, I don't know exactly what is the Left, and the ideology
of the Left, in the actual situation. In any case, let's now
leave the problems of the definitive justification of values.
Probably we agree on certain fundamental values, social
values, which we both conceive in the same way.

ELDERS :

But what, in your opinion, are the values of the Left?

KOLAKOWSKI :

The Left, such as it is—what is now called the Left?

ELDERS:

Is it not true that you have written an essay on "The Concept of the Left"?

KOLAKOWSKI:

Yes, that's true, but it was fifteen years ago. I can't refer to an essay which was written under particular circumstances.

So you believe there is a possibility of another urban society which is being outlined within our existing society, and which is opposing itself to existing society in a way which I, perhaps, haven't really grasped? Did you say that the difference between the two societies consists in this, that this new society must reintroduce the idea of leisure as a dominant value?

LEFÈBVRE:

The idea of non-work. I haven't said leisure; I have said non-work, which is made possible by automation.

KOLAKOWSKI:

What is the difference between leisure and non-work?

LEFÈBVRE:

That is an issue for sociology. Leisure is a time of recovery, in which one regains the strength to work.

KOLAKOWSKI:

Ah, leisure as rest.

LEFÈBVRE:

Non-work is not necessarily rest, it's something completely different. I am thinking of the citizen of Athens; he didn't work. We will find again, on a world scale, the possibilities of a new Greece, that is to say of the free man.

KOLAKOWSKI:

By replacing slaves with machines?

LEFÈBVRE:

Yes, it is possible today through the complete automation of work and of the production processes. That doesn't mean within a fortnight, but it is possible today.

KOLAKOWSKI:

Yes, that's exactly the idea of Marx.

LEFÈBVRE:

One finds this idea in *Capital*.

KOLAKOWSKI:

So, you think in terms of the possibility of free time which can be used in a creative way.

LEFÈBVRE:

Yes, yes, that's utopian, but concrete.

KOLAKOWSKI:

Yes, I agree, I don't know if it is concrete or utopian, but I agree to use the word "utopian", not necessarily in a pejorative sense.

LEFÈBVRE:

Oh yes, absolutely. Only in a completely optimistic sense.

KOLAKOWSKI:

Okay. I only ask myself in what sense you define this imaginary or utopian society which is being outlined as an urban society. The principal idea of Marx developed from a feeling current in the first half of the nineteenth century, and the source of which was opposition to the mechanisation of life, the dehumanisation resulting from industrial society: that is, the opposition which arose at exactly the moment when industrialisation began in the societies of Western Europe. It is the feeling that we are deprived of direct contact with each other, that there is a crisis of communication among individuals. Romanticism was an attempt to return to pre-industrial society. Marx nourished the more optimistic idea that industrial society would by-pass itself by virtue of a self-negation, of an internal dialectic; this society would it-self produce the powers which would enable us to eliminate these destructive aspects. That is to say, industry, the machine, will by-pass themselves and put aside the disasters which they have brought upon us. This is the idea of Marx, isn't it?

LEFÈBVRE:

Yes, I believe so. I am faithful to the thought of Marx, but Marx hadn't completely foreseen a series of new factors. He hadn't foreseen electronics, information systems, computers, and so on, which are now productive forces.

KOLAKOWSKI:

Yes, certainly. But he had foreseen automation.

LEFÈBVRE:

He had foreseen automation, but not the modalities of automation in concrete terms. Well, that is very important. I think it's very important.

KOLAKOWSKI:

We all experience the same feeling—which doesn't neces-sarily come from Marxist ideology—that industrial society with its machinery and its industrial and political bureau-cracy, has deprived us, so to speak, of the possibility of direct communication. There is a sort of nostalgia for the village.

LEFÈBVRE:

Yes, I think ...

KOLAKOWSKI:

Nostalgia for tribal communication, direct communication.

Which explains, for example, the unheard-of success of a writer as bizarre and trivial as McLuhan.

LEFÈBVRE :
Trivial!

KOLAKOWSKI :
Trivial, yes. But his success is due to the fact that he expresses the hope that modern technology will enable us to return to the village, to a form of tribal, direct communication which we will find again in a world which resembles a village. It is the same nostalgia which expresses itself in the ideology of the hippies.

LEFÈBVRE :
They are profoundly right in the idea of non-work, which is now the real meaning of work. The real meaning of work is to reach non-work, and not to maintain work. This is something new, in my opinion, and it takes us very far.

KOLAKOWSKI :
It is rather the idea of American industry : putting an enormous amount of effort into saving effort.

LEFÈBVRE :
Yes, only there results a vicious circle of undefined productivity, nevertheless.

KOLAKOWSKI :
Yes.

LEFÈBVRE :
Well, it has to do precisely with breaking this vicious circle of undefined productivity in order to give meaning to productivity in the organisation of a society where non-work could exist.

KOLAKOWSKI :

But non-work in the name of what? Marx, as you know, believed that the goal of society is to liberate itself from necessary work in the name of the free creativity of the individual, and at the same time he believed that it is work which permits man to realise himself, to express himself.

LEFÈBVRE :

Exactly. There now appears to be a sort of contradiction on this point in Marx.

KOLAKOWSKI :

The question is whether there is a contradiction or not. I am not sure.

LEFÈBVRE :

Oh, I think so.

KOLAKOWSKI :

You think so.

ELDERS :

When you say that the meaning of work is non-work, there is a relation between the means and the goal, but do you still make a distinction between the two?

KOLAKOWSKI :

Yes, inevitably.

ELDERS :

Then the problem arises of how to realise your utopia? What are the social and ideological factors contributing to this transformation of society? I ask it because you are Marxists, more or less, or meta-Marxists. Does that mean you are philosophers of the praxis?

KOLAKOWSKI :

Pre-Marxists or post-Marxists, it doesn't matter.

ELDERS:
One can always find good means of defending oneself. But when it has to do with a philosophy of praxis, then it seems to me very important that you indicate the means and the social strata, perhaps the group of intellectuals or of technicians, through which these processes of transformation will be realised.

LEFÈBVRE:
Yes.

ELDERS:
What are the possibilities?

LEFÈBVRE:
First of all there are those possibilities which develop from the practical, concrete problems, which are presented to this society. American society, which hasn't yet known a profound crisis, has already entered an urban crisis, which is a radical crisis of the organisation of space in the name of industry and of industrialisation. I don't use the words "city" or "urban" in their restrictive meanings. I am talking about the general organisation of space, which is now called the "environment", an official term, captured by those in positions of power. It's an extraordinarily serious matter. And European society is on the same road: it finds itself confronted by problems which it cannot resolve without a profound transformation of the methods of thought, action, and political power. Furthermore, I believe that socialism itself is in the process of changing profoundly in meaning. It is very possible that towards the year 2000 there will be a world socialist power which will manage what I call the new scarcities, that is to say water, air and light: the environment, as they say—a catch-all word. This socialism will be completely different from the old socialism which aimed, with Marx, at transforming the old scarcities, bread, clothing, into abundance. Today, this kind of socialism has been

achieved. The old scarcities, bread, food, clothing, have become abundant, at least in all the industrialised countries.

ELDERS:

Does this change also imply that the role of the working class as envisaged by Marx has changed for you?

LEFÈBVRE:

The working class and the class struggle already achieve new significance and a new scope in this sense. As I have just indicated, the working class has already chosen to press for qualitative claims which concern its daily life, the redistribution of activities in space, transportation, and so on. These claims concern the totality of daily life, so the working class plays a role in this transformation, but it's not alone in doing so. There are other strata or classes or fractions of classes of society which are involved but not all at the same time, and not all in the same way. For example, at a certain moment, women are in the vanguard of those involved in the transformation of life; at other times, it's youth, or students, and so on. It's not necessarily the working class. Ultimately the key phrase, which I adopt completely, is "to change life" with the idea that transforming society does not only consist of changing the government, or the state or the political regime, but is the changing of life itself. Again and again, different strata and classes of the population realise this, and sometimes abandon it, a little disappointed, but afterwards the idea is taken up again by others. And this is true for the entire world, including, for example, Latin America or Africa, with their widely differing modalities.

ELDERS:

Yes, but there are philosophers like Chomsky and Marcuse who believe that intellectuals have a special responsibility in these processes. Do you share this opinion?

KOLAKOWSKI:

No, I don't think that from this point of view the intellectuals are in a position other than that they have always
been in. They force themselves to articulate ideas, utopias,
opinions, sometimes to express the tendencies of classes or
social strata. Of course, they bear a particular responsibility,
but it is not specific to our time.

LEFÈBVRE:

If you don't mind my saying so, it seems to me that you have
a slightly restrictive concept of the intellectual. Is an architect an intellectual? I think so. His is a liberal profession
and, in his way, he is an intellectual. And, moreover, he has
an intellectual interest, that is to say, he has to know what
he is talking about. He also articulates ideas and projects.
And he is directly interested and concerned in this transformation, and his relationship with people also involves him.
And so he is brought to pose problems which are the same
as those I pose. Architecture is a social practice.

KOLAKOWSKI:

Not necessarily in words, but also in images.

LEFÈBVRE:

And in acts. An architect produces space; he is engaged in a
particular production, the production of space, which seems
to me to be of capital importance today. Neither the urbanist
nor the city planner who finds himself facing housing problems will succeed in resolving them, if he thinks only in
terms of undefined industrial growth.

ELDERS:

I don't agree with your idea, Mr. Kolakowski, because intellectuals and technicians have a very strong and powerful
role compared with their limited numbers. For example, in
Holland there are, I think, two hundred thousand intellectuals, but their influence is much greater than their num-

bers. So this seems to me to prove that intellectuals have a special responsibility.

KOLAKOWSKI:

Yes, that's what I just said. I merely say that it isn't exceptional to our time.

ELDERS:

I don't know, because as soon as the sciences are turned into practice, they change the world, and you couldn't say that until the seventeenth century: the sciences were in a domain apart. But since that time, science has entered into the realm of physical and social reality. So now it transforms society and even nature more effectively than any other force.

KOLAKOWSKI:

Surely.

ELDERS:

So this implies that intellectuals also have a responsibility which is strongly related to this state of affairs, not only theoretically, but also practically.

KOLAKOWSKI:

Oh yes, surely, but intellectuals are important for society not as those who control technology, including the technological application of the sciences, but as those who formulate, and articulate, and propagate human values concerning, among other things, the application of the sciences. In this sense, their role doesn't differ from that of a priest.

LEFÈBVRE:

There are propositions and projects, and it seems to me that today one can elaborate a strategy of knowledge which will be distinct from political strategy, but which will sometimes be able to fight political strategy, sometimes to agree with it,

as suits the moment and the contingencies. I am quite prepared to believe in the possibility of a strategy of knowledge, based in fact on the importance of intellectuals, in the
broadest sense of the word. And I can't see how these famous
problems of the environment—and once again this word has
to be taken with the greatest reserve—will be resolved without the contribution of all the sciences. And for scholars
that includes the possibility of a strategy that takes them
into account, and into the political arena.

It is technology itself which is going to fight the consequences of technology.

KOLAKOWSKI:
Yes, that's what I wanted to say. One always has to
emphasise that one can't direct technology, in a certain
sense, without having an idea of human values to define this
direction.

ELDERS:
And for you this strategy and this ideology are more to the
Left than to the Right? Or doesn't it make much difference?

KOLAKOWSKI:
Frankly, it's very difficult for me to use this concept. I don't
really know now how to define the Left, unless I make a
definition for myself.

ELDERS:
Will you define your concept of the Left?

KOLAKOWSKI:
I would say quite simply that the Left can define itself, as it
has always defined itself, as those who assume as theirs the
cause of the oppressed, of the workless, of people that suffer
from hunger and oppression, who don't have the right of
choice, who don't have the right of speech. In this sense,
it's extremely broad and, I admit, rather vague.

LEFÈBVRE:

Yes, for myself, I don't know.

KOLAKOWSKI:

I don't give a political definition, no.

LEFÈBVRE:

No, it's not completely the idea that I would present of the Left. On the contrary, I believe that the Left still and always has to assume the transformation of society, and not simply to care for the fate of the oppressed. It is one thing to care for the fate of the oppressed, but the oppressed can turn society over and modify it from top to bottom. Well, as far as the French Left is concerned, I must say that it is not very interested in the totality of problems, which costs it a lot. All problems, the most important as well as the most incidental escape it, from decentralisation to the problems of the transformation of space under the pressure of the technocrats. It seems to me that the Left should take these problems in hand, and by doing so it will renew itself. The new Left hasn't yet been renewed. It really needs to be renewed by adopting new strategies and new objectives. It risks becoming short-sighted, and it has become short-sighted until by now it is no longer the Left. But I believe that what one calls the Right is irremediably closed to these new problems. Their people don't resolve the problems of decentralisation, urban problems, and so on in France, they merely deal with them in a completely empirical, provisionary, momentary and finally inefficient way. And I believe that the Left will be obliged, sooner or later, to transform itself profoundly and find new objectives and a new strategy.

KOLAKOWSKI:

Moreover, if the Right doesn't interest itself or interests itself only a little in these questions, the Left doesn't either. So you say what the Left should be.

LEFÈBVRE:

In the fact that only the Left is sensitive to theoretical problems. It can deny them, it can be blind to them, but it still retains the sensibility or the capacity to perceive political problems on a theoretical level.

KOLAKOWSKI:

The major conservatives are also able to do so.

LEFÈBVRE:

Ah, I don't think so.

KOLAKOWSKI:

I believe so. It is the privilege, so to speak, of the Left and of the major conservatives, to think in terms of their period. On this point they meet each other.

LEFÈBVRE:

Perhaps, after all. But at last, our conservative-in-chief is dead now ...

KOLAKOWSKI:

You're thinking of whom?

LEFÈBVRE:

Of the General, of course! The conservative-in-chief has disappeared ...

ELDERS:

But do I have to conclude from what you've said about the Left, that the potential for the real political, ideological, social and cultural power doesn't exist at this moment? Or only as a possibility?

LEFÈBVRE:

As a possibility, I'm afraid.

ELDERS:
Is that all?

LEFÈBVRE:
I'm afraid so, yes. But here and there, there are openings, points where something a little different is appearing. Unfortunately, even today the ultimate goal of planning is still to maintain the norm of growth; in the last resort the Left, in its way, retains the ideology of the Right, that is to say, undefined growth. Only the Right hardly thinks about it, whereas the Left thinks a great deal about maintaining undefined growth with an ameliorated norm of growth in relation to the realisations of the powers of the Right.

KOLAKOWSKI:
One thinks of growth to the extent to which it corresponds to felt needs. Therefore, it's the idea of need which has to be redefined.

LEFÈBVRE:
The ideology of undefined growth maintains itself by not taking needs into account. They are created.

KOLAKOWSKI:
Indeed, one creates them, but as soon as they are created, they are there. The question is: do we have the right to say that there are needs that don't deserve to be satisfied, because they are, as one often says, "artificial", or artificially created? It is not evident that we have criteria to distinguish between needs that are authentic or true and others which are artificial. There aren't criteria for such a distinction, to eliminate such and such a need.

LEFÈBVRE:
We know, and it has also been said in America, that it is unthinkable that American families have two, three, four, five, six, seven or eight cars, ten, twenty or thirty televisions.

If that is the aim of unlimited growth, it is absurd.

KOLAKOWSKI:
It must seem absurd, but perhaps there are needs which we also feel, and which seem absurd to people who are now dying of starvation.

LEFÈBVRE:
Yes, and on the other hand, there are the needs of the third world to be satisfied, and finally there are many needs to be satisfied which are public needs, social needs, urban needs.

KOLAKOWSKI:
If I refuse to admit this distinction, it is quite simply because I don't know how to make it. I don't feel the need to have four or five cars, but I also have to admit that I have needs which already belong to the realm of luxury in the eyes of someone who is starving, or needs which may seem artificial to him. I feel the need for freedom of speech; but to an analphabetical Indian from Brazil, that may seem a really chimerical need. Still I don't want someone to tell me that it is artificial.

LEFÈBVRE:
But no one has said that: I simply said that it is impossible to maintain growth as an objective. Undefined growth, the norms of the growth of the economy ...

KOLAKOWSKI:
... as absolute criteria, yes, I agree .

LEFÈBVRE:
... with the productivist ideology, I say that it is impossible to maintain it! It is the general strategy of capitalist governments on the one hand, and on the other hand it is also the strategy of the technostructure in nearly all countries, if not in all. All this comes to a crisis, which is no

longer the classical crisis envisaged by Marx, which is a crisis of another kind, but a crisis of civilisation, a crisis of society, a crisis of space, what I call the urban crisis, to take up my terminology again.

KOLAKOWSKI:

But don't you think that the duty of people who are opposed to this tendency should consist first of all in redefining the notion of needs in order to exert an ideological influence in the sense of explaining that we can without difficulty limit our material needs?

LEFÈBVRE:

No, that is orientating production towards non-satisfied needs, especially when social needs in relation to individual needs are still very largely unsatisfied. Against the ideology of in-definite growth, in terms of individual needs, which are themselves growing indefinitely, I propose the idea of a different orientation of production. But I must add that undefined growth with its ideology is coming to a crisis. Notice that to maintain undefined growth, you resort to the armament industry which feeds the growth, and you come back sooner or later to the use of armaments. Well, that is the crisis of a complete society!

KOLAKOWSKI:

Agreed, but one has to take into account that this sort of change in production, orientated more to social than to individual needs, implies the growth of bureaucracy.

LEFÈBVRE:

I think that this implies an anti-bureaucratic revolution, be-cause bureaucracy is particularly interested in maintaining indefined growth under its direction.

KOLAKOWSKI:

Not necessarily, there is that bureaucracy which is based

precisely on the idea of the satisfaction of social needs.

ELDERS:

I'd like to interrupt here and suggest that you come back to your last question, which was also the question at the beginning of the debate. You have both been expelled from the Party. You feel that you are Marxist philosophers who have been disarmed outside the Party, without a political organisation, so that you have come to a fairly precarious situation. You haven't a definite political or ideological centre. So you have ended up, in my opinion, in a fairly strong kind of relativism. How do you feel being in this position, at the end of the debate?

KOLAKOWSKI:

It depends on what you understand by the word "disarmed". "Disarmed" means "deprived of arms"; but which arms?

ELDERS:

Are you content with the arms you have used until now?

KOLAKOWSKI:

Oh no, I wouldn't say that, but that doesn't come from the fact that I don't belong to any political party. On the contrary: I am only disarmed in the sense that I don't have sufficient intellectual means to resolve the problems which I would like to resolve, but not in the sense that belonging to a political party would give me more means with which to think. The contrary is true, exactly the contrary.

LEFÈBVRE:

Theory only becomes a force when it penetrates the masses, as Marx more or less said. But the means of penetrating the masses are diverse. It is not only a question of the party. Lenin said, effectively, that the role of the party is to let theory enter the masses, but it happens that the role of the party has changed a lot since Lenin said this. But the possibilities for theoretical ideas and critical theoretical analyses entering the masses are numerous. For example, one has to say that at certain times, in certain contingencies, students have been particularly sensitive to the contribution of critical ideas. I would like to remind you here that what has distinguished the French student movement from, for example, the American is that it hasn't tried to create micro-societies or marginal societies, but has attacked society itself in its entirety and in its totality. And that is its complete, specific character. I would like to recall in passing that I teach sociology at the literary faculty of Nanterre, and that a certain number of the student leaders in 1968 were students of sociology at the literary faculty of Nanterre.

ELDERS :

Is there another question which you would like to discuss to conclude the debate?

KOLAKOWSKI :

It's up to you to ask the questions!

ELDERS :

This *is* the last question, and you are completely free to put forward any problem to the audience.

KOLAKOWSKI :

No, don't ask us this. We came here without preparation. You surprise us with your question. We do our best to find answers to quite difficult questions. I willingly admit that it is necessary, but to ask us to replace you, that's too much!

ELDERS :

No, but now I am giving you complete liberty!

LEFÈBVRE :

We already had liberty! No, but I think that most of the questions which have been asked demand lengthy answers, as Kolakowski said just now. As a result, I imagine that the audience remain, as one says in France, *sur leur faim et sur leur soif*, that is hungry and thirsty. You will have to excuse us, but it would be a very good thing if we had given you hunger and thirst.

ELDERS:
Thank you. Do you agree, Mr. Kolakowski?

KOLAKOWSKI:
I agree.

ELDERS:
Well, I would like to thank you very cordially on my part and also for the audience.

LEFÈBVRE:
Thanks.

ELDERS:
You are liberated!
    Is there anyone who wants to ask a question?

QUESTION:
I would like to ask one. Mr. Lefèbvre, you talk about the concrete utopia, and you, Mr. Kolakowski, talk about science and mythology. I would like to know what is the objective or even subjective basis of value for one's taking a social position? A revolutionary position, in brief?

KOLAKOWSKI:
I don't think that there is a contradiction between the notion that Lefèbvre used, that of the concrete utopia, and the one which I just mentioned. If I understand him properly, the concrete utopia, as opposed to the abstract utopia, means a utopia based quite simply on the possibilities of existing society; and this is in contrast to a completely imaginary

idea which doesn't take into consideration what society is and isn't capable of producing. I don't think that there is a contradiction between this notion and the notion of mythology which I have just employed, because his last notion, in the sense in which I use it, says simply this: that the ultimate foundations of these values which we accept cannot be put into terms of scientific and rational thought. That is in no way opposed to the idea that we are capable of analysing the possibilities of society such as it is, and that we can ask ourselves what is possible or not, starting from the present situation. I don't see any opposition: they are completely different questions. The discussion between us about values concerned the possibility or impossibility of the definitive justification of values. I deny such a possibility, therefore I believe that we have to find our refuge in mythology. I in no way give a pejorative meaning to the words "myth" or "mythology". On the contrary, I believe that myth is a necessary and indispensable stratum of our consciousness.

QUESTION:

Yes, but this definition of mythology is very important. Is the definition nearly the same as Althusser's definition of ideology?

KOLAKOWSKI:

No, Althusser doesn't give any definition of ideology. He simply says that ideology is opposed to science, but defines neither of them. He says that Marx passed from the state of ideology to the state of science without defining either term.

LEFÈBVRE:

I think that your question concerning criteria incorporates the impossibility of its answer. And one doesn't have to put the problem that way, for it is precisely as follows: either revolutionary action, or the self-destruction of the world. So that the answer to your question isn't for tomorrow morning or the day after tomorrow, but in the sequence of events, it's a matter of revolution or death.

QUESTION:

Mr. Lefèbvre, you have written many things on the new type of revolution. You have said in an interview with *L'Express* that the type of revolution until now has been the nineteenth-century type, and that now a type of urban revolution has begun. What organisation can create this new type of revolution?

LEFÈBVRE:

But the question has already been asked during the debate. It has been asked by our friends, by both of them. The social and political powers which are able to take charge of this transformation are in fact still in a state of dispersion and disarray. I think they are trying to reunite and constitute themselves into new political forces, and that the mutation, as one says, of society will be undertaken by them. We are in a critical period, which is that of the mutation; and it is also the critical period for those social and political forces which can intervene. And when this critical period is on the point of terminating itself, the assemblage of theoretical and practical capacities able to take charge of the transformation will be in the process of developing. I think that all this is at the level of the possible and of the conflict between the possible and the impossible, and therefore I call it a concrete utopia.

All this is still impossible today. But its very impossibility becomes transparent the moment we put aside the obstacles and the veils of immediate and given reality. Today we either bow before reality such as it is, such as it is presented to us, in which case one is considered a realist and all these possibilities disappear; or one puts aside the veils, one criticises society, and then in spite of all the difficulties and the obstacles which one still has to go round or break down, the possibility of something else appears. And there is even more than the possibility, there is the criterion which I have just been trying to formulate, which amounts to either the self-destruction of the world, or the surmounting of those obstacles which stand in the way of what is possible today.

QUESTION:

Do you think that the communist parties at this time can help to realise this new type of revolution?

LEFÈBVRE:

I'm afraid not.

QUESTION:

Because of historical reasons? Or dogmatism, or immobility?

LEFÈBVRE:

All of them.

QUESTION:

All of them?

LEFÈBVRE:

I don't think that one hinders the other. I have many friends who thought that they would be forces of renewal in the communist movement; and until now I must say that they haven't succeeded, especially in France. And I infinitely regret it.

QUESTION:

You regret it, but do you see any organisations for revolution at the present time?

LEFÈBVRE:

To the extent that where new problems have been posed in France, they have been posed by the gauchists, the leftist movements, and especially by those movements of Maoist origin which have a tendency to liberate themselves from a certain Maoist dogmatism. A great deal of revolutionary youth sides with them, and I think that there we have something very interesting, because they are able to pose new problems. For example, they have carried out exemplary actions, such as taking over a reception centre for foreign workers, which has called the attention of French opinion to the situation of three million foreign workers who work in France, and that is of a considerable political importance. These are young people who come out of the Maoist movement, but have been freed from a certain dogmatism, which was the infantile characteristic of this movement.

QUESTION:
Mr. Kolakowski, do you see any possibilities for this new type of revolution about which Mr. Lefèbvre has talked?

KOLAKOWSKI:
Frankly, I don't believe as strongly as perhaps Lefèbvre does in a revolution which, in the capitalist societies, could with one blow change the whole orientation of society. I am more reformist than that.

QUESTION:
Reformist in what sense?

KOLAKOWSKI:
As far as the two types of society are concerned. I don't deny that the pressure of the working class, of intellectuals and of technicians can ultimately result in change. I say this without necessarily believing in the global revolution which, for me, is a romantic idea.

LEFÈBVRE:
I would like to add a little word to what Kolakowski has just said. There's an idea current in many socialist countries, although it is little expressed, that the struggle of the classes hasn't yet begun; that until now there have been national struggles, struggles for the independence of people, and that only now, in the course of the industrialisation of those coun-

tries which have gained their national independence, the class struggle can or will begin. It is a thesis which is common to quite a number of tendencies among young Trotskyites, Maoists and others, who don't accept that the *status quo* can maintain itself indefinitely in the so-called socialist countries.

QUESTION :

Mr. Lefèbvre, I would like to ask you two questions. Firstly, you said that there is only one solution, only one alternative : revolution or death.

And my second question : you have spoken about non-work. It would be a new ideal, wouldn't it ? You would agree, I hope, that youth and the whole world are searching for new ideals. Wouldn't it be better to talk of the ideal of rest ? To stop the economy a little now ? I didn't really understand your notion of non-work : it's a little bit negative. And it's rather paradoxical, when looking for a new ideal, to talk about non-work.

LEFÈBVRE :

Well, first question : I think that when I say, "revolution or death", this doesn't mean today or tomorrow morning. It means from here to the end of the second millennium, and perhaps I will appear to you as a millenniarist if I say that the years between now and the year 2000 will be terrifying years from any point of view. If we are thinking from the point of view of the environment, or that of the destiny of the Third World, where the gap with the industrial developed countries threatens to grow, or that of the choice between the automation of production or of management, the risks of catastrophes, including the risks of world war will not cease to grow and to be aggravated in the years to come. Consequently what I would like to say is "revolution or death", but if you understand by evolution a process which can extend itself over decades, if you want to speak about evolution, I don't see what one gains by it: I prefer my alternative which is clear, precise and brutal.

To take your second point: I believe that the ideal, work as an ideal, is used archetypically, and that we have had enough of it, and that evidently the notion of non-work is a difficult one. Philosophers as well as some science-fiction writers have already asked themselves what we will do when we don't work any more. I repeat that the situation of the free citizen in Athens will be reproduced on a world scale ...

QUESTION:
Mr. Kolakowski, you said that you can't analyse values in a scientific way. I don't think that's true: can one not analyse the social function of values in history?

KOLAKOWSKI:
Surely. That is exactly what I didn't say. I said the contrary, that values can be analysed as social and psychological facts, but that they don't let themselves be justified. The analysis of functions, of changes, of the social and psychological significance of values never leads us into justifying them as values. It's rather banal. I agree that this statement belongs to the positivist tradition. Yes, I admit that.

ELDERS:
Are you satisfied?

QUESTION:
No. You say that if you choose a certain value or policy, you can't justify its choice rationally. I don't agree.

KOLAKOWSKI:
Why not?

QUESTION:
Because one can still analyse or foresee the effect a little.

KOLAKOWSKI:

Yes, one can foresee, at least partly, the effects of our choices. But that doesn't allow us to justify or to reject the values which we admit at all. Because to evaluate the effects, we need also value judgements.

QUESTION:

When there is someone who chooses on a basis which will lead to the destruction of the world, you are still going to say that one can't justify an alternative, because we act in an arbitrary way?

KOLAKOWSKI:

The question is rather dramatic, because there are values on which we agree perhaps. Perhaps there are even values which are not historical in this sense, in that they maintain themselves through all human history. I don't believe, it is true, that there are many moral norms which have maintained themselves throughout all human history, except the forbidding of incest, perhaps.

But it's certain that if you now offered people the choice between the destruction or the salvation of the world, you would not find any disagreement, yet even though we are able to foresee the effects of our acts or of our choices, we haven't yet got an instrument for evaluating these effects.

ELDERS:

I imagine that the young lady wanted to say that there are some values which are more rational than others. You have both spoken about economic growth. One can easily analyse the rational or irrational effects of unlimited growth, which is senseless in itself.

KOLAKOWSKI:

Of course, I don't deny that I admit certain values by opposing them to others. What I deny is that I could, or anybody could, justify a value in an absolute way, that is to say, without referring to other more general values.

LEFÈBVRE :

Now you are alluding to an economic fact which has been
given values and presented as rational, namely economic
growth, which at a certain time reveals its irrationality. It
was rational for a certain period, but rationality does not
always remain the same. In our Western society, economic
growth was at first a little-known fact, and remained so
until economists analysed it. With the development of political economy, economic growth was recognised as a rational
fact and given values, and was considered as such until
now. I think that there has recently been a fundamental
modification of this point : in other words, the principle
has revealed itself as irrational.

KOLAKOWSKI :

But perhaps it's necessary for the solution of the problem
of values to redefine the principle of rationality ?

LEFÈBVRE :

Do you want to be here all night ?

KOLAKOWSKI :

No, no !

Postscript by FONS ELDERS

When I was an eight-year-old boy, walking down the main street of a village in North Holland, I made the discovery that to be distracted and to forget time and place in fact implied the opposite, in that all one's attention was concentrated on a particular train of thought to the exclusion of all else. Yet people often referred to this kind of concentration as absentmindedness. Another discovery at the same age was that of playing alone with a ball in a church, and knowing that He would like it, even though pious people would condemn such behaviour severely.

I began to realise that reality was not just a question of everyday appearances or common sense, even though I was not able to defend my intuitive knowledge of this, and to be aware of the existence of different layers of reality. The war, which had lasted four years already, actually strengthened, rather than undermined, my own sense of good and bad, true and false. Some German soldiers were stationed in our village. Everyone hated them, but at the same time we had to conceal our hatred to some extent. To disobey the German authorities became a virtue, a lesson that was easily applied to all authority.

Many people can tell stories of this kind, and they are important in that they can provide us with a key to our most basic ideas and feelings: in undergoing such experiences one realises the necessity of defending one's own beliefs in some detail. In my own case, as with some other people, this took a theoretical form. In addition I had been influenced by a living religious education, as a result of which I had been given the answers to such questions as the beginning and the end of the world and the nature of the cosmos; the origin of good and evil; free will and dependency; the value of ritual and dead languages, such as Latin; and life after death. I had been told that all personal acts have consequences, that prayer has power and efficacy, even at a distance; that something like a universal moral order exists, but that we are not doing wrong if we really believe in our own good intentions.

Philosophy is concerned with exactly these problems, with the very important addition, that among its main tasks are those of researching into such questions as the truthfulness of our knowledge and the consistency of reasoning, and of making basic suppositions both conscious and explicit. It is essential that some people should go as far as possible in formulating and justifying their intuitive knowledge of truth and reality; and very often we call these people philosophers.

What follows is an outline of some of my experiences with the philosophers who take part in *Reflexive Water*. My aim was to understand their philosophies as fully as I could. In doing so, one is sometimes in danger of losing one's own identity, at least if one takes matters seriously. After completing my work with the International Philosophers' Project, I wrote a series of fourteen television lectures on systematic philosophy, ranging from semantics and the theory of knowledge to questions about the body, mind and soul, metaphysics and the state, in which I formulated and justified my philosophy. During this time these eight philosophers, and others as well, kept coming into my mind whenever a difficult problem arose, all of them arguing for or against certain theories. As soon as I felt that a particular formulation could withstand the barrage of their arguments, I wrote it down. I felt I was better able to formulate my own ideas systematically than I had been before I studied and met "my" philosophers.

The risk of drowning in a sea of theories can ultimately have a refreshing and reassuring effect on the mind, if one totally immerses oneself in every idea and every argument. The masters become the helpers, and the helpers become friends.

During this process I realised an interesting difference between the philosophical and the psychological approaches to a problem. To take a simple but typical example of the psychological approach: if someone is greatly concerned with questions of identity or causality, one can concentrate primarily on his motives for researching into the subject. Why is he so interested in questions of identity, and does this interest imply that he has identity problems of his own? Or alternatively, is he so concerned with the problem of causality, and does this imply a need to fix incidents in his mind?

The philosophers, from their side, often try to reduce psychological questions to a more fundamental level; the truth of a theory of probability, or the argument for the existence of God does not depend on one's motives, but only on one's arguments. Roughly stated, the reasons why one is or is not interested in certain problems does not provide a solution to those problems. But one's solutions have everything to do with one's methods of thinking and one's interpretation of evidence, for the moment we open our mouths, the statements which come out may be lies or may be the truth, but they are *our* statements.

Many people see this problem as one of objectivity and subjectivity, but this opposition is a pitfall. First of all, there is a logical interdependence between both words: just as the word "father" implies the word "child", or the word "creator" implies the word "creature", objectivity implies subjectivity and *vice versa*. Secondly, every statement implies suppositions, as every language implies the rules for the statements about this same language. Thirdly, if someone utters a truth, it *is* the truth, it is *his* truth. I think that the distinction between subjectivity and objectivity can only be meaningful if one understands the logical and empirical unity behind all kinds of distinction.

As to the relationship between the philosophical "systems" of the debating philosophers, the differences prove to be partly superficial, in that they are not talking about the same problems; partly they are deeper differences, without being mutually contradictory; and they are partly mutually exclusive, in that if one theory is right, another cannot be. In *Reflexive Water* one can find these differences on all three levels. The criticisms of society made by Lefèbvre or Foucault are both very severe, and both have a Marxist background, yet at the same time they have nothing in common. They neither include nor exclude each other. They do not refer to society from the same angle. Similarly the dualism of Kolakowski, manifesting itself in the opposition between science and mythology, two ever-conflicting layers of consciousness, and the dualism of Popper, showing itself in his belief that man is not rational but ought to be, are not the same kind, neither do they actually contradict each other.

On the other hand, the empiristic philosophy of Ayer and the linguistics of Chomsky do exclude each other, as Ayer himself agrees. Chomsky challenges a good many empiristic presuppositions, using methods and criteria which many empiricists take seriously, even though they threaten their basic philosophy. At this level their differences are extremely interesting and important, not only because one world-view is trying to replace another, but also because of their long-range implications. For example, there is the distinction between theory and praxis, which radical empiricism implicitly justifies by trying to make a "clear-cut distinction" between statements that can be verified and statements that cannot, in other words, all normative statements. This distinction dominates not only most scientific theories, but also political and social practice. Thus a schizophrenic approach is implicit both in theory and in practice and between theory and practice. Empiricism justifies what is practised in everyday life, without questioning its own suppositions too hard.

The question of how one can approach all these systems of thinking is unavoidable. I tried to understand why a philosopher defended a particular theory and on what grounds; to go as far as possible *on his own terms* until I could go no further. At this crucial point, one has to analyse one's own suppositions, to decide if they are, in fact, more tenable than the other person's. This approach follows through the thinking in both systems, based on the simple idea that a truth is a truth for everyone. It does not matter a great deal who finds or formulates the truth. There are two criteria that must be applied. Firstly, how consistently is a philosopher reasoning on the base of his own assumptions: for example, Eccles defends Popper's falsifiability-criterion as the best means of obtaining progress in science, yet at the same time he has to put aside this principle when speaking about the immortality of the soul, since the means of falsifying a statement about life-after-death are not at his disposal. He has to separate this particular issue from the criteria he would apply to science.

Secondly, how many phenomena and areas of debate can a theory explain: if it can explain regularities and changes it is richer than one which can explain only certain regularities. For example, Foucault can describe certain historical periods, but the transition from one period to another remains unclear. Both criteria of consistency and range of application do not make a theory true, since they are purely internal criteria—in other words, they can be applied to every theory and world view, even animistic ones. It is necessary to get a clear understanding of the basic suppositions of a philosophy, since it is these assumptions which underlie any attempt to organise "reality" in a meaningful and useful way, and provide the metaphysical element in everyone's thinking. By metaphysics, I mean the theories philosophers hold about the "ultimate" structure of "reality", which are, by definition, not falsifiable. That such metaphysical theories are unavoidable is made apparent in every theory of knowledge and every methodology. An illustration of this is the famous verifiability-principle of the Vienna Circle, a group of philosophers in the late twenties and thirties for whom metaphysics and meaningless statements were synonymous. The empirical or logical positivists who made up its members believed that a principle is metaphysical if it is neither empirical nor analytical, in other words if it neither relies on knowledge based on experience nor a self-validating truth. All statements about reality have to be verifiable. According to the verifiability principle, all statements which can be verified as true or false are meaningful statements; all statements which cannot be verified as such are meaningless statements. But this criterion of meaningful and meaningless is not verifiable in itself, but a normative principle. The verifiability-principle is neither an empirical nor an analytical statement, and should therefore belong to the realm of metaphysics according to the Vienna Circle's own criteria.

The unavoidability of metaphysics is a result of man's inability to define "reality". No one can do that, at least not according to a definition which indicates its characteristic elements, as opposed to one that merely says that something exists. But even in the latter case, the reasoning is circular. If "reality" means the same as "everything that exists", we know no more than we did before. The word "reality" has to do with "everything that exists", without saying anything concrete about it; to try to say something concrete provides us with statements about certain aspects of a part of reality, rather than reality as a whole. Perhaps reality as a whole is an empty concept, but it is a necessary one, since otherwise every attempt to define what are vaguely called real things would prove to be impossible. If it is impossible to put the whole of reality into words, this may also be the reason why we are unable to define the truth. If the truth has to correspond with reality, and we are not able to know reality in its totality, but at the most only kinds of part-realities, then our truth is a series of part-truths.

If this analysis is correct, it implies an awareness of the unknown truth, since man has not been able to grasp reality in its full meaning, at least until now. This makes the differences between theories understandable, as, for example, the way in which Chomsky defends a real notion of justice, whereas Foucault tries to narrow the notion of justice to a concept bounded by time and class.

One can never sufficiently emphasise that there is no difference between academics and non-academics, or between professional philosophers and the man in the street, when it comes to elementary questions such as justice, human nature, and conceptions of the truth.

Naess tells us how he learned from housewives and schoolgirls that something is *if* it *is* so; it is true *if* it *is* so, it is false *if* it *is not* so. This hypothetical awareness of reality and truth is the expression of an awareness of the unknown truth, which is the truth that is most frequently overlooked by philosophers. Belief in the progress of science and civilization, manifesting itself in the theory of the unlimited growth of production and consumption, has been characteristic of the thinking of Western culture over the last two hundred years. Its main characteristic is its blindness, or as Kant expresses it, *"die zweckvolle Zwecklosigkeit"*, the aimful aimlessness. This absence of meaningful goals makes Western culture rather like a powerful, busy computer which is abundantly well provided as far as means are concerned, but underdeveloped when it comes to self-knowledge and goals to aim for. It is up to philosophers to occupy themselves with these and similarly vital questions.

I

Arne Naess skiing, Arne Naess sitting in the bath, Arne Naess climbing mountains, Arne Naess boxing, Arne Naess living alone in his mountain home, Arne Naess playing the comic, Arne Naess writing about scepticism :

> I was close to the logical empiricists in 1934 and 1935 before I became a professor, and I was close to American pragmatism in opposition to Bertrand Russell, for instance, who was more intellectual.... But then I asked myself more closely whether I could support empiricism as a total system, and I realised that was impossible. So, I came to a kind of scepticism, believing that it was possible to adhere to any kind of system, and this then led me to a philosophy of the diversity of life-styles and the diversity of life conceptions, and to opposition to the belief that there should or could be a scientific world-view. There will be no definite world-view in the future, I hope.

Arne Naess is a radical pluralist. It is clear that this is more difficult than climbing mountains; for climbing high mountains is surely something, but to climb several mountains at the same time, even if they are smaller, is trying to tempt God himself. And that is what Arne Naess is definitely trying to do. What does it mean to be a radical pluralist? It means that one defends every coherent system without claiming that its relation to reality is the definite one: one does not say that this *is* reality, but *if* this is reality. This appears to be the ultimate insight into the relationship of consciousness to reality. But this point of view takes for granted the word "if" as an *a priori* category. This radical philosophy is still within the idealist tradition that has developed since Descartes. What does this acceptance of different life-conceptions involve? Can one in principle take all systems equally seriously? It is impossible to say if it is right or wrong to do this, but I think the concept of plurality only makes sense if one assumes a unity within the different life-conceptions. I have sometimes wondered how Arne Naess would have reacted to all the philosophers of *Reflexive Water*. His philosophy would have prepared him to meet each of them on his own terms, but without accepting a final "truth" in any of their systems. I think that the only way to read and to talk with philosophers, and people in general, is to accept that they try to speak the truth, and that what they say *can* be the truth. I got the impression that Naess approaches everyone, from the beginning, on the assumption that they are going to be both right *and* wrong.

I told him of my plan to write about each of the eight philosophers in a postscript, giving my impressions of their philosophies and their personalities. I also expressed my fear that to do so it might create some misunderstandings at a personal level, and that I might lose the friendship or trust of some of them. He predicted that this would happen; that probably none of the eight would like what I was writing, but that I should go ahead, if I felt it to be right. I liked Naess' answer because it is at the heart of his philosophy to approach situations in a radical pluralist way, just as it is at the heart of my own philosophy, and those of Ayer, Popper, Kolakowski and the others, to take risks and to prefer making mistakes to not expressing oneself; to show that what seems obvious may not be obvious at all, and that what seems to be quite natural and evident, may be very doubtful, as Kolakowski says. It is always easier to express such a truth than to realise it, and to realise the truth is equally difficult for everyone. This is a major point of Naess' philosophy.

In his debate with Ayer he defends the non-existence of facts, to put it in the most extreme way. The empiricist assumption that a fact is a fact and that a value is a value, and that these are different realities, is torn to pieces by Naess' analyses and deductions. He takes his arguments so far that not only reality, but also the truth itself becomes conditional: *if* it is so, then it is so; *if* it is true, then it is true. Reality, and with it, the truth, hangs on a silver thread of "if's". Finally, the "if's" become a system; they form a circle. Circles look convincing, but an over-convincing system of doubt doesn't deal any more with reality, but only with itself.

An element of Naess' psychology comes in here: Naess is not as integrated, and probably cannot be as integrated as his philosophy demands that he should be. How can one take seriously every different kind of philosophy without ending up like a king looking down from the top of a mountain? Naess has undergone this temptation: prompted by the desire to climb the highest mountains in Nepal, he wrote a letter to the King of Nepal in 1970, in which he asked the King to declare all mountains above a certain height to be holy mountains. These mountains would be closed to mountaineers above that height. In this way, Naess wanted to strengthen the feeling of the untouchable:

The Great Mountains have since remote antiquity been the objects of religious cults. They have been the symbols of the Highest, the Imperishable, the Unsurpassable and Unreachable, and of course, symbols of the Deity. Those who look upon the Great Mountains as temples, may not hesitate to climb them, only they do it with an attitude acceptable in or on a temple. But those who rather feel them as symbols of the Highest and the Unreachable tend to reject climbing to their summits. It only shows the vanity, the impudence and also the dullness of mankind to carry out an act symbolising the dethronement of God and the conquest of the Unreachable.

I don't imagine the King of Nepal ever reacted to this letter : one either takes such a letter seriously or one doesn't, and in any event the best answer lies in action rather than in words.

Naess himself likes to stress the relative and the provisional in his dealings with the outside world : it is part of his debating style. He likes to play; he likes to take risks in defending highly improbable theses; but, above all, he likes to win. This is in sharp contrast with Ayer, who also likes to play; who also takes risks in defending common sense empiricism; who likes to win, but whose first concern is still to play. Naess' primary objective is to win. When one thinks of the philosophies of the two men, one would rather expect the opposite.

Naess makes up for this desire to win by putting forward a theory of active non-violence, and he wrote a book about Ghandi in which he developed this view. He defends boxing for teaching one not to be afraid, a vital condition for active non-violence. Naess would rather be killed himself than kill someone else. Only a radical can defend such a thesis, in which Self with a capital S is pushed into the foreground.

Naess is an extraordinary thinker in Western philosophy. He went through many phases trying to synthesise various different systems into his pluralism of always true and never true. But I believe that ultimately one cannot accept all these systems; otherwise one spends all one's time emptying the ocean with buckets. The water is not the problem, but the many buckets are. The water is its own undivisible reflexive life.

2

The first time I visited Sir Alfred Ayer to ask him to join us, I left his home at Regent's Park Terrace after only ten minutes. Everything had been arranged in this short time : whom Ayer wanted to debate with (Arne Naess and *not* Herbert Marcuse); the money; the film profile. When at the end of those ten minutes he asked me if I had any more questions to ask, I was so surprised at the efficient and, I felt, rather cool way in which he had talked things over and made up his mind, that I was unable to start a discussion.

The next time I visited him was to interview him for the film portrait. I predicted to Louis van Gasteren, the film-maker, that Ayer would not want to spend more than fifty minutes on a fifteen minute profile. When Ayer asked how long the profile would last on television, I didn't want to give him a precise answer, but Van Gasteren did. Ayer's reply was: "Then we need only fifty minutes".

With none of the philosophers did I have to revise my initial impressions and feelings so much as I did with Ayer. To know him is to love him. I know no philosopher whose personal behaviour is as integrated as that of Freddie Ayer. It is tempting to assume the same must be true of his philosophy, but nothing could be more erroneous: often a philosophy is quite at variance with the psychology of its proponent.

Both Ayer and Naess are, in my opinion, classic examples of this paradoxical relationship: the integration which Naess defends philosophically is not matched by an equal integration at the emotional level, while the emotional integration shown by Ayer does not correspond to an equally integrated philosophy. Many philosophers seem to develop a philosophy to counteract their psychological make-up instead rather than as an elaboration, justification, or coherent cosmology based on and expressive of their whole life-style. And here I suppose I must acknowledge that this remark betrays my own monistic view of philosophy and life. Ayer brought me to this self-discovery by citing *Pragmatism*, by William James, which gives clear-cut categories of monistic and pluralistic philosophy.

Characteristic of Ayer's pluralism, and by implication of his empirical positivism, is the division of statements into categories. One can summarise all statements in four categories. The first of these is analytical and covers *a priori* statements, such as "if p then q; if *not-q*, then *not-p*" or "the mother is fertile". These statements are true, apart from observation, for the truth is included in the relationship between the terms themselves.

Wittgenstein said statements of this kind are true because they are tautologies $(x=x)$, even if this is not apparent from the beginning, and Ayer agrees with him. In this context analytical means that the truth follows directly from the analysis, which is therefore *a priori*. Ayer always uses these terms, *a priori* and analytical, in combination.

The second category covers synthetic-empirical statements such as "snow is white". This statement becomes true only after observation of snow. It is logically feasible that snow could be black. The term "synthetic" means that the statement connects different aspects; the term "empirical" covers everything that falls within the domain of experience. Again Ayer always uses these terms in combination.

The third category includes emotional statements such as "You are a scoundrel". It derives its meaning from the fact that we know how A thinks about B, but such a statement cannot be affirmed or denied without reference to a value system. Such a value system is a factual datum, and as such, one can analyse it in what is called "meta-ethics"; but it is not testable. Like all the empirical positivists, Ayer believes that there are no criteria for such an evaluation, because any value system can be replaced by another. This implies that the whole field of acting and loving, of ethics and aesthetics, and even of politics, falls under this category.

"A circle is a square" and "the imperialism is white" are examples of the fourth category, nonsensical statements. The construction of such statements may be grammatically correct, but they are semantically meaningless.

Occasionally one comes across philosophical statements which it seems impossible even after decades, or centuries, to place in any of the four categories. *"Das Nichts nichtet"* ("the nothing nots") of Martin Heidegger is such a statement. Ayer rejects such statements outright, as becomes clear in the debate. I see them as an example of our incapacity to express ourselves fully through language, although I don't really see the meaningfulness of Heidegger's statement.

However Ayer takes a stand here. His mind is basically

"commonsensical", even if he takes seriously every argument against common sense: after all, the reason why Ayer takes scepticism seriously is simply in order to defend common sense more thoroughly. His scepticism is theoretically rather than emotionally radical, and, as a result, it is not carried to extremes. As a publisher once said, his mind works like "a bacon-slicing machine": a beautiful instrument, but not suited to reviewing books of certain philosophers, which he cuts into small pieces.

The distinction between testable and non-testable statements which Ayer takes for granted means that he limits the area of philosophy to a certain category of "facts" to the exclusion of another category of "facts": he divides facts from values, while facts and values are only separable to a certain degree, as Naess makes quite clear.

His approach to language is too limited to its surface structure, in other words, to its grammatical level. Ayer says that it is a logical consequence of the rules which govern our use of language that I cannot say: "I feel your toothache." But to accept this logic too normatively can easily result in overlooking the principles underlying these rules. As Chomsky points out, grammar can be read in another way.

The basic assumptions of Ayer's philosophy rely on the distinctions between the different categories of statements which I have already described. What is the reason for distinguishing between statements? What authority provides us with the criteria to do so? How can Ayer defend his belief that ethics come under the heading of emotional statements, a belief that is based on the argument that moral judgements are matters for decision? Why should philosophy have nothing to do with decisions? This is to presume that decisions—in other words, all our actions—lack any connection with theoretical knowledge. Is the "I" only a crossing point? Does the act of thinking become involved with the emotions, with desire, hate or love, at some stage moving invisibly from the realm of facts to that of values? And what is one to think about Spinoza's concept of "intellectual love"? The distinction between values and facts is not only vague, but sterile and dangerous. Its conception of reality is essentially arbitrary in its attempt to make firm distinctions on the basis of an ever-changing common sense and a *tabula rasa* theory of the human mind, which assumes that certain rules of grammar can lead us to the final truth.

A Zen master once asked three visiting monks: "Is that large stone over there inside or outside your mind?" One of them then answered "According to the Buddhist view, it is inside our mind". The Zen master then replied "Your head must feel very heavy". If the monk had answered "Outside the mind, because my head feels light", the Zen master would probably have asked "Do you think your head is a stone?"

I give the Zen master's possible alternative answer so as not to allow Ayer to feel too easily that his approach corresponds closely with that of the Zen master. One's mind feels neither heavy nor light if one consciously looks at a big stone: the stone is inside and outside the mind. The relation between the inside and outside reality of the stone has been interpreted too much by empiricists solely in terms of an exclusively outward existence.

The story of the Zen master and the stone makes me realise how little progress, if any, has been made to the understanding of one of the most elementary of all problems: who conceives what? These three small words are hardly explicable: *who conceives what?*

> Honesty? Don't you understand what honesty is? I think honesty is just telling the truth as you see it. And, well I mean, two things: not deceiving others, and what is perhaps in some ways harder, not deceiving yourself. First of all, telling the truth as you see it, not being afraid to do so, and secondly, I suppose, trying to be clear about your own motives and prejudices.

These words could be taken as Freddie Ayer's self-portrait: but an even nicer portrait is that of Ayer among children. An English newspaper was carrying a piece about philosophers, under the title of "The Thinkers". Lady Ayer tells this story:

> One (philosopher) was in a rowboat in the middle of a lake and one was in his study, all alone at his desk, you know, and another one was standing looking over the mountains or something and only Freddie, of all the philosophers, he was photographed out front here, in front of the house and he had all the neighbourhood children around him and they all wanted to be in the picture and they all came and crawled all over him and they said: Can we be in the picture, too?
>
> There was a marvellous big headline that said: "The Thinkers"—and then there were all these silly little children. That was very nice.

3

One of the first things I learned from Sir Karl Popper was to call him Sir Karl and not Sir Popper. After the initial cordialities, he remarked on his allergy to smoking. Precision and allergy are both characteristic of Popper. The precision is evident everywhere in his philosophical work; and so too are the allergies, theories with which he doesn't agree providing the irritation. Popper is not easy on his opponents. If he seriously disagrees with them, he can treat them in the way that a friendly, self-conscious grandfather treats his grandchildren. This may explain the refusal of some philosophers, such as Marcuse, to debate with him.

However, the essence of Popper is silence, even if he defends his philosophy with an unbroken and unbreakable energy, making a sharp contrast with his physical appearance. Truth and freedom are his highest values, for the sake of which he will never compromise either with himself or with anyone else.

We can get nearer to the truth, but we will never reach the truth. This remark of Popper provides us with a key to his whole philosophy: to the falsifiability-criterion, emphasis on the fallibility of man, and the three-world theory, in which there is even room for false theories.

There is no need to summarise Popper's philosophy here. He

did so himself, precisely and lucidly, in the debate—which turned out, in fact, not to be a debate. What was the reason for this?

It was not because Sir John Eccles and Popper agreed on all points; the differences between them are not inconsiderable, as the careful reader will discover for himself at several stages in the debate. During a preparatory meeting between Popper, Eccles and myself, they sometimes found themselves disagreeing with each other a good deal. The reason why there was no real debate between them was because both explicitly wanted to talk together before the public as friends rather than as debaters, and to speak about their most fundamental insights and values. Although I regretted this at the outset, I agreed because I was not able to convince them otherwise, and because I felt this would suit them better than a straightforward debate. Still, there is a paradox here. Both men staunchly believe in the virtue of killing ideas instead of people, and both formulate this belief in the falsifiability-criterion: but, as far as I know, Popper has never falsified any of his theories in his whole life. However, as he himself believes, man is fallible. Popper's defence of rationality is closely connected with his notion of the fallibility of man: so, even if he does not demonstrate his falsifiability-criterion in this debate, at least he explains it theoretically.

Popper belongs to that tiny group of philosophers who are conscious of the suppositions on which their philosophy is founded. Some of these assumptions can be summarised as follows: man does not know the truth, but ought to seek it; there is no such thing as the essence of philosophy; philosophers do not need to be specialists; the growth of human knowledge can be best studied by the growth of scientific knowledge; scientific knowledge can only be an extension of common sense; one has to try to refute one's hypotheses with all possible means; people are rarely rational; there is only the choice between reason or violence, because violence leads to more violence; the state is a necessary evil; there is no such thing as a reasonable society, but there is always a more reasonable society than the existing one; the decision for reason is not an intellectual decision, but a moral one; our lack of knowledge is unlimited. These assumptions can be grouped under the title of "dualistic monism".

Popper is a monist insofar as he believes in the absolute truth, but his monism is dualistic in that he simultaneously claims that man cannot know the truth. His defense of the falsifiability-criterion follows on logically from his concept of the unknown absolute truth, because if the absolute truth is unknown we can only falsify our false theories. It also implies that we can falsify every theory, but not the falsifiability-criterion itself.

Standing at the airport in Amsterdam, Sir Karl told me that "If I am praised, it seems to me exaggerated and unjust; if I am attacked, I ask myself, what have I done to deserve this." He is a David among Goliaths. He will survive in his third world, the world of true and false theories, the world of the products of the human mind, for many generations to come, even if his three-world theory should prove to be false.

4

Sir John Eccles is the only one among this group of philosophers who does not consider himself to be and is not considered a philosopher. He refers to himself as a brain scientist. The relationship between him and Sir Karl Popper led to his participation in the International Philosophers' Project. Eccles applied Popper's trial-and-error method to his own field, neurophysiology, with a great deal of success, as he explains clearly in the debate. Eccles has always been very interested in the philosophical basis of his science, a subject he touches on in his preface to *Brain and Conscious Experience* (1966), a book edited by him which resulted from a study week at the Pontifical Academy of Science in Rome in 1964. At this study week Eccles had been responsible for relating psychology to the neuro-sciences, and in the preface he writes:

I should mention that I was not able to invite any professional philosophers to the Study Week. Early in the planning I was instructed by the Chancellor that "the Academy by its constitution has for aim to promote the study and progress of physical, mathematical and natural sciences and their history. Thus the discussion of philosophical questions is excluded." I replied, "I fear that some of your concern derives from the different linguistic usages that we have. For example, to me all sciences have a philosophical basis and it is generally agreed that there is a philosophy of science which is in fact basic to all scientific investigations and discussions. Certainly when one comes to a Study Week devoted to brain and mind it is not possible to exclude relations with philosophy, though I agree that there are certain philosophical questions which the Academy would be well advised to avoid. I do not think that any of the proposed subjects fall into this category.

It would be interesting to know just which questions they would be well-advised to avoid. In any event, just how closely neuroscience and philosophy are interrelated becomes clear from this quotation, which reflects in a gentle way a sharp conflict between Eccles and the Pontifical Academy.

Eccles' philosophy is dualistic. The primary reality is the consciousness or the conscious experience, which is synonymous with the concepts of "mind", "mental", and "mentality". The personal identity, the "I" or the "Self", is the only reality which is known by direct apprehension: according to Eccles all else is a second order or derivative reality.

In clear opposition to the physicalists, he believes that conscious experiences are more than the operation of the physiological mechanisms of the brain: "The evidence ... shows that these events in the material world are necessary but not sufficient causes for conscious experiences and for my consciously experiencing self". Reasoning further on this basis, he comes to the religious concept of the soul and its special creation by God. With Thorpe, he sees science as a supreme religious activity. When I asked him why he could not convince Popper of his view of science in this aspect, he told me: "I don't think if you get him off the record that he would be so different; he does not express it this way. He has a belief that there is a deep spiritual meaning in life, but he does not use the word 'God', because he thinks it is a misused word. He has a feeling that it is something transcending any concept we can get by the use of such a word. This is what he believes in."

Eccles believes that brain research is the ultimate problem confronting man. A better understanding of the brain is likely to lead man to a richer comprehension both of himself and of the world he lives in—a statement to which his friend McKay shrewdly reacted by saying that this was much the same as saying that you cannot appreciate Beethoven until you understand the physics of the ear.

Eccles' use of science to support his beliefs about the soul, free will, God, beauty—in short, the so-called personalistic philosophy—is ambivalent. On the one hand he uses his authority as a neurophysiologist and arguments from neurophysiology to defend these views; on the other hand, he turns this argument around and defends these same views by claiming that contemporary physics and physiology are as yet too crude to solve these problems. But such a procedure does not solve the question of the relationship between the brain and consciousness. It is an inconsistent way of reasoning, in which different kinds of motives play a part.

Eccles' dualism is not only philosophical. His political and social philosophy is marked by sharp contrasts. His strong anti-communist position leads him into generalisations, about, for example, Communist China: "So far as I know there is almost no science coming out of China, except in special channelled fields, and no imaginative insights." Such a remark, from *Facing Reality* (1970), sounds prejudiced. Its only quality is that it can be falsified.

His remarks in the same book about "so-called" intellectuals, about "the meaninglessness and formlessness of so much so-called modern art", about the revolt of youth, about black students who want their own university, are all very extreme and very black-and-white. To defend segregation, and to say, in my interview with him, that "if a Negro child is brought up and forced to do a great deal of mathematics or chemistry to get on in this industrial world, he will realise that what he is reading and working on is something which is entirely European. The Negroes made no contribution to this. They have been grafted onto another society to which they feel alien. And some can do it, but I think on the whole it is not good. At least, if you are going to do it, you should do it slower, with more faculties and understanding" would seem to contradict a statement in *Facing Reality* in which he says that "The most glaring of all these tragedies is the efforts of the black students to have courses devoted to black history, culture and power and not to mathematics, engineering, medical science, and the physical sciences."

Eccles defends a democratic culture, yet speaks at the same time about the urgent need for ivory towers, "else all civilisation is lost in the market place." This sounds like a direct contradiction of democratic culture. In the epilogue of *Facing Reality*, Eccles begins by saying that: "It can be claimed that the philosophical position outlined in this book has the merit of encompassing in principle all experience. Also, it has the merit of being based on the present scientific understanding of the brain." This is to assume that knowledge of the functioning of the brain is identical with all knowledge and experience, yet at the same time, according to Eccles, this knowledge cannot even explain the functioning of free will. Eccles places too much emphasis on a knowledge of the working of the brain without explaining how such knowledge could be the key to all understanding. His own approach to many problems does not provide convincing evidence.

5

After visiting Sir Karl, I flew to Paris to meet Michel Foucault, professor at the Collège de France. I bridged the gap between London and Paris with a large Havana cigar, calculating that one could fly round the world on five cigars.

From reading Foucault I knew that it would be a good idea to be punctual, but I was delayed by the absence of names on the doors of French apartment houses. When I apologised for arriving five minutes late, he said it was a pity: there were only twenty-five minutes left. He had planned on exactly half an hour.

Foucault's reaction is fairly characteristic of one aspect of his personality. His style conjures up images of a general of the Ming dynasty or a Count Dracula. He likes to reject any expression of emotion. In reply to an attempt to obtain more biographical information for his film portrait, he wrote the following letter:

Sir,

I don't wish that in a television broadcast, which you want to dedicate to me, space should be given to biographical data. I consider, indeed, that they are without importance for the subject dealt with.

Sincerely yours,
Michel Foucault.

He is deeply convinced that all forms of modern subjectivity, as manifested in existentialism and humanism, rest on illusion and self-deceit. When a man excludes his personal life as of no importance to his philosophy, a closer scrutiny of that relationship becomes necessary.

His philosophy demands, or at least, justifies, his golden, cold thesis that his personal life does not exist. Foucault's ambivalence towards himself and his cultural environment resembles that of Nietzsche. In Foucault, Nietzsche's statement, "we are tired of the man", at times reaches the limit of self-destruction:

I do not say things because I think them; I say them rather with the aim of self-destruction, so that I will not have to think any more, so that I can be certain that from now on, they will lead a life outside me, or die the death, in which I will not have to recognise myself.

When one combines this statement with the theory about the "grille", which dominates every period of history, it becomes clear that there is a close connection between the so-called absence of personal life and Foucault's philosophy of history.

But there is another Foucault who does not want to meet his colleagues in Amsterdam after eight o'clock in the evening, but only people under thirty years old. As a guest at a philosophy congress, he can listen by day to lectures which he finds fairly boring about the difference between such sentences as "the window is open", and "open the window", but can then spend two long evenings in the Milky Way, a centre for underground culture, and like it a good deal. These were the days in which we had to make his film profile. We were sitting in a café in the old centre of Amsterdam one Saturday afternoon, and although we had previously made an appointment to leave by private plane, Foucault did not want to do the profile at all that day. I tried to convince him of the necessity for making the film, knowing that a cab and a plane were already waiting for us. He did not react at all to my remarks. I became more and more worried, wishing that I hadn't involved myself in the whole project just as Foucault was probably cursing himself for having promised to take part when he clearly disliked doing so. I felt humiliated. Deciding not to talk any more, I started to read Foucault's book, the *History of Madness*.

The result was like a Beckett play : two men sitting at a table, not speaking, while one of them reads a book written by the other. Outside a cab and a plane are waiting. They had to wait for three-quarters of an hour.

Foucault's psychology has a lot to do with his philosophy. He denies being a structuralist, but this does not tell us much because structuralists, like Dadaists or Provo's, often like to provoke and to disturb people, only in complicated language. His philosophy is strongly infused with structuralist influences.

He believes he has two goals in common with the structuralists: like them, he analyses the constant relation (structure) between the changing elements of a totality (whole), for example in the seventeenth and eighteenth centuries, and he attacks the almighty authority of the subject, the ego-centred attitude of the individual. Individuals are the changing, more or less haphazard elements within a pattern of constant relations.

In *La Quinzaine Littéraire*, number 5 (1966), Foucault made this statement:

What is the anonymous system that thinks without a subject? The "I" is disturbed. What matters now is the discovery of the *"es gibt"* ("there is"). There is a "one". In a certain sense we return herewith to the point of view of the seventeenth century with the following distinction: that we do not put man in the place of God, but an anonymous thinking, knowledge without a subject, the theoretical without an identity. Sartrean freedom is an illusion.

This view comes near to self-destruction. One is entitled to ask if this is the basic assumption of Foucault's philosophy: I do not think so. The ultimate assumption of Foucault's philosophy lies in the question which was not answered in the debate, about rules and freedom, about universal knowledge without any form of repression.

It makes sense to examine this question more closely. Chomsky, for example, could not understand it, and it proved very difficult for me to explain it to him. The clarity of a question depends on the possibility of its being answered. The answer to this particular question is very uncertain, but nonetheless intriguing. Foucault paraphrased it himself in an interview I had with him: "Can we conceive of a form of civilisation, which would be sensitive to that universality of knowledge which we have collected for centuries, and in such a way that it would not become a repressive civilisation. The problem is essentially there."

By repression, Foucault means the exclusion of certain ideas and experiences, a defining characteristic of every "grille". He believes that there are two optimistic themes in Western culture of the last two to three centuries: on the one hand, the belief that knowledge will liberate man, and that the more universal our knowledge the more free we become, and on the other hand the belief that freedom from taboos, obligations and prohibitions will lead to universal knowledge. These two affirmations taken together form a circle, and according to Foucault, a vicious one. One has to reverse them: man can only know everything on the condition that he is not free; or he has to discover that to be free, he has to sacrifice knowledge.

"In any case, our age is discovering that in order to obtain knowledge, the degeneration of a moral system, of a society such as ours and of capitalism has been necessary." Foucault said this in the same interview with me. His analysis of Western culture takes up once more the myth of Paradise: how can man enter Paradise once again and eat of the tree of knowledge without losing his freedom and his happiness.

When a member of the audience said to Popper, "You said that freedom is the most important thing for man," he replied "I did not actually say that. I said that freedom is more important *even* than happiness. I do not know what is the most important thing for me ... that depends on the situation." Foucault and Popper are speaking about freedom in metaphysical terms. Kolakowski would say that these are religious questions disguised.

I admire Foucault for his courage in getting rid of a good deal of moralistic thinking in philosophy, which often has more to do with hypocrisy and fear than with morality in a universal sense. He would perhaps laugh at my belief in universal morality, but I use the term in the same way as he uses the terms universal knowledge and freedom.

Foucault is a philosopher who has absorbed and ordered so many existing streams in Western philosophy in an engaged, intelligent, erudite way, that—like our culture itself—he nearly succumbs under them.

More than any other contemporary philosopher, Foucault

embodies, with his ambivalence and his polarities in thinking and behaviour, the theoretical and moral problems we must solve before we can breathe quietly again.

6

At eleven forty-five, on the morning of Friday, May 29th, 1970, I walked into Massachusetts Institute of Technology (MIT) to meet Noam Chomsky for the first time.

In the hall there is a notice listing the offices of the Defense Department, such as the Army Signal Corps, the Air Force Office of Development Command, and the Office of Naval Research. Politics, defence, and the sciences work together here.

As I waited in Chomsky's room, I became increasingly intrigued by him. I was surrounded by a life-size picture of Fidel Castro, his head bowed and his hands in his pockets; a picture of Fred Hampton (1948-69), the assassinated Black Panther; a folder from Agitprop, in London, an information and communication service for the Left; and cartons of books on the floor and on the table, the titles ranging from biology, chemistry, literature (Updike) and philosophy (Quine) to Free Press and Mouton editions.

Chomsky entered, greeted his secretary and me, asked if there were any new books and accompanied me to another room where he worked. The door remained open. Everyone called each other by their first names. Chomsky has the look of a rather frail, physically unimpressive man. In a dark, clean suit he would make a perfect bank clerk. He speaks softly and quickly, listens quietly to everything that is said, and gives direct answers. His way of speaking does not differ from his way of writing: extremely radical suppositions are defended with numerous empirical arguments, while at the same time he indicates without hesitation or self-defence the short-comings in his arguments.

After initially rejecting my proposal through lack of time, he made a complete turnabout and agreed to everything. The question of money was not important to him.

The picture of Bertrand Russell hanging over his desk made

me realise that Chomsky is the heir to Russell, both on the philosophical level, not as a radical empiricist, but as a radical rationalist, and on the political level in his continuous efforts for peace in Vietnam, social justice, and local self-government. He showed no fanaticism or aggression, just intellectual receptivity, with nothing standing in the way of his quick and functional reactions to concrete situations. Overall, he seemed a combination of clarity, quiet, organisation and sensitivity.

When I told Chomsky how depressed I had been by his essays in *American Power and the New Mandarins* because of the insight they gave into the political, moral and economic plight of the Western world, he reacted, saying that I was the first person to tell him so, but that he felt the same. He devotes probably most of his time to politics, which is quite something for a man who has achieved a revolution in linguistics that may be comparable to those of Newton and Einstein in physics.

As I left the room I saw that his door, leading on to a bare wooden corridor, was next to that of the campus police; a year later, I entered by the door that led into the police room to find that Chomsky's room had been enlarged accordingly. The old portrait of Russell, destroyed during a break-in, had been replaced by a new one. Strong nerves and a hard skull are prerequisites for political action in the United States, at least for someone on the Left.

Although Noam Chomsky and Michel Foucault share common interests in the seventeenth and eighteenth centuries, in their desire to uncover the deeper layers of thinking and in their political criticisms, especially of capitalism, there are irreconcilable differences between them.

At the end of the debate Foucault expressed his amazement that "finally, this problem of human nature, when put simply in theoretical terms, hasn't led to an argument between us; ultimately we understand each other very well as far as these theoretical problems are concerned. On the other hand, when we discussed the problem of human nature and political problems, then differences arose between us". But Foucault deceives himself. Even at the theoretical level they are opposed to each other.

Chomsky's revolution in linguistics stems from a different conception of the human mind to the empiricist belief that the mind is a *"tabula rasa"*, a blank which is shaped by all the impressions and influences of the external world. This challenge-response theory was not seriously challenged in linguistics, biology, history or psychology prior to Chomsky's investigations, with the result that—to use its own terminology—new responses were not forthcoming.

Chomsky has brought about a major change in linguistics by ordering into a coherent system a mass of data, which had hitherto been considered devoid of mutual relationships.

He asked a question which every mother must ask herself, namely how can one explain the ability of every child to generate new sentences which are both grammatically correct and meaningful, without having heard these same sentences before. Further, how is it that every child can learn every language, and that it is far easier for a child than for an adult to learn a second language. Behaviourist linguistics cannot explain language-capacity. Chomsky's research into the structure of language has, in fact, proved to be research into the origin of language, research that was for decades as taboo in linguistics as rejection of the growth theory still is in economics. But the results of his work are literally bursting with consequences, implying neither more nor less than the existence of a universal human nature in which innate structures explain the universally-present capacity for language.

The clash beween Chomsky and Foucault centres on this universal human nature : is human nature common to all people irrespective of time, place, class, religion, race, and so on? Or is the notion of human nature a limited construction dating from a certain period in history such as the seventeenth and eighteenth centuries, when Newtonian physics were applied to men with little understanding of the facts?

Chomsky defends this classic conception of the human

mind's innate capacities : it is not difficult to be reminded of the American Constitution or the Charter of the United Nations, both of which are replete with clichés about a universal human nature. Politicians' speeches are often full of such idealistic talk. What does it mean?

The *tabula rasa* theory of empiricism was accepted, for example, by Darwin in his theory of evolution; by structuralism with its classification systems, suitable for archaeological museums; and by Marxism with its deification of classes and means of production. Belief in a universal human nature was eroded long ago as a result.

Furthermore the cultural equality implicit in this hypothesis has been sacrificed to a scientific élite with a monopoly on knowledge, which pays more attention to money than to a morality that would be meaningful to all. The failure of philosophy to develop a coherent system with a broad range of applications based on clear and audacious assumptions is, I believe, connected to the systematic violence of the capitalist world, as manifested particularly in the Third World. Everyone has the right to reject such a statement because it says nothing and yet everything. But it is just such theories as Chomsky's that help us to realise how ill-equipped existing theoretical structures are for the exploration and explanation of simple but fundamental questions.

In an interview in number 57 of *New Left*, Chomsky was asked if his work in linguistics was in some way connected through the use of such concepts as "freedom", "spontaneity", "creativity", and "renewal" to his political views. In his opinion, a Marxist-anarchist perspective is justified, and can be kept apart from the issue of linguistics. But he agrees that the relationship has significance for him. It is clear that one cannot speculate at this stage on any logical connection between Chomsky's linguistic and political views : this is something that will need many years of research. However, I believe that the relationship between the hypotheses he uses in linguistics and his ethical-political convictions is a strong one.

One of the most urgent problems of our time has been the

enormous growth in the amount of power at our disposal which is not matched by any correspondingly greater fundamental insight into human nature—or, still worse, is accompanied by a one-sided, relativistic man-and-society theory. If the views of Chomsky on the universal structure of language and the fundamental freedom and creativity of man are applied to the social and political sciences, they can be the beginning of a revolution in social sciences.

7

"Moi, j'aime touts les manifestations de la vie, les femmes, le plaisir, le vin, tout, tout, tout y est, tout ce qui concerne la jeunesse, tout ce qui concerne ..." ("I love all the manifest-ations of life, women, pleasure, wine, everything, everything there is, everything that concerns youth, everything that con-cerns ...')

To learn about Lefèbvre, one has to go to three places : to the Rue Rambuteau in the third *arrondissement* of Paris, one of the oldest quarters around the former Halles, where he lives; to Nanterre, near Paris, one of the main centres of the 1968 Cultural Revolution, where he teaches; and to Mourenx, not far from Pau in the south of France, where he lives during the holidays in a big, old house, a family inheritance, and where one can find student Maoists working on dissertations.

Lefèbvre wrote his slightly romanticised autobiography *La Somme et le Reste*, in which he indicates the decisive phases and experiences of his life. He writes about his youth in terms which cannot be misunderstood: "I remember only a youth that was crushed by devotions, feelings of shame, a sickly anxiety for sex, false mysteries".

At the age of twenty he underwent an experience which was not altogether surprising in such an atmosphere, and which still permeates his philosophy, or meta-philosophy. Walking along a road in Landes, by the side of which stood crosses decorated with thorns and wreaths, he had an overwhelming experience—to use a current phrase, a "mind blower". He felt himself to be a crucified sun : in practical terms, he felt he had to free himself from his surroundings and fulfill his vocation.

The need to fulfill a vocation has become a permanent feature of his philosophy, which for that reason he calls a "metaphilosophy"; in other words, a philosophy which will realise itself in daily life.

Another important theme in his autobiography is, naturally, his membership in the French communist party. He became a member in 1929, at the cost of his relationship with the *Centrale Surrealiste* of André Breton. After the death of Stalin in 1953, tensions increased in communist parties everywhere. In 1955, he gave a lecture on George Lukàcs at a congress in honour of his seventieth birthday. The lecture was disavowed by the French communist party under penalty of expulsion. Yet the expulsion itself came three years later, after he had been subjected to a cross-examination, to which he could only respond with "yes" or "no".

Lefèbvre rather naïvely describes his amazement at his own long-standing membership of a party which demands such discipline and self-negation of its members. It is difficult for him to understand how he subjected himself to such a régime for so long.

I imagine that this experience was of importance to him in that he wanted to free himself from all his old ties and felt a strong need for clear goals, guidance and solidarity, sometimes at the cost of his intellectual doubts. However, his assimilation into the Stalinistic party apparatus was never so complete as to impair his own intellectual position. The first indication of this was the attack made by orthodox communists on his *Critique de la Vie Quotidienne. Introduction, Vol. 1 (Critique of Daily Life)*, written in 1947. His expulsion was a logical consequence. Obviously this was not a question of mere formalities, but of too great a deviation from doctrine, as happened later to Roger Garaudy.

It is not easy to come to grips with Lefèbvre's social philosophy. On the whole he does not follow a line of a logical argument on the basis of clear assumptions, but tries to synthesise a totality of actual and future developments in abstract concepts, such as the concept of "the possible". He uses such concepts as if they referred to an actual reality, whereas they are *abstract* concepts. Lefèbvre has never liberated himself from a naturalistic or naïve realistic theory of knowledge, as a result of which he can use abstract terms as if they reproduced what already exists, or will exist in the future. A fascinating analysis results when he attacks concrete situations such as the problem of the automobile: for Lefèbvre, the car has become an independent sub-system, living its own life. The car is the Object-King, the Thing-Pilot, a symbol of circulation instead of living. In the circulation of cars, people and objects mingle without encountering each other: each element remains isolated in its container. Traffic lights are signs without reference; signals order conduct and condition the sense to automatic reactions without external meaning (*Befehl ist Befehl*). Daily life is degraded to one dimension: aimless movement. Movement has become a goal in itself. The car is the last means of adventure, the substitute for erotic pleasure, symbol of social stratification. Its practical function in the city disappeared long ago. The car does not conquer and determine the shape of society, but daily life; and the philosophy of daily life is Lefèbvre's main concern. It is linked to his love of the man in the street, the cafés, the traditions of daily life in France, but applied to the problems of the megalopolis.

If the growth theory becomes dogma, it will, according to Lefèbvre, destroy the cyclical sense of time and replace it with a linear sense of time. The moment that the cyclical time-order is destroyed, the essentially cyclical order of daily life is thrown out of balance. It is in this perspective that the slogan, borrowed from Rimbaud, of "*Changez la vie!*" has to be understood. The alienation involved in our daily life cannot be overcome or a new order introduced without a radical development of urban life towards self-government, which was one of the demands made by students and workers during the Cultural Revolution. The subjection of city life to industrial development is one of the causes of urban crisis: the cultural order no longer determines daily life, whereas the economic order does, over which most people have no influence at all.

Many of Lefèbvre's analyses are a combination of sociological analyses from a Marxist viewpoint, in which he is not so much concerned with the renewal or justification of a theory as with its practical implications. His eagerness to influence and to change too often seduces him into the use of a manic terminology, which has to both embrace and solve all the contradictions involved, and which defends dialectics as the only way to the final synthesis; and to do so he resorts to an unconvincing distinction between formal logic and dialectic logic. Over twenty-five years ago Lefèbvre wrote that he literally does not expect proof of a philosophical discourse which could be completely justified by the verification of its claims, by researches into the validity of its concepts, and by explanations for its meanings. He expects proof only from history. Now he talks of the future instead of the past. But neither the past nor the future are self-evident. By putting them within a theoretical framework, Lefèbvre articulates the feelings and desires of many people. The alienation and frustration that exist everywhere are no longer treated as something transitory or accidental, but as fundamental to the present economic and cultural system.

8

"After the debate let's all get drunk," Leszek said to me during dinner, just before the debate with Henri Lefèbvre. Later, in the Lutheran church in Amsterdam, he laid his head on his arms on the table, for rest or concentration, unaware that the cameras were already taking pictures. And even if he had known, it would not have altered his behaviour.

I will never forget Kolakowski's behaviour before a camera he hated and a public he wanted neither to shock nor to please. Kolakowski and his philosophy are inseparable. His whole bearing reflects a close connection between thinking and feeling, the more remarkable because it is not an easy relationship.

I remember a meeting with some people in Utrecht at which

Kolakowski was present. There was a friendly, official talk, and I could see he did not care for it, and found it rather boring. Suddenly it struck me that Kolakowski talked like a man who has built a cage for himself, closed the door, and thrown the key as far away as possible. I told him this. The people round us were shocked by my remark, but he was not at all. On the contrary: it marked the beginning of our friendship.

Kolakowski is full of a subtle humour. When about to speak to theologians of the Catholic University of Nijmegen last year, he told me on the telephone that he would try to convert them to Catholicism, while he knew that they were waiting for Marxist slogans, in which he does not believe. Perhaps I should add, in which he no longer believes.

His scepticism has a hard, historical background. It has much more to do with his own personal experiences—especially in Poland, which he loves with all his heart—than is the case with the scepticism of Arne Naess.

He has gone through numerous theoretical and political phases, and he has paid for it with a "free" exile. To give some examples: having defended at a very young age Stalinistic dogma about the difference between bourgeois and proletarian science, he attacked this same dogma in 1956 together with Eilstein. That same year he attended the Twentieth Party Congress, at which Khruschev opened the attack on Stalin. Like many other young intellectuals, Kolakowski played an important role in the events leading to the Polish "October" of 1956 which gave power to Gomulka. Ten years later he was expelled from the Communist party for his beliefs. In 1968 his books were banned by the Party; he lost his appointment at the University after administrative hassles over the course of study between 1966 and 1968.

He has been attacked, like Chomsky and Socrates, for corrupting youth through his support of student revolts.

His relativism and scepticism are related to his knowledge of Marxism both as it is officially professed in theory and practised in fact. His allergy to slogans, as used by the students of Berkeley while he was teaching there, stems from his ex-

perience of the use by the Right wing in Poland of such slogans
as "self-government by the people" to conceal "government by
a political apparatus". Such scepticism is apparent in every
page of the debate.

But there is also a more philosophical background to his
thinking, namely his dualism. He calls this the "via Spinoza":
a thorny path, in which one is involved in a ceaseless struggle
with finiteness of one's thinking. In his dissertation about
Spinoza he says that Spinoza tried to overcome the idea of
death without taking refuge in the illusion of immortality. An
individual has to find a way to keep in contact with the infinite

> ... as an organism keeps contact with its heart. Only if the
> two can live together, and only by such a cohabitation, can
> human loneliness be conquered; it cannot be really con-
> quered by connections with a finite being. Man becomes
> only seemingly rooted in existence, because he has his own
> family, his own country, his own nation, his own religion
> and his own god. In its final conclusion Spinozism reveals
> that man does not have a family, nor a country, nor a nation,
> nor a god, nor a religion. But only Spinoza could, because of
> his own life, live through the final consciousness of this
> situation, which is a universal human situation, masqueraded
> by the apparent forms of daily life ... If Spinoza's solution
> to the two main problems of life, on which philosophy has
> to give an open or hidden answer—the problem of freedom
> and the problem of death—is fictive, it is the most beautiful
> fiction of the many fictions with which philosophy has
> nourished the human mind throughout the ages.

I will not apologise for this long quotation, because it tells us
so much about Kolakowski himself.

Kolakowski did not develop his own philosophical system:
he would be unable to believe in it if he had. But in all his
essays or lengthy historical studies, such as *Les Chrétiens sans
Église*, in which he studies the fate of the numerous religious
sects of the seventeenth century, an outline finally emerges
through which he puts his own philosophical stamp on the

whole story, in a discrete, almost concealed way. For example, he concludes that the chances of reviving true belief inevitably fail in highly organised communities of believers. They are usually unable to co-ordinate the collective and hierarchical forms of religious life with radical beliefs. The acceptance of a realistic, rationalistic structure denies the starting point of radical protest, and vice versa. At best, the radical religious sects can be pressure groups. In a manner analagous to his views on these religious sects, he defines the Left, not as an organised political movement, but as the negation of the existing world and social order. Negation is not the opposite of construction; it is merely the opposite of the *status quo*.

Everything touched by Kolakowski is changed, sometimes barely visibly, but changed all the same. Whether he is speaking or writing, it is clear that Somebody is passing. Kolakowski is always passing, even if he would prefer not to be observed.

He did not want to see his own profile. He would have been happier if we had burned the film; he did not see his own debate on television. He only made the necessary corrections and gave permission for this publication of the debate out of friendship. And it can hardly be chance that the corrected manuscript was lost in the mail the first time he sent it, and so he had to do it again. Such accidents can only strengthen his scepticism about reality.

He would like to surrender to the lures of monism, the desire to explain the world by one sweeping principle or theory, and in all events as a unity; but he describes this as philosophical monarchism, and tries to take the more difficult path of dualism —to examine the differences between the world of myths and values and that of science and facts, and the impossibility of justifying oneself while being unable to rid oneself of the need to do so.

Once, when we were eating at an Indonesian rice-table, I mixed all the different dishes together and started to do the same for him. I was not successful. He preferred to eat them one at a time, and we discovered that a philosophy manifests itself even in eating habits.

About the Contributors

ARNE NAESS was born in Oslo, 1912. He studied philosophy and psychology at the Universities of Oslo, Vienna and Paris. Since 1939 he has been Professor at the University of Oslo.

Some of his major publications are:
Interpretation and Preciseness: A Contribution to the Theory of Communication, Oslo, 1953.
Democracy, Ideology and Objectivity, Oxford, 1956.
Ghandhi and the Nuclear Age, Totowa, N. T., 1965.
Communication and Argument, Elements of Applied Semantics, London, 1966.
Four Modern Philosophers, London, 1968.
Scepticism, London, 1969.
The Pluralist and Possibilist Aspect of the Scientific Enterprise, London, 1972.

ALFRED J. AYER was born in London, 1910. He was educated at Eton, then at Christ Church College, Oxford, where he studied philosophy. He is presently Wykeman Professor of Logic, and a Fellow of New College, Oxford. He was awarded a knighthood in 1970.

Some of his major publications are:
Language, Truth and Logic, London, 1936.
The Foundation of Empirical Knowledge, London, 1940.
Philosophical Essays, London, 1954.
The Problem of Knowledge, London, 1956.
Logical Positivism (editor), London, 1959.
The Concept of a Person, London, 1963.
Metaphysics and Common Sense, London, 1967.

The Origins of Pragmatism: Studies in the Philosophy of Ch. S. Pierce and William James, London, 1968.

Bertrand Russell and G. E. Moore: The Analytical Heritage, London, 1971.

NOAM CHOMSKY was born in Philadelphia, Pa, in 1928. He studied linguistics and philosophy at the University of Pennsylvania. He is at present Ferrari P. Ward Professor in Modern Languages and Linguistics at Massachusetts Institute of Technology. In recent years he has attracted national attention through his leadership of *Resist*, a national draft-resistance movement, and through his criticisms of American political life.

Some of his major publications are:

Syntactic Structures, New York, 1957.

Aspects of the Theory of Syntax, Cambridge, Mass., 1965.

Cartesian Linguistics, London, 1966.

Language and Mind, New York, 1968.

Sound Pattern of English (with Morris Halle), London, 1968.

American Power and the New Mandarins, London, 1969.

At War with Asia, New York, 1970.

Problems of Freedom and Knowledge: The Russell Lectures, New York, 1971.

Studies on Semantics in Generative Grammar, New York, 1972.

For Reasons of State, New York, 1973.

MICHEL FOUCAULT was born in Paris, 1926. He studied history, philosophy and psychology at the University of Paris. He is now Professor of History and Systems of Thought at the Collège de France, and Visiting Professor at the State University of New York at Buffalo. He is a member of the Groupe d'Information sur la Prison (G.I.P.).

Some of his major publications are:
Maladie Mentale et Personnalité, Paris, 1954.
Folie et Déraison; Histoire de la Folie à l'Âge Classique, Paris, 1961, translated under the title: Madness and Civilization, London, 1973.
Raymond Roussel, Paris, 1963.
Les Mots et les Choses, Paris, 1966.
Archéologie du Savoir, Paris, 1969.

KARL RAIMUND POPPER was born in Vienna, 1902. He studied mathematics, physics and philosophy at the University of Vienna. In 1936 he was appointed senior lecturer at Canterbury College, Christchurch, New Zealand, and in 1949 Professor in Logic and the Philosophy of Science at the London School of Economics, where he taught until his retirement. He was knighted in 1964.

Some of his major publications are:
Logik der Forschung, Vienna, 1934, reprinted in English under the title: The Logic of Scientific Discovery, London, 1959.
The Open Society and Its Enemies, 2 vols., London, 1945.
The Poverty of Historicism, London, 1957.
Conjectures and Refutations; The Growth of Scientific Knowledge. Collected Essays, London, 1963.
Karl Popper's Life and Scientific Work, Library of Living Philosophers (to be published).

JOHN C. ECCLES was born in Melbourne, Australia, 1903. He studied physiology at the Universities of Melbourne and Oxford. He is at present Distinguished Professor of Physiology and Biophysics at the State University of New York at Buffalo. He was knighted in 1958, and in 1963 received the Nobel Prize in Physiology and Medicine.

Some of his major publications are:
The Neurophysiological Basis of Mind : The Principle of Neurophysiology, Oxford, 1953.
Physiology of Nerve Cells, Baltimore, 1957.
The Physiology of Synapses, New York, 1964.
Brain and Conscious Experience (Editor), Berlin, 1966.
The Cerebellum as a Neuronal Machine (In collaboration with Drs. Szentagothai and Ito), Berlin, 1967.
The Inhibitory Pathways of the Central Nervous System, Liverpool, 1969.
Facing Reality, London, 1971.

HENRI LEFÈBVRE was born in Hagetnau, France, 1905. He studied philosophy at the University of Aix-en-Provence. He is at present Professor of Sociology at Nanterre. He was a member of the French communist party from 1929 to 1955.

Some of his major publications are:
Hitler au Pouvoir, Bilan de Cinq Années de Fascisme en Allemagne, Paris, 1938.
Le Matérialisme Dialectique, Paris, 1940.
Critique de la Vie Quotidienne : Introduction, I, Paris, 1947.
Critique de la Vie Quotidienne : Fondements d'une Sociologie de la Quotidienneté, II, Paris, 1962.
Le Marxisme, Paris, 1948.
Logique Formelle : Logique Dialectique, Paris, 1947; 1969.
La Somme et le Reste, Paris, 1959.
Marx Philosophie, Paris, 1964.
Métaphilosophie, Paris, 1965.
Le Langue et la Société, Paris, 1966.
Position : Contre les Technocrates, Paris, 1967.
Le Droit à la Ville, Paris, 1968.
Le Manifeste Differentialiste, Paris, 1970.
Au-delà du Structuralisme, Paris, 1971.

LESZEK KOLAKOWSKI was born in Radom, Poland, 1927. He studied philosophy at the University of Lodz. After World War II he became a member of the communist party of Poland until his expulsion in 1966. He was Professor at the University of Warsaw until 1968, the year his writings were proscribed by the Party. In 1969-70 he was guest-professor at Berkeley (U.S.A.). Since 1970 he has been Professor at All Souls College at Oxford.

Some of his major publications are:
Essays on Catholic Philosophy, Warsaw, 1955.
Philosophy and Everyday Life, Warsaw, 1957.
Jednostka i Nieskonczonosc (The Individual and Infinity, dissertation on Spinoza), Warsaw, 1960.
Les Chrétiens sans Église : [La Conscience Religieuse et le lien Confessionel au XVII e siècle] published in Polish, Warsaw, 1965; in French, Paris, 1969.
The Alienation of Reason : A History of Positivist Thought, New York, 1968.
Toward a Marxist Humanism : Essays on the Left Today, New York, 1968.
Die Gegenwartigkeit des Mythos, 1973.

FONS ELDERS was born in Bovenkarspel, Holland, 1936. He studied philosophy and history at the Universities of Amsterdam, Paris and Leiden. He lectures at the Academy of Physical Education, the Academy of Architecture, Rietveld Academy and at the Theatre School in Amsterdam. He is presently a member of the Council of the University of Amsterdam.

His major publications are:
Philosophy as Science-Fiction. Seventeen Debates with Dutch Philosophers, Amsterdam, 1968.
Analyze-Decondition, An Introduction to Systematic Philosophy, Amsterdam, 1972.
A Series of Monographs for the International Philosophers Project, Amsterdam, 1971-73.